Introduction to Crime Psychology

Introduction to Crime Psychology

Edited by
K.C.Dubey

OMEGA PUBLICATIONS
NEW DELHI-110 002 (INDIA)

OMEGA PUBLICATIONS
4378/4B, G-4 JMD House
Murari Lal Street, Ansari Road
Daryaganj, New Delhi - 110 002
Phone : 011-23278062,9811787417
e-mail : omega_publications@yahoo.com

Edition : 2025

Price - 1295/-

ISBN : 978-81-8455-135-8

PRINTED IN INDIA

Published by Mahender Garg for Omega Publications, New Delhi-110 002
Printed at Suman Printers, Delhi-110093

Introduction to Crime Psychology

by K.C.Dubey

Preface

Crime psychology is the study of the wills, thoughts, intentions and reactions of criminals. It is related to the field of criminal anthropology. The study goes deeply into what makes someone commit crime, but also the reactions after the crime, on the run or in court. Criminal psychologists are often called up as witnesses in court cases to help the jury understand the mind of the criminal. Some types of Psychiatry also deal with aspects of criminal behavior.

A major part of Criminal psychology, known as offender profiling, began in the 1940's when the United States Office of Strategic Services asked William L. Langer's son Walter C. Langer, a well renowned psychiatrist, to draw up a profile of Adolf Hitler. After the Second World War British psychologist Lionel Haward while working for the Royal Air Force police, drew up a list of characteristics which high-ranking Nazi war criminals might display, to be able to spot them amongst ordinary captured soldiers and airmen.

One can view criminalization as a procedure intended as a pre-emptive, harm-reduction device, using the threat of punishment as a deterrent to those proposing to engage in the behavior causing harm. The State becomes involved because they usually believe costs of not criminalizing (*i.e.* allowing the harms to continue unabated) outweigh the costs of criminalizing it (*i.e.* restricting individual liberty in order to minimize harm to others). Criminalization may provide future harm-reduction even after a crime, assuming those incarcerated for committing crimes are more likely to cause harm in the future.

Criminalization might be intended as a way to make potential criminals pay for their crimes. In this case, criminalization is a way to set the price that one must pay (to society) for certain actions that are considered detrimental to society as a whole. In this sense criminalization can be viewed as nothing more than State-sanctioned revenge.

The major topics dealt in this book are : *Basic Facts; Anthropological Criminology; Criminal Behaviour; Psychiatric Research; Treatment for Offenders; Developmental Psychology; Developmental Psychobiology; Psychology and Research Methods; Thinking Psychology; Psychology of Abnormality; Social Process;* etc.

No doubt, these will serve the purpose of trainees and trainers, professionals and policy planners in the field. Since the sources of information are all secondary, we express our gratitude to the scholars whose works are cited or substantially made use of. We are thankful to all those who rendered ready help and cooperation while working on this project.

We express our gratitude to various scholars, teachers and friends for their assistance and guidance. Finally, we thank our publishers for bringing out this book in very limited time.

—Editor

Contents

1

Basic Facts

Crime psychology is the study of the wills, thoughts, intentions and reactions of criminals. It is related to the field of criminal anthropology. The study goes deeply into what makes someone commit crime, but also the reactions after the crime, on the run or in court. Criminal psychologists are often called up as witnesses in court cases to help the jury understand the mind of the criminal. Some types of Psychiatry also deal with aspects of criminal behavior.

A major part of Criminal psychology, known as offender profiling, began in the 1940's when the United States Office of Strategic Services asked William L. Langer's son Walter C. Langer, a well renowned psychiatrist, to draw up a profile of Adolf Hitler. After the Second World War British psychologist Lionel Haward while working for the Royal Air Force police, drew up a list of characteristics which high-ranking Nazi war criminals might display, to be able to spot them amongst ordinary captured soldiers and airmen.

In the 1950's, US psychiatrist James A. Brussel drew up what turned to be an uncannily accurate profile of a bomber who had been terrorizing New York.

The fastest development occurred when the FBI opened its training academy, the Behavioral Sciences Unit (BSU), in Quantico, Virginia. It led to the establishment of the National Center for the Analysis of Violent Crime and the violent criminal apprehension program. The idea was to have a system which could pick up links between unsolved major crimes.

In the United Kingdom, Professor David Canter was a pioneer helping to guide police detectives from the mid 1980's to an offender who had carried out a series of serious attacks, but Canter saw the limitations of "offender profiling"- in particular, the subjective, personal opinion of a psychologist. He and a colleague coined the term investigative psychology and began trying to approach the subject from what they saw as a more scientific point of view.

Among the most notable people who criticized how psychology and psychiatry treated crime as an identity is French philosopher Michel Foucault in Discipline and Punish. Foucault showed how, since its birth, the prison had been criticized by a reformist movement, which showed that it created a class of professional criminals (recidivists), separated from the popular classes, and often used by the police as informants and to carry out shady acts for the act. In other words, far from stifling criminality, the reformist movement showed that prison created and perpetrated a class of professional criminals. Henceforth, Foucault concluded that the prison's alleged failure (in rehabilitating criminals) was in fact its success, and that it was used as a disciplinary technology to control the population. Foucault also showed that, if the penal system in Early Modern Europe punished the crime in itself, the act itself, the new disciplinary system punished the person, and not the crime. It did not ask: "what did you do?" (as in the classical school of criminology; *i.e.* Cesare Beccaria and Jeremy Bentham), but "who are you?" (as in the Italian school, Cesare Lombroso, etc.) In this frame, the role of criminal anthropology, psychiatry, etc., became evident as a tool used to create the notion of "dangerous people"

Crime

Societies define crime as the breach of one or more rules or laws for which some governing authority or force may ultimately prescribe a punishment.

When society deems informal relationships and sanctions insufficient to establish and maintain a desired social order, there may result more formalized systems of social control imposed by a government, or more broadly, by a State. With the institutional and legal machinery at their disposal, agents of the State can compel individuals to conform to behavioral codes, and can punish those that do not.

Authorities employ various mechanisms to regulate behaviour, including rules codified into laws, policing people to ensure they comply with those laws, and other policies and practices designed to prevent crime. In addition, authorities provide remedies and sanctions, and collectively these constitute a criminal justice system. Not all breaches of the law, however, are considered crimes, for example, breaches of contract and other civil law offences.

The label of "crime" and the accompanying social stigma normally confine their scope to those activities seen as injurious to the general population or the State, including some that cause serious loss or damage to individuals. The label is intended to assert an hegemony of a dominant population, or to reflect a consensus of condemnation for the identified behavior and to justify a punishment imposed by the State, in the event that an accused person is tried and convicted of a crime. Usually, the perpetrator of the crime is a natural person, but in some jurisdictions and in some moral environments, legal persons are also considered to have the capability of committing crimes.

Definition

A normative definition views crime as deviant behavior that violates prevailing norms–cultural standards prescribing how humans ought to behave normally. This approach considers the complex realities surrounding the concept of crime and seeks to understand how changing social, political, psychological, and economic conditions may affect the current definitions of crime and the form of the legal, law-enforcement, and penal responses made by society.

These structural realities remain fluid and often contentious. For example: as cultures change and the political environment shifts, societies may criminalise or decriminalise certain behaviours, which will directly affect the statistical crime rates, determine the allocation of resources for the enforcement of laws, and (re-)influence the general public opinion.

Similarly, changes in the collection and/or calculation of data on crime may affect the public perceptions of the extent of any given "crime problem". All such adjustments to crime statistics, allied with the experience of people in their everyday lives, shape attitudes on the extent to which the State should use law to enforce any particular social norm. There are many ways in which behaviour can be controlled without having to resort to the criminal justice system.

Indeed, in those cases where no clear consensus exists on a given norm, the use of criminal law by the group in power to prohibit the behaviour of another group may count as an improper limitation of the second group's freedom, and the ordinary members of society may lose some of their respect for the law in general — whether the disputed law is actively enforced or not.

Legislatures pass laws (called mala prohibita) that define crimes which violate social norms. These laws vary from time to time and from place to place: note variations in gambling laws, for example. Other crimes, called mala in se, count as outlawed in almost all societies, (murder, theft and rape, for example).

Criminalization

One can view criminalization as a procedure intended as a pre-emptive, harm-reduction device, using the threat of punishment as a deterrent to those proposing to engage in the behavior causing harm. The State becomes involved because they usually believe costs of not criminalizing (*i.e.* allowing the harms to continue unabated) outweigh the costs of criminalizing it (*i.e.* restricting individual liberty in order to minimize harm to others). Criminalization may provide future harm-reduction even after a crime, assuming those incarcerated for committing crimes are more likely to cause harm in the future.

Criminalization might be intended as a way to make potential criminals pay for their crimes. In this case, criminalization is a way to set the price that one must pay (to society) for certain actions that are considered detrimental to society as a whole. In this sense criminalization can be viewed as nothing more than State-sanctioned revenge.

States control the process of criminalization because:

- Even if victims recognize their own role as victims, they may not have the resources to investigate and seek legal redress for the injuries suffered: the enforcers formally appointed by the State have the expertise and the resources.
- The victims may only want compensation for the injuries suffered, while remaining indifferent to a possible desire for deterrence (see Polinsky & Shavell (1997) on the fundamental divergence between the private and the social motivation for using the legal system).
- Fear of retaliation may deter victims or witnesses of crimes from taking any action. Even in policed societies, fear may inhibit reporting or co-operation in a trial.
- Victims, on their own, may lack the economies of scale which might allow them to administer a penal

system, let alone to collect any fines levied by a court (see Polinsky (1980) on the enforcement of fines). Garoupa & Klerman (2002) warn that a rent-seeking government has as its primary motivation to maximize revenue and so, if offenders have sufficient wealth, a rent-seeking government will act more aggressively than a social-welfare-maximizing government in enforcing laws against minor crimes (usually with a fixed penalty such as parking and routine traffic violations), but more laxly in enforcing laws against major crimes.

- As a result of the crime, victims may die or become incapacitated.

History

The idea of crime has a long history. Some religious communities regard sin as a crime; some may even highlight the crime of sin very early in legendary or mythological accounts of origins—note the tale of Adam and Eve and the theory of original sin. What one group considers a crime may cause or ignite war or conflict. However, the earliest known civilizations had codes of law, containing both civil and penal rules mixed together, though not always in recorded form.

The Sumerians produced the earliest surviving written codes. Urukagina had an early code that does not survive; a later king, Ur-Nammu, left the earliest extant written law-system, the Code of Ur-Nammu, which prescribed a formal system of penalties for specific cases in 57 articles. The Sumerians later issued other codes, including the "code of Lipit-Ishtar". This code, from the 20th century BCE, contains some fifty articles, and has been reconstructed by comparison among several sources.

The Sumerian was deeply conscious of his personal rights and resented any encroachment on them, whether by his King, his superior, or his equal. No wonder that the Sumerians were the first to compile laws and law codes.

Successive legal codes in Babylon, including the code of Hammurabi, reflected Mesopotamian society's belief that law derived from the will of the gods (see Babylonian law). Many states at this time functioned as theocracies, with codes of conduct largely religious in origin or reference.

Sir Henry Maine (1861) studied the ancient codes available in his day, and failed to find any criminal law in the "modern" sense of the word. While modern systems distinguish between offences against the "State" or "Community", and offences against the "Individual", the so-called penal law of ancient communities did not deal with "crimes" (Latin: crimina), but with "wrongs" (Latin: delicta). Thus the Hellenic laws treated all forms of theft, assault, rape, and murder as private wrongs, and left action for enforcement up to the victims or their survivors. The earliest systems seem to have lacked formal courts.

The Romans systematized law and applied it across the Roman Empire. Again, the initial rules of Roman Law regarded assaults as a matter of private compensation. The most significant Roman Law concept involved dominion. The pater familias owned all the family and its property (including slaves); the pater enforced matters involving interference with any property. The Commentaries of Gaius on the Twelve Tables treated furtum (in modern parlance: theft) as a tort.

Similarly, assault and violent robbery involved trespass as to the pater's property (so, for example, the rape of a slave could become the subject of compensation to the pater as having trespassed on his "property"), and breach of such laws created a vinculum juris (an obligation of law) that only the payment of monetary compensation (modern "damages") could discharge. Similarly, the consolidated Teutonic laws of the Germanic tribes, included a complex system of monetary compensations for what courts would now consider the complete range of criminal offences against the person, from murder down.

Even though Rome abandoned its Britannic provinces sometime around 400 AD, the Germanic mercenaries–who had largely become instrumental in enforcing Roman rule in Britannia – acquired ownership of land there and continued to use a mixture of Roman and Teutonic Law, with much written down under the early Anglo-Saxon Kings. But only when a more centralized English monarchy emerged following the Norman invasion, and the kings of England attempted to assert power over the land and its peoples, did the modern concept emerge, namely of a crime not only as an offence against the "individual", but also as a wrong against the "State"

This idea came from common law, and the earliest conception of a criminal act involved events of such major significance that the "State" had to usurp the usual functions of the civil tribunals, and direct a special law or privilegium against the perpetrator. All the earliest English criminal trials involved wholly extraordinary and arbitrary courts without any settled law to apply, whereas the civil (delictual) law operated in a highly developed and consistent manner (except where a King wanted to raise money by selling a new form of writ). The development of the idea that the "State" dispenses justice in a court only emerges in parallel with or after the emergence of the concept of sovereignty.

In continental Europe, Roman law persisted, but with a stronger influence from the Church. Coupled with the more diffuse political structure based on smaller State units, various different legal traditions emerged, remaining more strongly rooted in Roman jurisprudence modified to meet the prevailing political climate.

In Scandinavia the effect of Roman law did not become apparent until the 17th century, and the courts grew out of the things—the assemblies of the people. The people decided the cases (usually with largest freeholders dominating). This system later gradually developed into a system with a royal judge nominating a number of most esteemed men of the parish as his board, fulfilling the function of "the people" of yore.

From the Hellenic system onwards, the policy rationale for requiring the payment of monetary compensation for wrongs committed has involved the avoidance of feuding between clans and families. If compensation could mollify families' feelings, this would help to keep the peace. On the other hand, the threat of feudal warfare was played down also by the institution of oaths. Both in archaic Greece and in medieval Scandinavia, the accused was released if he could get a sufficient number of male relatives to swear him unguilty. This may be compared with the United Nations Security Council where the veto power of the permanent members ensures that the organization is not drawn into crises where it could not enforce its decisions.

These means of restraining private feuds did not always work, and sometimes prevented the fulfillment of justice. But in the earliest times the "state" did not always provide an independent police force. Thus criminal law grew out of what is now tort; and, in real terms, many acts and omissions classified as crimes actually overlap with civil-law concepts.

The development of sociological thought from the 19th century onwards prompted some fresh views on crime and criminality, and fostered the beginnings of criminology as a study of crime in society. Nietzsche noted a link between crime and creativity–in The Birth of Tragedy he asserted: "The best and brightest that man can acquire he must obtain by crime". In the 20th century Michel Foucault in Discipline and Punish made a study of criminalization as a coercive method of State control.

Natural-law Theory

Justifying the State's use of force to coerce compliance with its laws has proven a consistent theoretical problem. One of the earliest justifications involved the theory of natural law. This posits that the nature of the world or of human beings underlies the standards of morality or constructs them. Thomas Aquinas said: "the rule and measure of human acts is the reason, which is the first principle of human acts" (Aquinas, ST I-II, Q.90, A.I), *i.e.* since people are by nature rational beings, it is morally appropriate that they should behave in a way that conforms to their rational nature. Thus, to be valid, any law must conform to natural law and coercing people to conform to that law is morally acceptable. William Blackstone (1979: 41) describes the thesis:

> "This law of nature, being co-eval with mankind and dictated by God himself, is of course superior in obligation to any other. It is binding over all the globe, in all countries, and at all times: no human laws are of any validity, if contrary to this; and such of them as are valid derive all their force, and all their authority, mediately or immediately, from this original."

But John Austin (1790-1859), an early positivist, applied utilitarianism in accepting the calculating nature of human beings and the existence of an objective morality, but denied that the legal validity of a norm depends on whether its content conforms to morality. Thus in Austinian terms a moral code can objectively determine what people ought to do, the law can embody whatever norms the legislature decrees to achieve social utility, but every individual remains free to choose what he or she will do. Similarly, Hart (1961) saw the law as an aspect of sovereignty, with lawmakers able to adopt any law as a means to a moral end.

Thus the necessary and sufficient conditions for the truth of a proposition of law simply involved internal logic and consistency, and that the state's agents used state power with responsibility. Dworkin (2005) rejects Hart's theory and argues that fundamental among political rights is the right of each individual to the equal respect and concern of those who govern him. He offers a theory of compliance overlaid by a theory of deference (the citizen's duty to obey the law) and a theory of enforcement, which identifies the legitimate goals of enforcement and punishment. Legislation must conform to a theory of legitimacy, which describes the circumstances under which a particular person or group is entitled to make law, and a theory of legislative justice, which describes the law they are entitled or obliged to make.

Indeed, despite everything, the majority of natural-law theorists have accepted the idea of enforcing the prevailing morality as a primary function of the law. This view entails the problem that it makes any moral criticism of the law impossible in that, if conformity with natural law forms a necessary condition for legal validity, all valid law must, by definition, be morally just. Thus, on this line of reasoning, the legal validity of a norm necessarily entails its moral justice.

One can solve this problem by granting some degree of moral relativism and accepting that norms may evolve over time and, therefore, one can criticize the continued enforcement of old laws in the light of the current norms. People may find such law acceptable, but the use of State power to coerce citizens to comply with that law is not morally justified. In more modern conceptions of the theory, crime is characterized as the violation of individual rights.

Since society considers so many rights as natural (hence the term "right") rather than man-made, what constitutes a crime is also natural, in contrast to laws (which are man-made). Adam Smith illustrates this view, saying that a smuggler would be an excellent citizen, "...had not the laws of his country made that a crime which nature never meant to be so."

Natural-law theory therefore distinguishes between "criminality" (which derives from human nature) and "illegality" (which originates with the interests of those in power). Lawyers sometimes express the two concepts with the phrases malum in se and malum prohibitum respectively. They regard a crime malum in se as inherently criminal; whereas a crime malum prohibitum (the argument goes) counts as criminal only because the law has decreed it so.

Distinctions

Religious sentiment often becomes a contributory factor of crime. Rioters set fire to many of Ahmedabad's buildings during the 2002 Gujarat violence.

Governments criminalise antisocial behaviour—and treat it within a system of offences against society—in order to justify the imposition of punishment. Authorities make a series of distinctions depending on the passive subject of the crime (the victim), or on the offended interest(s), in crimes against:

- personality of the State
- rights of the citizen
- public administration
- administration of justice
- religious sentiment and faith
- public order
- public economy, industry, and commerce
- public morality
- the person

- honour
- patrimony

Or one can categorise crimes depending on the related punishment, with sentencing tariffs prescribed in line with the perceived seriousness of the offence. Thus fines and noncustodial sentences may address the least serious crimes, and lengthy imprisonment or (in some States) capital punishment the most serious.

Types

Researchers and commentators may classify crime into categories, including:

- violent crime
- property crime
- public order crime

Analysts can also group crimes by severity, some common category-terms including:

- felonies (US and previously UK)
- indictable offences (UK)
- misdemeanors (US and previously UK)
- summary offences (UK)
- infractions

U.S. Classification

In the United States since 1930, the FBI has tabulated Uniform Crime Reports (UCR) annually from crime data submitted by law enforcement agencies across the United States. Officials compile this data at the city, county, and state levels into the Uniform crime reports (UCR). They classify violations of laws which derive from common law as Part I (index) crimes in UCR data, further categorised as violent or property crimes. Part I violent crimes include murder and criminal homicide (voluntary manslaughter), forcible rape, aggravated assault, and robbery; while Part I property crimes include burglary, arson, larceny/theft, and motor-vehicle theft. All other crimes count as Part II crimes.

For convenience, such lists usually include infractions although, in the U.S., they may come into the sphere not of the criminal law, but rather of the civil law. Compare tortfeasance.

Booking arrests requires detention for a time-frame ranging 1 to 24 hours.

Crimes in International Law

Crimes defined by treaty as crimes against international law include:

- crimes against peace
- waging a war of aggression
- crimes of apartheid
- piracy
- genocide
- war crimes
- the slave trade

From the point of view of State-centric law, extraordinary procedures (usually international courts) may prosecute such crimes. Note the role of the International Criminal Court at The Hague in the Netherlands.

Religion and Crime

Socially accepted or imposed religious morality has influenced secular jurisdictions on issues that may otherwise concern only an individual's conscience. Activities sometimes criminalized on religious grounds include (for example) alcohol-consumption (prohibition), abortion and stem-cell research. In various historical and present-day societies institutionalized religions have established systems of earthly justice which punish crimes against the divine will and specific devotional, organizational and other rules under specific codes, such as Islamic sharia or Roman Catholic canon law.

Military Jurisdictions and States of Emergency

In the military sphere, authorities can prosecute both regular crimes and specific acts (such as mutiny or desertion) under martial-law codes that either supplant or extend civil codes in times of war.

Many constitutions contain provisions to curtail freedoms and criminalize otherwise tolerated behaviors under a state of emergency in the event of war, natural disaster or civil unrest. Such undesired activities may include assembly in the streets, violation of curfew, or possession of firearms.

Employee Erime

Two common types of employee crime exist: embezzlement and sabotage.

The complexity and anonymity of computers may help criminal employees camouflage their operations. The victims of the most costly scams include banks, brokerage houses, insurance companies, and other large financial institutions.[13]

Most people guilty of embezzlement do not have criminal histories. Embezzlers tend to have a gripe against their employer, have financial problems, or simply an inability to resist the temptation of a loop-hole they have found. Screening and background checks on perspective employees can help in prevention; however, many laws make some types of screening difficult or even illegal. Fired or disgruntled employees sometimes sabotage their company's computer system as a form of 'pay back'. This sabotage may take the form of a Logic bomb, a computer virus, or creating general havoc.

Some places of employment have developed measures in an attempt to combat and prevent employee crime. Places of employment sometimes implement security measures such as cameras, fingerprint records of employees, and background checks. Although privacy-advocates have questioned such methods, they serve the interests of the organisations using them. Not only do these methods help prevent employee crime, but they protect the company from punishment and/ or lawsuits for negligent hiring.

●●

2

Anthropological Criminology

Anthropological criminology (sometimes referred to as criminal anthropology, literally a combination of the study of the human species and the study of criminals) is a field of offender profiling, based on perceived links between the nature of a crime and the personality or physical appearance of the offender. Although similar to physiognomy and phrenology, the term criminal anthropology is generally reserved for the works of the Italian school of criminology of the late 19th century (Cesare Lombroso, Enrico Ferri, Raffaele Garofalo). Lombroso thought that criminals were born with inferior physiological differences which were detectable. He popularized the notion of "born criminal" and thought that criminality was an atavism or hereditary disposition. His central idea was to locate crime completely within the individual and utterly divorce it from the surrounding social conditions and structures. A founder of the Positivist school of criminology, Lombroso hereby opposed social positivism developed by the Chicago school and environmental criminology.

History

The physiognomist Johann Kaspar Lavater (1741-1801) was one of the first to suggest a link between facial figures and crime. Victor Hugo referred to his work in Les Misérables, about what he would have said about Thénardier's face. Franz Joseph Gall then developed in 1810 his work on craniology, in which he alleged that crime was one of the behaviors organically controlled by a specific area of the brain. The philosopher Jacob Fries (1773–1843) also suggested a link between crime and physical appearance when he published a criminal anthropology handbook in 1820.

The Italian School

However, criminal anthropology per se refers to the Italian school of criminology, whose most famous member was Cesare Lombroso. The Italian criminologists rejected the Classical school of criminology (Cesare Beccaria, Jeremy Bentham) who had developed a "rational choice theory" before the letter. They considered that crime was attributed to a specific nature, and that essential type of criminals could be found.

Lombroso divided for instance Northern Italian and Southern Italians in two different "races," and claimed that "Southern Italians were more crime-prone and lazy because they were unlucky enough to have less Aryan blood than their northern countrymen." Enrico Ferri, a student of Lombroso, considered Black people to be of an "inferior race" and more prone to crime than others.

Mugshot and Fingerprinting

On the other hand, Alphonse Bertillon (1853–1914) created a mugshot identification system for criminals prior to the invention of fingerprinting. Hans Gross (1847–1915), leading worker in the field of criminology was also involved in the development of the theory.

Social Darwinism

The theory of anthropological criminology was influenced heavily by the ideas of Charles Darwin (1809-1882). However, the influences came mainly from misconceptions of Darwin's theory of evolution, specifically that some species were morally superior to others. This idea was in fact spawned by Social

Darwinism, but nevertheless formed a critical part of anthropological criminology.

The work of Cesare Lombroso was continued by Social Darwinists in the United States between 1881 and 1911.

The Theory

In the 19th century, Cesare Lombroso and his followers performed autopsies on criminals and declared that they had discovered similarities between the physiologies of the bodies and those of "primitive humans", monkeys and apes. Most of these similarities involved receding foreheads, height, head shape and size, and based on these Lombroso postulated the theory of the 'born criminal'. Lombroso also declared that the female offender was worse than the male, as they had strong masculine characteristics.

Lombroso outlined 14 physiognomic characteristics which he and his followers believed to be common in all criminals: unusually short or tall height ; small head, but large face ; fleshy lips, but thin upper lip ; protuberances (bumps) on head, in back of head and around ear ; wrinkles on forehead and face ; large sinus cavities or bumpy face ; tattoos on body ; receding hairline ; bumps on head, particularly above left ear ; large incisors ; bushy eyebrows, tending to meet across nose ; large eye sockets, but deep-set eyes ; beaked or flat nose ; strong jaw line ; small and sloping forehead ; small or weak chin ; thin neck ; sloping shoulders, but large chest ; large, protruding ears ; long arms ; high cheek bones ; pointy or snubbed fingers or toes.

Rejection

During Lombroso's life, British scientist Charles Goring 1870–1919 was also working in the same area, and concluded that there was no noticeable physiological differences between law abiding people and those who committed crimes. Maurice Parmelee, seen as the founder of modern criminology in

America, also began to reject the theory of anthropological criminology in 1911, which led to its eventual withdrawal from the field of accepted criminology research.

Modern Times

Despite general rejection of Lombroso's theories, anthropological criminology still finds a place of sort in modern criminal profiling. Certain studies into tattoos in particular have been made with the result that some rehabilitation programs promote the removal of tattoos to help individuals disassociate themselves from criminal organizations. Studies have also been made of a link between general physical attractiveness and crime.

Historically (particularly in the 1930s) criminal anthropology had been associated somewhat with eugenics as the idea of a physiological flaw in the human race was often associated with plans to remove such flaws. This was found particularly in America, with the American Eugenics Movement between 1907 and 1939, and the Anti-miscegenation laws, and also in Germany during the Third Reich where 250,000 mentally disabled Germans were killed.

Criminal anthropology, and the closely related study of Physiognomy, have also found their way into studies of social psychology and forensic psychology. Studies into the nature of twins also combines aspects of criminal anthropology, as some studies reveal that identical twins share a likelihood of criminal activities more so than non-identical twins. Lombroso's theories are also found in studies of Galvanic skin response and XYY chromosome syndrome.

Psychiatry

The word psyche comes from the ancient Greek for soul or butterfly. The fluttering elusive insect is in the coat of arms of Britain's Royal College of Psychiatrists.

Psychiatry is a medical specialty devoted to the treatment, study and prevention of mental disorders. The term was first coined by the German physician Johann Christian Reil in 1808.

Psychiatric assessment typically involves a mental status examination and the taking of a case history; and psychological tests may be conducted. Physical examinations may be carried out and on occasion neuroimages or other neurophysiological measurements taken. Diagnostic procedures vary. Official criteria are listed in manuals, the most widely available being the ICD from the World Health Organization and the DSM from the American Psychiatric Asso iation.

Psychiatric medication is currently a central option, often in conjunction with one of the many varieties of psychotherapy. In extreme instances, currently less favored techniques such as electroconvulsive therapy may be used. Treatment is available on an inpatient or outpatient basis. With the necessary legal sanction, this may be applied involuntarily. Research and the clinical application of psychiatry are conducted on an interdisciplinary basis involving various sub-specialties and theoretical approaches.

In the West, treatment of emotional and cognitive disfunction may be said to have its origins at least as far back as the 5th century BC. The first hospices for the mentally ill appeared in the Middle Ages. The early 19th century saw the development of psychiatry as a recognized field. Mental health institutions came to utilize more elaborate and, over the course of time, more humane treatment methods. The 19th century saw a huge increase in the number of patients.

The 20th century saw an upsurge of biological understanding of mental disorders, as well as the introduction of more systematic disease classification, and the advent of sophisticated psychiatric medication. An anti-psychiatry movement, hostile to most of the fundamental assumptions and practices of the discipline, emerged in the 1960s. A shift in emphasis in several Western societies led to the dismantling of state psychiatric hospitals in favor of more community-based treatment.

Theory and Focus

"Psychiatry, more than any other branch of medicine, forces its practitioners to wrestle with the nature of evidence, the validity of introspection, problems in communication, and other long-standing philosophical issues"

The term psychiatry, coined by Johann Christian Reil in 1808, comes from the Greek (soul or mind) and (healer or doctor). It refers to a field of medicine focused specifically on the mind, aiming to study, prevent, and treat mental disorders in humans. It has been described as an intermediary between the world from a social context and the world from the perspective of those who are mentally ill.

Those who practice psychiatry are different than most other mental health professionals and physicians in that they must be familiar with both the social and biological sciences. The discipline is interested in the operations of different organs and body systems as classified by the patient's subjective experiences and the objective physiology of the patient. Psychiatry exists to treat mental disorders which are conventionally divided into three very general categories; mental illness, severe learning disability, and personality disorder. While the focus of psychiatry has changed little throughout time, the diagnostic and treatment processes have evolved dramatically and continue to do so. Since the late 20th century, the field of psychiatry has continued to become more biological and less conceptually isolated from the field of medicine.

Scope of Practice

While the medical specialty of psychiatry utilizes research in the field of neuroscience, psychology, medicine, biology, biochemistry, and pharmacology, it has generally been considered a middle ground between neurology and psychology. Unlike other physicians and neurologists, psychiatrists specialize in the doctor-patient relationship and are trained to varying extents in the use of psychotherapy and other therepautic communication techniques. Psychiatrists also differ from psychologists in that they are physicians and the entirety of their post-graduate training is revolved around the field of medicine. Psychiatrists can therefore counsel patients, prescribe medication, order laboratory tests, utilize neuroimaging in a research setting, and conduct physical examinations.

Ethics

Like other professions, the World Psychiatric Association issues an ethical code to govern the conduct of psychiatrists. The psychiatric code of ethics, first set forth through the Declaration of Hawaii in 1977, has been expanded through a 1983 Vienna update and, in 1996, the broader Madrid Declaration. The code was further revised in Hamburg, 1999. The World Psychiatric Association code covers such matters as patient assessment, up-to-date knowledge, the human dignity of incapacitated patients, confidentiality, research ethics, sex selection, euthanasia, organ transplantation, torture, the death penalty, media relations, genetics, and ethnic or cultural discrimination. In establishing such ethical codes, the profession has responded to a number of controversies about the practice of psychiatry.

Subspecialties

Various subspecialties and/or theoretical approaches exist which are related to the field of psychiatry. They include the following:

- Biological psychiatry; an approach to psychiatry that aims to understand mental disorder in terms of the biological function of the nervous system.

- Child and adolescent psychiatry; a branch of psychiatry that specialises in work with children, teenagers, and their families.
- Community psychiatry; an approach that reflects an inclusive public health perspective and is practiced in community mental health services.
- Cross-cultural psychiatry; a branch of psychiatry concerned with the cultural and ethnic context of mental disorder and psychiatric services.
- Emergency psychiatry; the clinical application of psychiatry in emergency settings.
- Forensic psychiatry; the interface between law and psychiatry.
- Geriatric psychiatry; a branch of psychiatry dealing with the study, prevention, and treatment of mental disorders in humans with old age.
- Liaison psychiatry; the branch of psychiatry that specializes in the interface between other medical specialties and psychiatry.
- Military psychiatry; covers special aspects of psychiatry and mental disorders within the military context.
- Neuropsychiatry; branch of medicine dealing with mental disorders attributable to diseases of the nervous system.
- Social psychiatry; a branch of psychiatry that focuses on the interpersonal and cultural context of mental disorder and mental wellbeing.

In the United States, psychiatry is one of the specialties which qualify for further education and board-certification in pain medicine, palliative medicine, and sleep medicine.

APPROACHES

Psychiatric illnesses can be approached in a number of different ways. The biomedical approach examines signs and symptoms and compares them with diagnostic criteria. However psychiatric illness can also be assessed through a narrative which tries to understand symptoms as a part of a meaningful life history and as a responses to external conditions. Both approaches are important in the field of psychiatry. A lack of consensus between these often opposing view has contributed in part to the biopsychiatry controversy. It has also played a role in controversies over specific psychiatric illness, such as ADHD and Multiple personalities.

Ancient Times

Starting in the 5th century BC, mental disorders, especially those with psychotic traits, were considered supernatural in origin. This view existed throughout ancient Greece and Rome. Early manuals written about mental disorders were created by the Greeks. In 4th century BC, Hippocrates theorized that physiological abnormalities may be the root of mental disorders. However further explorations of this perspective ceased shortly thereafter following the fall of the Roman Empire. Religious leaders and others returned to using early versions of exorcisms to treat mental disorders which often utilized cruel, harsh, and other barbarous methods.

Middle Ages

The first psychiatric hospitals were built in the medieval Islamic world from the 8th century. The first was built in Baghdad in 705, followed by Fes in the early 8th century, and Cairo in 800. Unlike medieval Christian physicians who relied on demonological explanations for mental illness, medieval Muslim physicians relied mostly on clinical observations. They made significant advances to psychiatry and were the first to provide psychotherapy and moral treatment for mentally ill patients, in addition to other forms of treatment such as baths, drug medication, music therapy and occupational therapy. In the 10th century, the Persian physician Muhammad ibn Zakariya Razi (Rhazes) combined psychological methods and physiological explanations to provide treatment to mentally ill patients. His contemporary, the Arab physician Najab ud-din Muhammad, first described a number of mental illnesses such as agitated depression, neurosis, priapism and sexual impotence (Nafkhae Malikholia), psychosis (Kutrib), and mania (Dual-Kulb).

In the 11th century, another Persian physician Avicenna recognized 'physiological psychology' in the treatment of illnesses involving emotions, and developed a system for associating changes in the pulse rate with inner feelings, which is seen as a precursor to the word association test developed by Carl Jung in the 19th century. Avicenna was also an early pioneer of neuropsychiatry, and first described a number of neuropsychiatric conditions such as hallucination, insomnia, mania, nightmare, melancholia, dementia, epilepsy, paralysis, stroke, vertigo and tremor.

Psychiatric hospitals were built in medieval Europe from the 13th century to treat mental disorders but were utilized only as custodial institutions and did not provide any type of treatment. Founded in the 13th century, Bethlem Royal Hospital in London is one of the oldest psychiatric hospitals. By 1547 the City of London acquired the hospital and continued its function until 1948.

Early Modern Period

In 1656, Louis XIV of France created a public system of hospitals for those suffering from mental disorders, but as in England, no real treatment was being applied. In 1758 English physician William Battie wrote the Treatise on Madness which called for treatments to be utilized in asylums. Thirty years later the new ruling monarch in England, George III, was known to be suffering from a mental disorder. Following the King's remission in 1789, mental illness was seen as something which could be treated and cured. By 1792 French physician Philippe Pinel introduced humane treatment approaches to those suffering from mental disorders. William Tuke adopted the methods outlined by Pinel and that same year Tuke opened the York Retreat in England. That institution became known as a model throughout the world for humane and moral treatment of patients suffering from mental disorders. It inspired similar institutions in the United States, most notably the Brattleboro Retreat and the Hartford Retreat (now the Institute of Living).

19th Century

At the turn of the century, England and France combined only had a few hundred individuals in asylums. By the late 1890s and early 1900s, this number skyrocketed to the hundreds of thousands. The United States housed 150,000 patients in mental hospitals by 1904. German speaking countries housed more than 400 public and private sector asylums. These asylums were critical to the evolution of psychiatry as they provided a universal platform of practice throughout the world.

Universities often played a part in the administration of the asylums. Due to the relationship between the universities and asylums, scores of competitive psychiatrists were being molded in Germany. Germany became known as the world leader in psychiatry during the nineteenth century. The country possessed more than 20 separate universities all competing with each other for scientific advancement. However, because of Germany's individual states and the lack of national regulation of asylums, the country had no organized centralization of asylums or psychiatry. Britain, like Germany, also lacked a centralized organization for the administration of asylums. This deficit hindered the diffusion of new ideas in medicine and psychiatry.

In the United States in 1834, Anna Marsh, a physician's widow, deeded the funds to build her country's first financially-stable private asylum. The Brattleboro Retreat marked the beginning of America's private psychiatric hospitals challenging state institutions for patients, funding, and influence. Although based on England's York Retreat, it would be followed by speciality institutions of every treatment philosophy.

In 1838, France enacted a law to regulate both the admissions into asylums and asylum services across the country. By 1840, asylums as therapeutic institutions existed throughout Europe and the United State.

Emil Kraepelin studied and promoted ideas of disease classification for mental disorders.

However, the new and dominating ideas that mental illness could be "conquered" during the mid-nineteenth century all came crashing down. Psychiatrists and asylums were being pressured by an ever increasing patient population. The average number of patients in asylums in the United States jumped 927%. Numbers were similar in England and Germany. Overcrowding was rampant in France where asylums would commonly take in double their maximum capacity. Increases in asylum populations may have been a result of the transfer of care from families and poorhouses, but the specific reasons as to why the increase occurred is still debated today. No matter the cause, the pressure on asylums from the increase was taking its toll on the asylums and psychiatry as a specialty. Asylums were once again turning into custodial institutions and the reputation of psychiatry in the medical world had hit an extreme low.

20th Century

The 20th century introduced a new psychiatry into the world. The different perspectives of looking at mental disorders began to be introduced. The career of Emil Kraepelin somewhat model this hiatus of psychiatry between the different disciplines. Kraepelin initially was very attracted to psychology and ignored the ideas of anatomical psychiatry. Following his acceptance for a professorship of psychiatry, and later his work in a university psychiatric clinic, Kraepelin's interest in pure psychology began to fade and he introduced a plan of a more comprehensive psychiatry. Kraepelin also began to study and promote the ideas of disease classification for mental disorders, an idea introduced by Karl Ludwig Kahlbaum. The initial ideas behind biological psychiatry, stating that these different disorders were all biological in nature, evolved into a new idea of "nerves" and psychiatry became a sort of rough neurology or neuropsychiatry. Following Sigmund Freud's death, ideas stemming from psychoanalytic theory also began to take root. The psychoanalytic theory became popular among psychiatrists because it allowed the patients to be treated in private practices instead of asylums. However the progress of psychiatry by the 1970s turned psychoanalytic theory into a marginal school of thought within the field.

Otto Loewi's work led to the identification of the first neurotransmitter, acetylcholine.

This period of time saw the reemergence of biological psychiatry. Psychopharmacology became an integral part of psychiatry starting with Otto Loewi's discovery of the first neurotransmitter, acetylcholine. Neuroimaging was first utilized as a tool for psychiatry in the 1980s. The discovery of chlorpromazine's effectiveness in treating schizophrenia in 1952 revolutionized treatment of the disease, as did lithium carbonate's ability to stabilize mood highs and lows in bipolar disorder in 1948. While psychosocial issues were still seen as valid, psychotherapy was seen to be their "cure." Genetics were once again thought to play a role in mental illness. Molecular biology opened the door for specific genes contributing mental disorders to be identified. By 1995 genes contributing to schizophrenia had been identified on chromosome 6 and genes contributing to bipolar disorder on chromosomes 18 and 21.

Anti-psychiatry and Deinstitutionalization

The introduction of psychiatric medications and the use of laboratory tests altered the doctor-patient relationship between psychiatrists and their patients. Psychiatry's shift to the hard sciences had been interpreted as a lack of concern for patients. Anti-psychiatry had become more prevalent in the late twentieth century due to this and publications in the media which conceptualized mental disorders as myths. Others in the movement argued that psychiatry was a form of social control and demanded that institutionalized psychiatric care, stemming from Pinel's thereapeutic asylum, be abolished. Incidents of physical abuse by psychiatrists took place during the reign of some totalitarian regimes as part of a system to enforce political control with some of the abuse even continuing to our present day. Historical examples of the abuse of psychiatry took place in Nazi Germany, in the Soviet Union under Psikhushka, and in the apartheid system in South Africa.

Electroconvulsive therapy was one treatment that the anti-psychiatry movement wanted eliminated. They alleged that electroconvulsive therapy damaged the brain and it was used as a tool for discipline. While there is no evidence that brain damage was a result of electronconvulsive therapy, there have been isolated incidents where the use of electroconvulsive therapy was threatened to keep the patients "in line." The prevalence of psychiatric medication helped initiate deinstitutionalization, the process of discharging patients from psychiatric hospitals to the community. The pressure from the anti-psychiatry movements and the ideology of community treatment from the medical arena helped sustain deinstitutionalization. Thirty-three years after deinstitutionalization started in the United States, only 19% of the patients in state hospitals remained. Mental health professionals envisioned a process wherein patients would be released into communities where they could participate in a normal life while living in a therapeutic atmosphere.

Transinstitutionalization and the Aftermath

In 1963, United States president John F. Kennedy introduced legislation delegating the National Institute of Mental Health to administer Community Mental Health Centers for those being discharged from state psychiatric hospitals. Later, though, the Community Mental Health Center's focus was diverted to provide psychotherapy sessions for those suffering from acute and/or mild mental disorders. Ultimately there were no arrangements made for actively ill patients who were being discharged from hospitals. Some of those suffering from mental disorders drifted into homelessness or ended up in prisons and jails. Studies found that 33% of the homeless population and 14% of inmates in prisons and jails were already diagnosed with a mental illness.

In 1972, psychologist David Rosenhan published the Rosenhan experiment, a study analyzing the validity of psychiatric diagnoses. The study arranged for eight individuals with no history of psychopathology to attempt admission into psychiatric hospitals. The individuals included a graduate student, psychologists, an artist, a housewife, and two physicians, including one psychiatrist. All eight individuals were admitted with a diagnosis of schizophrenia or bipolar disorder. Psychiatrists then attempted to treat the individuals using psychiatric medication. All eight were discharged within

7 to 52 days. In a later part of the study, psychiatric staff were warned that pseudo-patients might be sent to their institutions, but none were actually sent. Nevertheless, a total of 83 patients out of 193 were believed by at least one staff member to be actors. Rosenhan's study concluded that individuals with no presence of mental disorders could not be distinguished from those suffering from mental disorders. While critics such as Robert Spitzer placed doubt on the validity and credibility of the study, they also conceded that the consistency of psychiatric diagnoses needed improvement.

Psychiatry, like many medical specialties, has a continuing, significant demand for research investigating its related diseases, classifications, origins, and treatments. Psychiatry falls into biology's fundamental belief that disease and health are different elements of an individual's adaptation to an environment. But psychiatry also recognizes that the environment of the human species is complex and includes physical, cultural, and relational elements. In addition to external factors, the human brain must recognize or organize an individual's hopes, fears, desires, fantasies and feelings. Psychiatry's difficult task is the attempt to envelop the understanding of these factors so that they can be studied both clinically and physiologically.

●●

3

Criminal Behaviour

In the united states and other free societies each man is allowed maximum freedom and protection. This is accomplished by rules and regulations protecting the individual's rights within the group. Although this at first seems incongruous, it actually means that we each give up a certain amount of freedom by obeying rules and regulations that protect other members of society in order to gain the maximum amount of freedom and protection for ourselves. Formalized rules or regulations reflecting the group desires are called laws. Thus criminal behavior becomes the breaking of a rule or regulation called a law.

We must note immediately that laws reflect man's knowledge about the world and his ethical system within this world. As civilizations change, ethics change. Thus laws must change with the passage of time. Because the norms, or expectations, of society are reflected in laws, these laws are relative or changing, but at the same time absolute. For example, an activity such as slavery or homosexual behavior is always morally wrong, but not always legally wrong. It is up to man in an evolving world to produce laws reflecting current moral ethics. This is often a slow process. Thus the effect is often accomplished by interpretation of laws by judges and other people in authority, rather than in the formulation of new laws.

The fact that crimes are committed in the United States is well known. Each year, the Federal Bureau of Investigation of the United States Department of Justice releases crime statistics for the entire nation. They reported that in. 1963 over 2¼ million serious crimes took place. This is a 10-percent increase over 1962 and a 40-percent increase over 1958 (Hoover, 1964). Statistics by themselves must always be questioned, and later in this chapter we discuss some specific points to observe when reading crime reports. However, over 2¼ million serious crimes is an obviously large number, and the increases from 1962 and 1958 are far greater than the yearly 1.5-percent increase in the general population during the same period. Crime, as reported by the police authorities in the United States, is increasing.

But what about criminal behavior that does not show up in statistical reports? Wilson (1951) stated, "One study estimates that the average citizen in one American city, considering himself entirely law-abiding, would unwittingly break sufficient laws to spend over 1,825 years in prison, and to accumulate fines in excess of $2,085,919.55, within one year of orderly living." Obviously then, laws, even though they reflect desirable social norms of the group, are not strictly adhered to by many members of our society, nor can they be, since most individuals simply cannot even know all of the laws.

Lindner (1955) suggested that criminal behavior is not adequately described as simply breaking a rule or regulation, but that different kinds or levels of criminal behavior must be noted. He indicated that behavior called law breaking is a form of legal transgression involving an unintentional action or a circumstance to which a person cannot make a rapid change. A second classification is habitual type offense, and it too is not real criminality, although such offenses take place relatively frequently. They are habits, which the transgressor is unable to change in conformance with the law when his old mode of response is no longer legally permissible. Finally real criminals are people involved in acting out unlawful behavior due to internal stress and pathological distortion, so that they can satisfy their own needs or motivations.

Those trained in the law profession have as their duty the understanding of laws pertinent to their activities. Their functions and the function of law is to control behavior. Behavior is also a major interest of psychologists. This and the following chapter will cover many topics of psychology as applied to law. A complete understanding of human behavior and prediction and control of that behavior represents all of psychology and all of law, so naturally, there is a great deal of mutual concern to the two professions.

The topics to be covered in this chapter generally pertain to identifying and evaluating criminal behavior. Although we readily agree that there is no such thing as a criminal type, we will discuss personal and environmental factors related to criminal behavior. In addition, we will discuss methods of detecting deception.

In our system of government a. person is guilty of a crime only after proven guilty. It is the duty of the prosecuting attorney to present enough information before a judge or a group of fellow citizens and a judge to absolutely prove that a defendant has committed a crime. The last major segment of this chapter considers the trial of the accused.

Identification of Criminal Behaviour

Some laymen and professional employees still persist in the notion that criminals are of a particular physiological or anthropometrical makeup. Work done by an Italian military physician in the late nineteenth century (Lombroso, 1911) is probably the basis for attitudes that criminals are of a certain type. Lombroso studied the physiognomy of 5,907 convicts and concluded that the typical criminal had a long lower jaw, flattened nose, a symmetrical cranium, and other physiological characteristics. Such a theory is unfortunately still accepted by many. The work of many other researchers since Lombroso has shown that there are very few physical characteristics of criminals that can be isolated and shown to be different from the general population. Some evidence seems to indicate that physical types are related to particular types of crimes, but even there, the evidence is rather scant. In general, criminals are not criminals because of certain physiological characteristics, but more likely because of psychological and environmental factors.

An individual may exhibit criminal behavior when he is exposed to a criminal influence, when he has a strong motivation to express aggressiveness, or when he has a desire for punishment due to guilt feelings. As yet, specific causes of criminal behavior are not isolated and most likely will not be as long as researchers equate criminal behavior with convicted or arrested individuals. Many sets of criminal behavior occur and do not result in conviction or arrest.

It seems quite evident that criminals develop through an interaction of their personality and psychological characteristics with their environment. Before we can discuss adequately the psychological and environmental factors, which seem to predispose an individual to criminal behavior, it is important to understand the shortcomings of crime statistics upon which our estimates of causes of crime are often based.

Statistics of Criminal Behaviour. In an attempt to get an understanding of the amount of crime in the United States, the Federal Bureau of Investigation annually collects statistics from local law enforcement agencies. Recognizing that good statistics are difficult to collect and analyze, the FBI established specific techniques for collecting the information for the uniform crime reports. Since 1930 the FBI has been collecting the uniform crime reports, and the local agencies have been using very specific techniques of reporting. Even so, variations and report procedures occur because 8,000 jurisdictions report to the FBI. Thus the FBI cautions that criminal acts as indicated in their reports are simply a first means of account of crime in the United States. They state that, "Not all crimes come readily to the attention of the police; not all crimes are of sufficient importance to be significant in an index; and not all important crimes occur with enough regularity to be meaningful in index." With these considerations in mind, the FBI reports crime classification in seven categories.

All serious crimes increased in 1963 as compared to 1962. The serious crimes are subdivided into crimes of violence (murder, forcible rape, robbery, and aggravated assault) and crimes against property (burglary, larceny of $50 and over, and auto theft). Crimes of violence increased about 5 percent, and crimes against property increased about 10 percent in 1963 as compared to 1962. About 92 percent of the total crimes in 1963 were against property (Hoover, 1964).

Indexes of crime rates are not absolute measures of crime frequency. The indexes are based on reports of crimes or arrest or commitments to prison and not on the number of people involved or occurrences of crime. Crimes such as stealing from an employer or friend do not show up in statistics if they are never reported to police. Statistics frequently show only major criminal behavior. For example, overtime parking, going through a stop sign, and so on, are illegal but usually 'not recorded in crime statistics. Reports of total amount of crime are of little use unless compared to another base such as the population at large or the number of people in the environment where crime occurred. For example, it would not be fair to compare the number of vehicle violations in 1920 against 1960 without comparing the total number of vehicles or miles driven. The number of crimes reported does not necessarily reflect amount of criminal behavior, because one crime may involve more than one person. For example, a burglary committed by five people may show up in a police record as one robbery.

Keeping aware of these difficulties in interpreting criminal statistics, we will examine the psychological and environmental factors related to crime rates. These statistics will aid us in evaluating possible causes of criminal behavior.

Earlier the psychologist's concept of behavior as primarily determined by psychological and environmental factors has been stated. At times the disparate views of psychologists and attorneys is the result of disagreements concerning free will and determinism. It is not essential to prove that an individual is not a free agent. However, it is important to recognize the responsibility for behavior. We accept the concept that an individual does not have free will in a particular situation but rather behaves as he does as the result of past experiences and innate characteristics. Complete knowledge of all the factors that will create a particular behavior is not now available. Psychology is not an exact science and cannot predict and control behavior precisely. On the other hand, most of our society accepts the concept that a mentally ill person needs help and cannot cure himself. The same concept must be carried over to criminal behavior. Criminal behavior is another form of abnormal or mentally ill behavior.

The individual who responds in a particular situation in a manner that is considered criminal does so as a result of environmental and personal factors. Our discussions of criminal behavior are concerned with these two categories. By and large, available evidence indicates very little general relationship between environmental or personal factors and criminal behavior. However, different individual factors seem to be related to particular types of criminal behavior. We examine a series of personal factors in the following sections.

Personal Factors

Age. Whenever we visit a prison and observe the inmates, we cannot help but note the apparent youthfulness of the inmate population. Without a complete statistical analysis, it appears that the prison populations are considerably younger than the population at large in the United States. Although crime reports are about known criminal behavior and are therefore primarily a measure of police activity, we must accept them for our study of age and criminal behavior. The FBI annually collects data concerning age, sex, and race of persons arrested for certain crimes. The percentage of total arrests in the United States during 1963 by various age groups for all offenses except traffic violations. It is quite obvious that the under-21 age group has a far higher arrest rate than the older groups. It is also disheartening to notice the large percentage (17.4) of total arrests of people under 18 years of age. During the calendar year 1963, arrests of persons under 18 years of age rose 11 percent over the 1961 data whereas the number of arrests for those 18 years and over decreased 0.7 percent in the same period. This upward trend in arrests for young people continued from previous year increases in all crimes except gambling. Particularly large increases in arresting rate were recorded for negligent manslaughter (up 24.8 percent) and embezzlement (up 27.1 percent). For the serious crimes committed in the United States during 1963, juveniles were involved in 46 percent of the total arrests.

A larger proportion of people in the younger age groups are arrested for serious crimes than are members of older groups of the population. Approximately 25 percent of known offenses are cleared by arrests, and about 29 percent of those arrested are eventually found guilty. Thirty-five percent of juveniles arrested are referred to juvenile court and thus do not show up on regular records as guilty or not guilty after arrest. Arresting does not indicate proof of guilt, and arrest rates do not indicate extent of crime, but such statistics do provide us with suitable information to use in comparing one age, sex, or race against another.

Perhaps it is unfair to suggest that the younger age groups are so involved in crime. The data that we are citing concerns those that were suspected or caught. It is conceivable that the person exhibiting criminal behavior at a later age in life has learned how to avoid being caught. Consequently statistics and observation of penal institutions may show a bias in the direction of overemphasizing youthfulness in criminal behavior. It is also likely that older people learn to live in their environment without resorting to criminal behavior or that some younger people who have been involved in criminal behavior "go straight" as they grow older.

Perhaps the most important point concerning juvenile delinquents is the known high rate of returning to prison after once serving a term. Recidivism for all criminals as a group is reported to be approximately 60 to 70 percent, meaning that of prisoners once incarcerated, 60 to 70 percent return. When a person starts his criminal behavior early in life, he has a great chance of repeating.

Earlier studies have also indicated that recidivism is a characteristic of juvenile delinquents. In fact, most juvenile delinquency guidance programs have had little or no effect on the overall recidivism rate.

Juvenile delinquency has increased at a alarming rate in the United States. Between 1948 and 1960, the juvenile courts experienced a 100percent increase in referrals. Programs to prevent such behavior did not seem to function adequately, and studies were completed to seek early identification techniques of people who would later become juvenile delinquents. Most studies indicated that home backgrounds and personality development of delinquents and non-delinquents could be differentiated. However, very few studies showed any statistically significant results in terms of predicting juvenile delinquency. For example, Kvaraceus (1962) studied children over a period of three years and found a significant relationship between teachers ratings of behavior and later juvenile delinquency records. Unfortunately he did not report the percentages of students who later became delinquents.

Studies that show juvenile delinquency rates are increasing also indicate that delinquency rates are higher in deteriorated or blighted sections of large cities than in suburban or less blighted urban areas. It seems that juvenile delinquency, and therefore age, is related to criminal behavior, but the relationship is confounded by the cultural system or way of life of the population where these young criminals reside. A particular sub-society may place emphasis on characteristics of behavior that are different from the usually acceptable norms of society and thus foster juvenile delinquency.

On the other hand, it must be remembered that the great bulk of individuals from poorer environments do not go astray. Thus there is something besides the physical and social environment and age of individuals that encourages antisocial behavior.

Sex. The differences in rate of criminal behavior of males and females is absolutely striking. Hoover (1964) reported that the ratio of male to female arrests in the United States during 1963 was about 8 to 1. However, female arrests continued to increase during 1963 at a faster pace than did the male arrests. As might be expected, arrest rates for females were higher than for males in some classifications of criminal behavior, such as commercialized vice, but in most classifications, males far exceeded female arrest rate.

The variance in arrest rate by sex is due to several factors. First of all the physical abilities of males and females are different. Secondly, most girls lead a more restricted life. Even in environments that breed criminal behavior, parents expect the female members of the household to stay nearer home, and they allow them less leniency than males. Finally there is generally more leniency given to females than to males in terms of arrests and convictions. Thus statistics are biased toward an indication of less criminal behavior on the part of women than men.

Race. Many comments have been made by sophisticated as well as naive observers that one nationality or racial group contributes more than their proportionate share to the crime rate in the United States. Negroes have particularly been blamed for an excessively high criminal behavior. Substantial evidence to support such concepts when other factors such as environment, socioeconomic status, income, age, and so on, are controlled is nonexistent. As a matter of fact, statistics concerning crime must always be carefully considered before drawing conclusions concerning cause-and-effect relations. On the other hand, statistics do provide leads for further investigation.

In a report concerning crime rate in the United States in 1963 (Hoover, 1964), the arrests made by police in some towns and cities are recorded by race. Cities numbering 3,951, with an estimated population of 116,952,000, reported such information. This group reported a total of 4,259,463 arrests during 1963. Of these arrests, 2,943,148 involved white and the remaining nonwhite offenders. In other words, almost 70 percent of arrests for all crimes involved white offenders, whereas 30 percent involved nonwhite offenders. Since it is estimated that the nonwhite population of the United States is about 14 percent of the total, it is obvious that this group contributed to arrest rates more than should be expected. However, again we note that arrest rate can very easily be biased information. In many cities a white person may be reprimanded or ignored by the police for an act that would result in an arrest of a nonwhite. Nonwhites frequently reside in environmental situations that are more likely to result in antisocial acts and consequent arrests. The role of the nonwhite as an inferior in society such that he does not have proper security and self-respect has been emphasized by many authorities in criminology. Unstable home and family life and exposure to criminal influences result in additional criminal behavior. These factors are more likely to influence a greater proportion of nonwhites than whites.

Intelligence. For years a good many criminologists and psychologists agreed that low intelligence was a major factor contributing to crime. For example, Goddard (1920) stated, "Every investigation of the mentality of criminals, misdemeanents, delinquents, and other antisocial groups has proven beyond the possibility of contradiction that nearly all persons in these classes, and in some cases all, are of low mentality-it is no longer to be denied that the greatest single cause of delinquency and crime is low-grade mentality, much of it within the limits of feeblemindedness."

Such concepts of intelligence as related to crime have long since been outmoded. Many studies have shown that criminals incarcerated for their antisocial activity have intelligence relatively near the general population. Although the studies generally show a prison population average IQ just below the average for the population at large, it is generally conceded that some of the more intelligent criminals are probably not apprehended and that the more intelligent ones are more capable in defending themselves in courtrooms and consequently are not as likely to be convicted and imprisoned.

The author has been particularly interested in the abilities and rehabilitation problems of the inmates of one prison. This is a county prison with a population of approximately 120 men. Although the prison handles all types of criminals, the majority of the inmates are incarcerated for relatively short sentences (under four years) rather than for long terms or life sentences. The Henmon-Nelson Test of Mental Ability was administered to 31 male inmates during the first half of 1964.

These men ranged in age from 18 through 41 years. Their average education was 9½ years. Their average (mean) IQ was 91. Considering their ages and level of formal education, it seems that the average prisoner is not below the average non-prisoner in intelligence.

A previously mentioned study by Kvaraceus (1962) evaluated the relationship between intelligence and juvenile delinquency. The correlations ranged from .028 to .217 and were statistically non-significant. Kvaraceus indicated, however, a higher relationship between intelligence of boys in special classes and later juvenile delinquency. This was a negative correlation, which seemed to indicate that children with higher intelligence placed in special classes were more likely to become juvenile delinquents than were their duller classmates in the mentally retarded classes. This very likely could reflect the discomfort or conflict on the part of the borderline learners who are placed in special learning centers.

The relationship between intelligence and general criminal behavior is not very firmly established; however, type of crime and intelligence seems to be related. Persons with higher intelligence generally commit crimes requiring more mental ability. (For example, embezzlement and fraud, well-planned robberies, forgery, and counterfeiting.) On the other hand, criminals with lower intelligence are more often involved in such activities as robbery, aggravated assault, and murder. Kahn (1959) reported on a study of two groups, one composed of murderers and the other composed of burglars. Both groups had been admitted to a psychiatric hospital for evaluation of legal sanity. In almost all cases they had pleaded not guilty by reason of insanity. The mean IQ obtained from the Wechsler-Bellevue Intelligence Test for the murderers group was 94.6 and for the burglary group 103.0. The difference between these mean scores was shown to be significant, suggesting that the burglary group functions at a somewhat higher inte1lectuallevel than the murderer group.

Variations in intelligence level in relationship to criminal activity are not surprising. Many studies have shown that intelligence is related to various levels of occupation. Consequently antisocial behavior might be expected to vary according to mental ability.

Personality. The gross personality characteristics of being fairly well balanced or normal personality versus mentally ill or abnormal personality will be discussed in a separate section considering mental stability. In general, the relationship between criminality and measured emotional disorder is not very high. However, certain personality characteristics do seem to be related to criminal behavior. A review of the available literature concerning personality factors in criminal behavior (Schuessler and Cressey, 1950) indicated that personality traits are distributed in the criminal population in about the same way as in the general population.

Since 1950, studies seem to show that specific characteristics of personality are related to criminal behavior. For example, Panton (1959) reported on the use of a new series of MMPI (Minnesota Multiphasic Personality Inventory) scales to measure male prisoners. He concluded that inmates scored in the direction of inadequacy on those scales designed to measure prejudice, responsibility, dominance, dependency, and ego strength significantly more than did non-prisoners.

In another study using the MMPI, a large group of ninth grade school children were tested and followed up two and four years later. Using a delinquency rating based on records of public and private agencies, the investigators (Hathaway and Monachesi, 1957) found that 33 of the 550 items on the MMPI differentiated significantly between the delinquent and the non-delinquent group. They concluded that a rather youthful exuberance, a love of danger, and a resentment of restrictions go with later juvenile delinquency.

Freedman (1961) reported a study that indicated different personalities in three classes of criminal behavior. Dr. Freedman and his coworkers investigated three classes of deviate behavior: sexual, aggressive, and acquisitive. Sexual behavior was defined as substantially concerned with erotic or genital stimulation, aggressivity had to do with forceful and harmful action directed at another person, and acquisitivity meant the illegal acquisition of property without aggression. They admitted that there couldn't be a clean-cut differentiation in the three kinds of behavior, but they diagnosed behavior in terms of the primary symptoms or characteristics. Dr. Freedman and his coworkers found that "the acquisitive offender is sexually a free-acting poly-focal being. The acquisitive offenders adjusted easily to externally imposed variability of available objects. The interchangeability and relative personal insignificance of his sexual objects as compared to the persistence of his sexual aims is matched by the human objectless-ness of his persistently acquisitive aims."

Dr. Freedman continued, "... the acquisitive offender is much more typically a sub-cultural phenomenon, in that there is variance in the values of his entire group and those of the dominant sanctioning community."

The results of Freedman's study showed that the acquisitive offenders are more group-oriented than the sexual and aggressive offenders. The latter two groups offended against society individually, whereas the acquisitives went along with a subculture that was somewhat opposed to the dominant culture. In other words, a group of offenders, the acquisitives, might be identified by their subculture with common personality characteristics, whereas the sexual and aggressive offenders are more individualistic and do not seem to have very many common personality characteristics.

Although several studies have shown positive relationships between personality attributes and particular types of criminal behavior, or criminals versus non-criminals, some studies have questioned such findings. For example, Scodel and Minas (1960) used a "prisoner's dilemma" game with prisoners and college students. The prisoner's dilemma game requires two people to work together toward the solution of a problem. If they do not collaborate, they cannot achieve as good a solution as if they do. The results of the two groups were about the same in that almost all showed no cooperation or collaboration but instead employed definite competitive strategy. Such a study shows that there is little difference between a college group and a prison population in the ideas of cooperativeness and certainly casts some doubt upon the "honor among thieves" concept.

In summary, evidence to date indicates that the personality of the nonconformist or the criminal is not a great deal different from that of the so-called average person. A few personality characteristics, particularly impulsiveness and difficulty in 6valuating himself and others, seem to be more common among criminals than non-criminals. As additional evidence is accumulated, it seems likely that personality factors will be valuable means for differentiating potential criminals and non criminals and types of crime committed.

Mental Disorders. Earlier chapters of this book discuss mental disorders in detail. Consequently, there is no attempt here to describe the various syndromes of mental abnormalities. However, we must point out that the once generally held concept that criminal behavior is predominantly a particular psychotic condition is somewhat questionable. It is probably realistic to think of all antisocial behavior as abnormal behavior and therefore a type of mental disorder. On the other hand, a true criminal psychosis is probably difficult if not impossible to define. Less than 5 percent of all prisoners are truly insane from a technical standpoint. Thus the classification "criminally insane" represents a rare group, accounting for very little of the crime in the United States.

The idea of criminal insanity developed when the study of psychology and behavior was relatively new and considerably different from today. Psychology and law vary in their concepts concerning prediction and control of behavior. In general law cannot be expected to keep up with all the most recent evidence gathered by psychology; on the other hand, the stability of the traditional systems would be in jeopardy if there was an attempt to change rules and regulations as rapidly as scientific evidence was unearthed. Even so, there are many places where psychology and laws vary to the irritation or people in both fields. Definitions of terms is one area. Admittedly the differentiation between normal and abnormal behavior is difficult to make. In the legal system, a criminal must be mentally healthy to be subject to legal punishment, whereas an insane person is not responsible for his behavior. Psychologists and psychiatrists have repeatedly questioned the concept that a person can be mentally ill and criminally responsible at the same time. If criminal behavior (breaking of moral or ethical codes of conduct or laws of the country) is considered mentally abnormal, it seems illogical to consider such behavior to be that of a legally responsible person.

One of the first legal definitions of insanity came in 1843, when a Scot by the name of McNaghten pleaded innocent of a criminal act on the grounds of insanity. The court acquitted him on the basis of the facts available at that time and that set the precedent for the so-called McNaghten rule, which lasted into the 1950's. According to this rule, it must be clearly proven that a person committing a criminal act was so disturbed at the time of doing the act that he did not know the nature and the quality of the act he was doing, or if he did know it, that he didn't realize that it was wrong. The McNaghten rule has been amended in many of the United States to include an irresistible-impulse clause to account for the possibility of a mental illness where the intellect appears good but emotions are uncontrollable. Although there have been a variety of different rulings, particularly toward more leniency concerning proof of insanity, the principle is still not clearly stated. If anything, the problem of deciding from a legal standpoint what is and is not insanity is becoming more confusing. Many specialists are suggesting that the decision can be made by the same technique that a person is decided guilty or not guilty.

It is quite true that there is nothing to be gained by suggesting that antisocial conduct of an individual indicates an internal maladjustment and then stating that since a person is psychologically maladjusted he performs an antisocial act. On the other hand, most antisocial behavior must be recognized as a poor adjustment on the part of the individual concerned. Thus the treatment of the offender must be in terms of his personality and psychological makeup rather than just in terms of the crime committed.

An individual with certain personality characteristics that cannot be expressed easily in normal society may learn to contain his urges and behave in a manner agreeable to society, or he may go to a society where his desired behavior is acceptable. For example, homosexual behavior is generally not acceptable in society, but in some subsections of society it is acceptable. In some subsections of society stealing from the employer or taking things from a display case is thought to be "big" or an outstanding activity. The individual that modifies his behavior to fit such a subsection of society is likely to continue such behavior in societies where it is not acceptable. Individuals adjusting their personality to their society or transferring from one subsection to another have difficult changes to make. The abnormal behavior of each person must be treated according to the abnormality rather than the criminal behavior.

Motivation. All behavior of humans must be considered in the light of motivating causes. Abrahamsen (1946) emphasized this point concerning criminals when he stated that the nature of motivation in criminal behavior does not differ from motivation in any other form of behavior.

Motivation is a condition of seeking to fulfill a need or imbalanced state. All humans are subjected to many different need states at all times. A criminal is no different than any other human in this manner.

The difference between criminal behavior and non-criminal behavior is in the method of satisfying the need situation. Motivation may be just as strong in criminals as in non-criminals. Non-criminals use socially acceptable behavior to fulfill their need states. Criminals have exhibited behavior that is not acceptable to society. The basic physiological changes of the body are important in causing motivation, but learned or derived needs are often of more importance. As discussed in other chapters, most physiological needs are filled relatively easily. The learned needs for status symbols, cooperation with the group, achievement within the group, specialized foods or beverages, are more difficult to fulfill and thus are frequently of importance in criminal behavior. The person who lives in an environment that accepts behavior to fulfill needs, even. If it is antisocial, is more likely to be involved in crime than the individual living in a different segment of society. For example, a boy who grows up in an environment that accepts stealing of apples or objects of minor value is more likely to accept the concept of car stealing to go for a joy ride than is the person brought up in an environment that has consistently maintained that "borrowing" without permission is wrong. Abrahamsen (1960) insisted throughout his book that the juvenile delinquent and later the criminal is not born to be a criminal, but has the same basic motivations as the non-criminal.

All children and adults experience their external environment through their receptor organs. Information is taken within them and is perceived according to past experiences. When the normal child is faced with new situations, he uses his reasoning process to evaluate them and to come up with a solution that is acceptable according to his past experiences. The juvenile delinquent, because of his early experiences, may be unable to integrate the new experiences properly or may respond with antisocial behavior. Such antisocial behavior may n6t be perceived as such in the perpetrator's own view.

Motivations are not easily determined. They are frequently buried deeply within the individual and even the most intelligent, law-abiding citizen may at times wonder why he does a certain thing. Criminals may find themselves in the same situation, wondering why they have committed a particular act. In fact, they may honestly be unaware or not able to admit to themselves why they do unsocial acts. For example, Sadler (1947) cited a case of a youth who did not want to admit that he stole automobiles to "get even with the old man," whom he subconsciously hated.

Considering motivation for particular criminal behavior, more information is available. It is well accepted that law enforcement agencies usually seek the motivation for a particular crime so that they may unearth the person who committed the act. There is a good deal of scientific evidence and well-founded reasoning behind such activity. When the motivation for a crime is known, police can narrow down the possible suspects. For example, a man and unmarried woman were found dead in bed together. Although the man was shot only once in the chest, the woman had been shot many times and her face badly marked by repeated blows. The man's wife was an obvious suspect, because she might have strong motivation for such an act.

Although we have discussed several personal characteristics related to criminal or asocial behavior, we have not professed to cover every possible personal characteristic that might be related to crime. These factors mentioned more often relate to specific types of criminal behavior than to criminal behavior in general. Unfor-tunately, there is little substantial evidence to differentiate the criminal from the non-criminal, particularly in a predictive manner. Some progress has been made toward understanding where criminals might develop in terms of environment. These factors related to crime are discussed in this next segment of this chapter.

Environmental Factors in Crime

Socio-economic Status. It is essential to remember that although socio-economic status and criminality are generally positively related, there are far more non-criminals growing up and living in low socio-economic environments than there are criminals. Thus, although rates of criminality are generally higher in low socio-economic environments than in high socio-economic environments, there are still many, many individuals who live socially acceptable lives in rather poor environmental conditions.

Socio-economic status refers to a standing within society resulting from the father's occupation, income of the family, education of the individuals in the family, and the neighborhood in which the family resides. Many studies indicate a relationship between socio-economic status and delinquency or criminal behavior. For example, one study showed that 50 percent of boys investigated in a state training school came from the lower socioeconomic levels and only 4.1 percent from the higher levels (Nye, Short, and Olson, 1958).

Kvaraceus (1959) suggested that the lower socioeconomic background associated—with a higher delinquency rate is very possibly only an indication of the real problem. The youth living in a female-based household, where the father is usually absent or rarely involved in the support and raising of the family, encounters more difficulty in personality growth than a child developing in a better socioeconomic home. Thus the youth in the poorer home may think of his father in a negative manner. He may be cautioned, "Don't be a bum like your father," and may develop a negative connotation toward the male adult role. When trying to gain identification, such a child will turn to his street comer gang and identify there rather than with his parents; consequently, in testing his new masculinity, he may turn to forms of norm-violating behavior.

Gardner (1959) also suggested that lower socioeconomic families are frequently broken families and that the economic burden of a child to the mother without the father creates real problems. The mother may eventually identify the child with the absent husband and especially with the bad faults or characteristics that he possessed. The child responds to his mother's behavior by further norm-violating behavior.

The majority of delinquent or criminal behavior comes from the population of deteriorated sections of larger cities. These cities are generally heterogeneous in background, often with lower moral requirements and lacking the facilities and activities for youth found in more favorable neighborhoods. Youth coming from low-income families have less chance of obtaining the initiative for social and economic success. They are often deprived and feel lacking in self-esteem, so that they devise new sets of values. These values are not always acceptable to society at large and thus result in norm-violating behavior. Poor socioeconomic conditions also provide youths with examples of norm-violating behavior by the parents and other respected figures. Consequently youths set up as an idol the more successful members of their subgroup who may be successful because of their norm-violating behavior (Kvaraceus, 1959).

Whether living in the low socioeconomic conditions causes criminal behavior or whether the low socioeconomic conditions and criminal behavior have a common cause is still questionable. Many years ago, at least one author emphasized this point when reviewing available evidence concerning socioeconomic conditions (Berrien, 1944). He stated: "It may be that poor success in the economic struggle and consequent drifting to slum neighborhoods is a reflection of inadequate motivation, lack of intellectual capacity, poor occupational training, or a twisted and distorted emotional life. These same factors in various combinations could conceivably be causative agents in criminal behavior as well." He went on to state that, "It cannot rightly be concluded from this that low economic status is the necessary cause of high criminal rates." Low socioeconomic conditions seem to be related to high criminal rates, and an attempt to upgrade the poorer socioeconomic status of many citizens is at least a step in the direction of reducing known criminal activity.

It seems that the relationships between socioeconomic status and delinquency and crime rate are the reflections of the factors creating low socioeconomic status, such as family breakdown, poor living conditions, impoverished environment, poor educational development, and so on. These factors must be considered in a discussion of crime.

Home and Family Situation. Two previously cited studies concerning economic conditions are also relevant concerning the family. It is fairly well established that a higher crime rate occurs among children from broken homes than from better adjusted families. When a family disintegrates, for whatever reason, children are often deprived of some of the normal contacts that help them to develop into law-abiding adults. Thus it is entirely possible for a delinquent gang or a group of nonconforming individuals to be especially attractive to a child from a broken home. Robinson (1947) suggested that the broken family resulted in the lack of family protection and was often important in juvenile delinquency. But he also reported that as far as his study was concerned, there were a few cases of juvenile delinquents who had been overprotected during childhood.

Although broken homes seem to be important in creating an environment that is conducive to nonconforming behaviour, there are other ways in which home conditions can produce criminal behavior. First, the environment may be such, within a non-broken home, that the child is forced to seek satisfactions elsewhere. For example, the parents may be over demanding or overprotective of their children or completely irresponsible in terms of providing training that enables the child to develop normal social behavior. Smith (1955) reported that in a study in Detroit in 1953, 81 percent of the delinquents came from families in which there were no serious quarrels, and 94 percent reported they liked their homes.

The influence of the home is undoubtedly important. The broad classification of broken homes versus unbroken homes is not as crucial as the treatment a child receives in the home. A series of pioneering studies by Sheldon and Eleanor Glueck has investigated the influence upon criminal and non-criminal behavior of different methods of rearing children. After 10 years of investigation, their work has been reported in a variety of sources (Glueck and Glueck, 1950, 1959). They showed that a scale describing parent-child relations as determined by interviews with the parents is a good indicator of future delinquent or non-delinquent behavior. Lack of affection and inconsistency in discipline in the home are related to delinquency.

We emphasize that the legally broken home is not necessarily the most dangerous in terms of creating criminal behavior. An individual from a psychologically broken home, where he does not receive understanding and sympathy, is more likely to do antisocial acts than a person from a well-adjusted home environment. Unfortunateiy the measurement of psychological breaks in the family seems to be almost impossible. The previously mentioned Glueck and Glueck scale is an attempt to measure this characteristic, but it is not perfect. Thus prediction of delinquent or criminal behavior is difficult if not impossible.

Occupational Status. As with many of the other factors related to crime, occupational status seems to be related to the type of the crime more than to criminal or non-criminal behavior. It is rather obvious that crimes of certain types can be perpetrated only by individuals in particular kinds of employment. For example, professional persons most often find themselves in positions where embezzlement, forgery, or fraud or perhaps grand larceny are possible, whereas unskilled or laboring workers find themselves in a position in which embezzlement is almost impossible. However, the latter group are more likely to be involved in vagrancy, abandonment of children, nonsupport, and so on. These differences seem to reflect the differences in criminal opportunities.

In a study of delinquents in one city, Kvaraceus (1945) found a definite relationship between occupation of parents and juvenile delinquency. He found a larger proportion of fathers either working as factory operators or laborers or unemployed among the juvenile delinquents' parents than among the general male population. Correspondingly there were fewer parents in the professions, proprietorships, and clerical or craftsman jobs among the juvenile delinquents' parents than among the gainfully employed workers in general. Thus there does seem to be a relationship between employment of the parent arid criminal versus non-criminal behavior. As previously discussed, this is probably an additional factor influencing the relationship between the socioeconomic environment and crime rate.

Climate. Crime rate in various climates is fairly uniform, but there is evidence that the type of criminal activity varies according to environmental conditions of temperature and humidity. There is a relationship between the kind of crime committed and climatic conditions. The environmental conditions may be the precipitating cause of the particular kind of criminal behavior. In very cold weather, crimes against property are more important for the offender. Crimes against other persons are more likely to occur because of emotionalized conditions more easily aroused in summer months, when the necessities of life, such as food and warmth, are more readily available.

Radio, Television, Movies and the Press. Although a great many comments have been made concerning the disadvantages of television, radio, newspapers, magazines, and movies to the upbringing of American children, little evidence indicates exactly what effect these media have. It is true that attitudes as measured by questionnaires and even behavioral changes can be noted after the presentation of a film or reading of certain materials. On the other hand, who is to say what material a child or a young person should be allowed to read? Even the story of "The Three Bears" can be questioned, because it might be inferred that it teaches a child that it is proper to walk into someone else's home, eat their food or porridge, and sleep in their beds.

Even though we are cognizant of the values of learning in predicting and controlling behavior, most of us do not realize how readily opinions or attitudes of people can be changed. Staats and Staats (1957) described how a meaning response to a word, such as a person's name, could be changed solely by language experience. Presenting nonsense syllables with no apparent emotional connotations to subjects at the same time that emotionally toned words were presented showed that the word meaning could easily be attached to the nonsense syllables. Apparently all that was needed was repeated exposure to the neutral stimulus (the nonsense syllables) at the same time that the emotionally toned words were presented.

Cohen (1964) questioned the work of Staats and Staats. His experimentation essentially replicated their work, but checked on the awareness of the subjects during the learning. He found that such learning could take place, but only for the subjects who were aware that learning was taking place. Thus it seems that attitudes can be changed rather rapidly by learning procedures if a person knows that such learning is to take place. If a person wants to learn something about crime from criminal reporting, he can. Combining names of people with negatively toned words may change a person's attitude toward the names of the people involved, or it may have little or no effect.

Individual films, television programs, stories, or radio programs may have an effect upon an individual. When specific details are given about how to commit a particular crime, it is obvious that some people may use such information to commit an antisocial act.

Some reporting may actually enhance criminal activity by glorifying the criminal. Most legitimate public media now recognize the fact that criminals are often seeking publicity by their criminal acts. Thus the reporting is done in such a manner that the individual criminal is shown to poorest advantage. Even a typical Hollywood melodrama inevitably ends up showing retribution for the criminal activity, in summary, we have to repeat that it is possible to influence behavior by mass media. Who is to decide what services media should and should not provide and on what basis such decisions are to be made is highly questionable.

Drugs and Alcohol. During 1963, 41.2 percent of the total arrests in the United States were for liquor laws violations, charges of driving while intoxicated, and drunkenness charges. Many rules and regulations of society are regularly broken by users of alcohol and drugs. Most of the offenses involving alcohol are less serious charges but occur in large numbers, On the other hand, narcotic drug law violations represented only 0.7 percent of the total arrests during 1963. The most important criminal result of the use of drugs is the behavior of the drug addict brought about by his financial need to purchase the drug. Thus the small percentage of arrests for narcotic drug law violations does not indicate the seriousness of the situation. Various estimates show that 90 to 98 percent of drug addicts are involved in other criminal acts at least partially to support their habit.

The problems of drug addiction are considerably more severe and less socially acceptable than the problems of alcoholism. Thus our discussion primarily concerns drug addiction. First we must define addiction. Bowman (1958) defined addiction as "*1.* An overpowering desire or need (compulsion) to continue taking the drug and to obtain it by any means; 2. A tendency to increase the dose; *3.* A psychic and sometimes a physical dependence on the effects of the drug." The drug addict has progressed to the point where all of his resources are directed toward obtaining the drug.

Usually drug addiction in the United States is to opium and its derivatives (heroin, paregoric, and codeine). Morphine is also derived from opium and with heroin makes up the two most commonly used narcotic drugs in the United States. In addition, cocaine, derived from coca leaves, and marijuana, derived from Indian hemp, are controlled under federal narcotic legislation but are not drug-addicting in the usual sense of producing a physical dependency. The most important characteristic of marijuana and cocaine is that they introduce the user to dependence on a stronger drug for a satisfactory adjustment to life. Likewise, alcohol may also do the same thing. In addition to the drugs just mentioned, the barbituates, such as the bromides, phenobarbital, and benzidrine, can lead to addiction, but these are not ordinarily considered narcotic drugs.

Drug addiction requires repeated dosage on the part of the user. Although there are differences of opinion about how much repeated use is necessary before a person becomes a drug addict, it seems that at least two weeks of daily usage is needed. It is relatively easy to establish the habit, and a tolerance to the use of the drug is rapidly established. Thus the user soon becomes aware of certain desirable physiological reactions after using the drug, but finds that with use, additional quantities must be taken in order to produce the same effects.

The first drug experience is rather temporary and may produce nausea, like the early stage of alcoholic drinking. After the first few dosages, there is usually no nausea and a feeling of goodness or euphoria takes place with the use of the drug. The narcotic drugs are depressants and generally result in a decrease of sexual desire, drowsiness, relief of physical pain, and a general feeling of relaxation and contentment. Many young people get "hooked" into the use of drugs because of an initial trial as a result of a dare or at the suggestion of the neighborhood gang. As the pleasurable effects are experienced they tend to increase the desire to repeat the dosage. After about two weeks of regular dosage, a physical dependence is established. This means that the drug must be consistently received in the body or strong withdrawal symptoms of a physiological nature will take place.

Coleman (1964) described typical withdrawal symptoms: "The first symptoms to be noted are yawning, sneezing, sweating, and anorexia, followed by increased desire for the drug, restlessness, psychic depression and feelings of impending doom, irritability, muscular weakness, and an increased respiration rate. As time passes, these symptoms become more severe; in addition there may be chilliness alternating with vasomotor disturbances of flushing and excessive sweating (this may result in marked pilomotor activity so that the skin of the addict resembles that of a plucked turkey), vomiting, diarrhea, abdominal cramps, pains in the back and extremities, severe headache, marked tremors. The patient refuses food and water, and this, coupled with the vomiting, sweating, and diarrhea, results in dehydration and in weight losses as great as 5 to 15 pounds in a day. Occasionally there may be delirium, hallucinations, and manic activity." The withdrawal symptoms increase in intensity for about 3 or 4 days and then disappear slowly with all acute symptoms usually gone in 5 to 7 days after the last intake of the drugs. Generally restlessness and insomnia may appear with an ordinary physical weakness for 3 or 4 months after the last intake of the drug. Because these withdrawal symptoms are so extreme, a person tends to stay hooked on the habit, and as the tolerance for the drug increases, has to maintain increasingly large dosages just to stay "normal." The drug becomes an indispensable element in the body equilibrium.

The extreme physical dependence upon drugs with the terrible withdrawal symptoms force the addict to purchase a supply continually. In the early 1960's, a drug addict in the United States often needed $60 to $100 worth of drugs per day to maintain a habit. Thus the drug addict is often forced into criminal behavior to obtain enough funds to purchase his needed drug. Perhaps this is far more important in terms of criminal behavior than the actual drug addiction. Because the person addicted to the drug is so busy seeking the drugs and even engaging in illegal behavior in order to obtain financial support for his habit, he rarely has an opportunity to lead a normal life or to develop a vocation.

Why a person turns to drugs seems to be questionable at this time. Many sociologists and psychologists who have studied drug addiction have suggested that psychological problems are the cause of drug addiction. Of course, many people have psychological problems and do not turn to drug addiction. But if a person in need of help tries drugs he may easily become addicted.

Taking the drug away from the person may result in a "cure" in that the person no longer uses the drug. Whether this is really a successful breaking of a habit is quite questionable. There is a general disinterest on the part of society in trying to provide facilities for drug addiction cure and rather unfavorable prognosis for treatment. Ausubel (1958), after discussing drug addiction from a psychological, physiological, and sociological point of view, suggested that many of the researchers in the field did not understand the medical aspects. He suggested that even a 35 percent cure rate would be quite optimistic. Considering that the persons involved in drug addiction have inadequate personalities that are being supported by drugs, Ausubel suggested that it is rather amazing that there is any cure rate at all. He stated that the average relapse rate of "cured" drug addicts is so high that only about 12-15 percent of addicts who receive specialized treatment may be expected to abstain from drug addiction over long periods of time.

Winick (1961) presented a little more optimistic view of drug addict treatment when he wrote that "There are addicts who do not revert to drug use for reasons which are not known because of the lack of adequate research. Only 40 percent of the patients at the hospital at Lexington come back more than once although some have come back for as many as 20 times. Some 14 percent of the patients at Lexington account for 42 percent of the total admissions. Some patients go to Lexington to withdraw so that they can re-establish their addiction at a lower dosage." Winick suggested that most addicts who do revert to the use of drugs seem to have longer and longer periods of abstinence between-drug usage. He goes on later to suggest that, "The poor results so far obtained with treatment of addicts should not be discouraging, any more than poor results in schizophrenia or cancer research are keeping us from an extensive program of research and treatment in these fields." He felt that the real problem in drug addiction is the lack of public interest in research and understanding of the problems.

Hopes for cures of drug ad4iction are better than they ever were before. Some researchers find that more and better treatment centers are reducing addiction and that relapse rate is lowered. More public understanding of the problem and additional research and treatment facilities will improve the prognosis for a drug addict and ultimately reduce the problem of drug addiction.

Dedecting Deception

Most criminal behavior is accomplished by people who do not want to be prosecuted or punished for their activity. Therefore evidence proving nonconforming behavior is generally collected from all possible sources including the criminal himself. Whether the individual is telling the truth or not is questionable, so that modem-day criminology uses lie detectors to help estimate whether a person is telling the truth or not. Unfortunately there is no such machine as a "lie detector." There are machines and techniques that allow specialists to estimate whether a person is becoming emotionalized more to some statements than to others. These are the so-called lie detectors.

The "Lie Detector". The "lie detector" is a machine that records a variety of physiological characteristics that may change during interrogation of a person. It therefore measures physiological changes that take place within an individual with concomitant changes in his emotional state. The use of such a technique is not completely new. Centuries ago, lie-detection measures were attempted. For example, it is reported that King Solomon established the maternity of a child by noting the extreme fear of the actual mother when he threatened to sever the child's body. Torture devices, particularly during the medieval years, were used as methods of forcing true statements. (A carryover of such torture known as the "third degree" is sometimes used by law enforcement employees in an attempt to obtain confessions.)

Modern methods of detecting lies from true statements measure blood pressure, pulse rate or amplitude, electrical conductivity of the skin, and breathing rate. These factors usually vary with the emotional condition of a person emotionalized conditions might be expected to change at the same time that a person lies. Thus an estimate of lying behavior is recorded by the measurement of concomitant changes in the body when emotional state changes. It must be recognized that the same changes in emotionalized conditions may take place as the result of a variety of things other than just the lying behavior. For example, a person may generally be upset and may respond to fear of others or factors in the environment. And some individuals simply do not make the same kinds of responses to fear that are made by the average person.

Machines record the physiological 'changes of the subject. The interrogator and expert evaluate the records of the machine, statements made by the subjects, and their own observations of the subjects to decide when lies were told.

Bood Pressure and Pulse Rate Changes. Many studies have shown that systolic blood pressure changes as a result of innervations from the sympathetic nervous system. This pressure of the blood at the moment when the valves of the heart are open can readily be measured, and changes in the pressure can be automatically recorded. When changes in blood pressure are correlated with the answers obtained during interrogation, an indication of whether a subject lies or tells the truth is obtained. An assumption is made that a person when telling a lie will have a change in innervation of the sympathetic nervous system. Modern apparatus can continuously record heart beat and systolic pressure. However, such records from regular criminal interrogation are difficult to interpret. A suspect who tightens his grip, tenses his legs, or otherwise creates muscular tension can obscure or make difficult the interpretation of the records. Apparently people familiar with lie detectors can bias their responses in such a way that lying and non-lying responses cannot be differentiated.

Pulse rate varies for about the same reasons as blood pressure. Thus apparatus for the measurement of pulse rate can show changes that can be interpreted as lying.

Respiratory Responses. A pneumograph is an instrument that measures and records breathing rate. The pneumograph consists of a rubber tube, connected around the chest of the suspect, with suitable apparatus to record the inspirations and expirations. The ratio of the time of inspiration and expiration changes with innervation from the nervous system. Although this is not an infallible system for detecting lying, it is another indication. Unusually deep breathing and irregular respiration follow the telling of lies.

Psychogalvanomic Responses. The psychogalvanomic responses may be measured in two ways. One method introduces a small amount of electricity to the surface of the skin at one point and measures the amount of that electricity available at another nearby point. Variations in the conductivity of the skin can be noted and are referred to as the psychogalvanomic response. Another method is the measurement of the actual electrical activity on the surface of the skin.

Both psychogalvanomic responses are extremely sensitive and difficult to record and interpret. They represent changes in the organism accompanying changes in the sympathetic nervous system and thus may indicate lying behavior.

Brain Waves. Some minute electrical currents are generated in the brain and may be measured by suitable apparatus. Measurement of the electrical results from the brain shows two wave patterns: *(1)* a slow rhythmical current, named the Alpha Wave, and *(2)* a much faster wave, called the Beta Wave, superimposed on the Alpha Wave. The Alpha Wave tends to disappear during states of emotional agitation. Thus measurement of brain, waves is another method for estimating lying, but it also involves very sensitive apparatus and difficult interpretation of records.

In addition to previously mentioned techniques, the eye movements of a subject have been measured as estimates of lying behavior. Berrien (1942) reported that judges could differentiate guilty from non-guilty suspects by observing their eye movements during and after interrogation.

Use of "Lie Detectors". Fear, anger, embarrassment, surprise, or strong stimulation from the environment can change any of the physiological measurements just discussed. Thus extraneous factors can corrupt the records of an interrogation. Even with these difficulties, the physiological changes that take place with emotionalized conditions provide information of value in estimating lying behavior.

The value of lie detection by the use of polygraphs (lie detectors) is somewhat questionable. Very few courts allow information collected by polygraphs to be presented in court as objective evidence. In some situations, testimony by an expert witness who has read the polygraph recordings and has been present at or has conducted the interrogation of a suspect may be brought into court as evidence. There have been studies indicating that polygraphs can measure lying. One rather elaborate program carried out for the Air Force Systems Command of the United States Air Force was reported by Kubis (1962). He concluded that there is sufficient validity in the experiments that he conducted to warrant confidence in the lie-detecting procedure as an aid to interrogation processes. Although he used a simulated test situation for the experiments, Kubis reported that trained personnel examining data from the lie detector were able to attain significant accuracy in identifying the thief, the lookout, and the innocent suspect. Even so, Kubis concluded that, "the intelligent suspect is capable of controlling his reactions to such an extent that he can elude detection in the ordinary lie detection procedure, provided that he has been trained in the use of effective countermeasures." He reported that the psychogalvanic response was the most effective measurement of those recorded. He also suggested that the research did not provide sufficient evidence to encourage the development of a computer connected to the lie-detecting apparatus to provide on-the-spot decisions on guilt or innocence of a suspect.

Exactly why there is a change in galvanic skin resistance is not known. A study reported by Johnson and Corah (1963) indicated that there are racial differences in skin resistance. They found that Negro subjects had higher skin resistance than a comparable white population. They suggested that a variety of other factors besides race must be included in the growing list of variables that determine skin resistance. Such variability increases the difficulty in interpreting the results, even though lie detection generally is interested only in variability of resistance rather than actual amount of resistance.

In the lie-detecting situation, the apparatus measuring respiration, psychogalvanic response, and breathing rate is used in conjunction with a special interrogation technique. A series of questions are asked or a word association technique requiring the response of a word to each stimulus word is used. The interrogation is carried on while the recordings of physiological changes are being made. Thus variations that occur can be pinpointed to the question, answer, or word spoken at the time of the variance of the lie detector records.

New Apparatus. New equipment for fighting crime is constantly being developed. One example of a new technique of measuring illegal behavior is the Breathalyzer. This machine indicates the alcoholic content of the blood and is particularly useful in estimating drunkenness, because symptoms of intoxication are similar to those of epilepsy, heart attack, diabetes, or overdose of insulin or tranquillizers. Such a machine is only one of many new scientific discoveries being applied to the study of criminal behavior. Scientific investigation of suspected criminal behavior is increasingly important in prevention and prosecution of antisocial behavior. Additional fascinating scientific technology was discussed by Kirk (1963) as it applies to a study of criminalistics. He showed that such things as the amount of gold, cobalt, manganese, and other rare minerals in human hair can be measured and used to identify positively the origin of the hair.

Courtroom Procedures

Now that we have discussed factors in criminal behavior and problems of detecting deception, we turn to proving guilt or innocence. In many countries of the world, including the United States, a suspect is considered innocent until proven guilty. Courts provide .a location for presentation of evidence of guilt and innocence and judgment thereof. Courtrooms are generally massive structures with quiet atmospheres. Court proceedings involve a great deal of ritual. The courtrooms and ritual help create the proper atmosphere for a serious investigation of the factors involved in the suspected antisocial act.

Before we further discuss courtroom activity, we must understand some commonly used terminology. There are two general types of court cases. Criminal cases involve prosecution of a person who has broken a rule or regulation of society. The prosecution is on the side of the people and prosecutes the defendant. It is up to the prosecuting attorney to prove the defendant guilty. The defense attorney does everything possible to show his client innocent. In civil cases, a plaintiff is a person who is seeking retribution for an alleged act of another. He asks a judge or jury to decide whether he has been unjustly affected by another person, and if so, to recommend some compensation for the damages incurred. The plaintiff is represented by an attorney who tries to prove by a preponderance of evidence that the plaintiff has been damaged, and the defending attorney tries to show that this was not so. Our discussions are primarily oriented toward criminal cases, although the principles also apply to civil trials.

The purpose of the courts is to protect the liberty and freedom of citizens. Because of this, it is the duty of the prosecutor in a criminal case to prove beyond a reasonable doubt that a defendant has broken a rule or regulation of society. The prosecution must convince a jury or a judge that the defendant is guilty. As Cohen (1961) suggested: "When the defendant appears in the court room, the jurors must consider him innocent, and it is the task of the prosecutor to remove from around the shoulders of the defendant 'beyond a reasonable doubt' this mantle of innocence with which the law has clothed him. 'Presumption of innocence' and 'proof beyond a reasonable doubt' creates psychological factors which favor the defendant. However, other factors inherent in the nature of the trial favor the prosecution."

The suspected criminal and the prosecutor are usually represented by specialists (attorneys). In criminal cases the prosecutor represents the people via a local, state, or federal governmental agency. Thus the trial is the people of the Commonwealth of Pennsylvania versus John Doe; or the United States of America versus John Doe. The prosecutor always stresses this point to show that he is on the side of the people, protecting them from the defendant. The case is usually tried before a well-respected citizen who has been elected or appointed as a judge, and in some cases, a peer group called a jury. The judge has usually been selected because of his education, experience, and knowledge of the law. It is his duty to hear both sides, make a judgment on the guilt or innocence, and pass sentence on the suspect, or in the case of a jury trial, instruct the jury, hear their decision, and then pass sentence.

We will consider psychology and the use of psychological knowledge by attorneys in the courtroom as related to the jury, witnesses, testimony, and judgments of the jury.

The Jury. In criminal cases, a suspect ordinarily has the right to request a jury or a non jury trial. If he requests a jury trial, his attorney as well as the prosecuting attorney has the right to select the jurors that will be hearing the facts of the case as presented by the two opposing sides. The choosing and functioning of the jury is an area where psychology is closely involved in legal activity.

The function of a jury is to determine, from the contradictions and assertions of two parties, the truth of the contested issue. The judge can then apply the law to the conclusions reached by the jury and see that the proper sentencing and legal procedures are followed.

Trial by jury originated to supplant a system that was less efficient. In early days the feudal lords or high-placed officials had absolute control over all other citizens. With the passage of time, it became apparent that a group of fellow citizens could do a better and a fairer job of evaluating the behavior of a suspected citizen. The jurors were selected because they knew the individual and the general circumstances involved in the litigation. Such a jury system worked rather well and avoided many of the injustices of the earlier systems.

In modern days the jury system has many shortcomings. For example, modern-day juries must decide which of the facts at issue are to be given the greatest weight. A jury may be asked to decide on a civil case involving liability, or a burglary case, or a homicide. Jurors must evaluate testimonies of all kinds of people from many specialties and varying educational backgrounds. It is impossible to collect jurors who can be competent to interpret all the testimony presented to them. However, this system is in use so we will describe some of the places where psychology comes into the selection of jurors and why this selection is important.

In some jurisdictions the judge questions prospective jurors and selects them for a particular trial. In most situations the prosecuting and defense attorneys have the authority to pass on jurors and therefore select from among an available jury list. The prosecuting and defense attorneys each have the right to waive from duty any person who shows a detrimental view to the proceedings. They each also have a limited number of peremptory challenges, which they can use arbitrarily. Thus they may excuse a juror from serving on a particular jury for reason or for no reason at all, if they feel so inclined.

Selecting jurors is difficult because each of the defense and prosecuting sides may question each prospective juror. This questioning is done in an attempt to select jurors who the questioning attorney feels are going to be favorably inclined toward his position, and to prepare them for some of the problems that may arise during the trial.

Apparently there is no experimentally proven best method of selecting jurors. Prospective jurors are often excused on the basis of specific information. For example, a particular religious background or attitude toward a problem may be important during the trial, so an attorney might excuse a prospective juror because of a prejudice that would influence the case. Attorneys during the examination and selection of jurors are creating impressions on the jury that may influence the trial. Thus they have to be very careful about the way they select members to the panel. If they have to excuse a person, they must do so in a manner that will not alienate the other jurors who might tend to identify with the unwanted juror. Most attorneys also like to create a good feeling on the part of the jurors that they do select and so question them in such a manner as to provide a positive attitude at the beginning of the trial. More specific evidence is needed as to exactly what is important in selecting jurors.

Juries decide facts or make decisions on the guilt or innocence on many factors other than the specific evidence presented during the trial. Thus it is important for the attorneys to keep in mind the nationality, educational level, experiences, backgrounds, and so on, of the witnesses, the defendants, the jurors and others when selecting jurors and during the trial. Biases on the part of the jury cannot readily be changed during a trial and are very likely going to be important when the balloting of the jury takes place.

In general, the American citizen is more willing to accept the view that the evidence should be used to decide guilt or innocence than might be expected. The problem is to find jurors who can listen to evidence and decide guilt or innocence according to the facts presented. Prejudices, attitudes, and mental sets color the process of decision and are strongly ensconced in the individual. Prospective jurors do not realize that they have the biases and that the biases may affect their perceptions of the evidence presented. It is up to the attorneys to be "psychologists" when selecting jurors to serve on the panel.

The jury trial ordinarily begins with an opening statement by the prosecutor addressed to the jury. He tries to help the jury understand what is going to happen during the trial. He usually does not engage in an emotional appeal but presents a straightforward picture of the proceedings that will take place to show the jury the kind of crime charged against the defendant. There is a good deal of "psychology" in presentation techniques used, but there is little scientific evidence available as to which of various forms of presentation are best.

After the prosecuting attorney presents his opening statement, the defense attorney has the option of presenting an opening statement or waiting until later. Usually the defense attorney gives his opening statement when presenting his first witness. The "psychological" reasons for this are not well validated, but the reasoning seems logically correct.

Witnesses. In a criminal case, it is the responsibility of the prosecuting attorney to bring in all the witnesses that can present information concerning the events that occurred. When a witness is brought to the witness stand, he ordinarily is sworn in by an oath. This procedure is based on the assumption that a person is a more reliable witness when he has sworn to tell the truth. Although strong oaths including kissing the Bible, and so on, are not as prevalent as they were at one time, there is generally a good deal of emotional appeal to the courtroom situation and the oath taking. Whether or not this increases the veracity of the statements made by the witness is questionable. One study (Burtt, 1951) indicated that in a laboratory situation, subjects that ordinarily gave testimony that was 20-25 percent incorrect gave only 10 percent incorrect testimony when placed under oath. Other laboratory studies are in general agreement with these findings. Unfortunately studies cannot be conducted in the courtroom situation, so objective, practical evidence is not available. Oath taking is apparently conducive to truth telling, especially when a witness has little at stake himself.

There is not much scientific evidence indicating which order of narration of evidence is most valuable for a prosecuting attorney. It is up to the attorney to use his own "psychology" to pick the witnesses and present them in the order that he thinks most valuable to his case. Often the prosecuting attorney picks as the first one a strong witness who he thinks will be able to stand up to strong cross examination by the defense counsel. He then uses the rest of his available witnesses to present the case in what he thinks is an organized manner, generally ending with a strong witness. This procedure is based on the assumption that the testimony of the last witness will be remembered most by the jurors when they adjourn for their deliberations. The order of presenting information has been studied in a laboratory. Such a study (Weld and Roff, 1938) showed that there were shifts in the judgment of guilt or innocence as testimony was presented to a group of "jurors." They also showed that not only the degree to which the jurors were certain of the defendant's guilt varied as the evidence was presented, but different orders of presentation of evidence produced different shifts of judgment of guilty and of a final verdict of the jurors. It does seem that the order of presenting evidence is important. A later study (Weld and Danzig, 1940) showed that the opening and closing statements of the attorneys on both sides were important in the attitudes of the jurors. However, no evidence specifically indicates which material should be presented at a particular time in the sequence to bring about a particular verdict by a jury.

The defense attorney does everything he can to show that the defendant is not as bad as pictured by the prosecuting attorney. Frequently emotional aspects are emphasized rather than the factual presentations of material. There are a variety of ways in which the defense counsel attempts to develop sympathy for his client. If possible, he tries to raise a doubt in the jurors minds about the guilt of the defendant and also tries to show that the defendant is a very nice person. The defense attorney may try to show that the prosecuting attorney is being unfair or that the injured party was a bad person in the first place. Humor may be brought into play in an attempt to discredit the opposing attorney's presentation.

Although these methods are used, there is apparently little scientific evidence proving one method is better than another or that any of the techniques work.

Cross examination has been mentioned as the only condition where the witness can be tested. Cross examination is the time when an attorney can ask questions of the witness provided by the opposition. In general, it is not appropriate to ask leading questions during direct examination, so that the prosecuting attorney, when presenting his case, must only ask general questions and let the witness present the information. If there are witnesses for the defense, direct examination must be conducted in the same manner. During cross examination, leading questions, trick questions, and attempts to discredit the witness are all legitimate. Thus cross-examination techniques receive a great deal of attention in the training of lawyers. Again, no specific scientific evidence seems to be available to support a particular cross-examination technique. Gair (1961) indicated what the attorney must do during cross examination: "The lawyer must know enough to stop while he is ahead, to let well enough alone. The cross-examiner must constantly sniff the atmosphere for signs of danger. It may be a paradox, but he is at once inwardly apprehensive and outwardly confident. He never cross-examines just to hear once more some evidence, which delighted him, either on the witness's direct or on his cross-examination. He may not hear it again. Only too often the witness may rephrase his answer so as to rob it of its original effect. He may guilelessly and with the jury's sympathy explain away his answer." It is fairly apparent that there is no specific way to best cross-examine in all situations.

In the typical courtroom situation, cross examination places a stress upon the witness. The topic of stress has been discussed in some detail by Gerver (1957), who concluded: "In our court system, it would appear that stressful witness behavior results from an interaction of the personal insecurities that the witness brings to the situation and those components of the courtroom situation which function to aggravate these personal insecurities. Ceremony, legal roles and their associated social relationships, public display of private inadequacies, the apparent inflexibility of the rules of evidence seemingly designed to frustrate the witness and limit his contribution, the domination of the proceedings by the lawyers, and that shadowy figure, the judge—all may be perceived by the witness as factors which stimulate and reinforce feelings of insecurity and emotional discomfort." There seems little doubt that the average witness is uneasy in the witness chair and that the stress of the situation may add to the questionable testimony as discussed in the next sections.

Testimony. Psychology as a science has produced a good deal of information concerning the interaction of man with his external environment. Among this data is information concerning how an individual perceives stimulation, interacts with it, and responds. This data is valuable for the courtroom situation. Testimony is the giving of a report by an individual about a specialized situation or series of events that earlier occurred in his presence. Thus the processes of perception, attention, reporting, and memory are involved in testimony.

It is rather unfortunate that relatively little psychological research concerning testimony has appeared since the First World War. Just before 1917, there was a flurry of interest in the problems of the psychology of testimony. From 1918 through 1960 relatively little work concerning this application of psychology appeared in print. Thus we begin our discussion of the factors affecting the accuracy of testimony with material presented by Berrien (1952).

"It is perfectly obvious that accurate testimony in court will depend upon the accuracy with which the initial observations are made. The factors that creep in to distort the original impressions are related, on the one hand, to manifest sensory illusions and defects studied in general psychology. On the other hand, influences not generally recognized also account for some inexact observations.

Sensory Factors—Vision. The courts and the general public are for the most part aware of the common visual defects that may prevent clear observation. Nearsighted persons, when not wearing corrective lenses, cannot be expected to give unimpeachable evidence of events occurring some considerable distance from them, the degree of reliability depending upon the degree of defect. Conversely, farsighted persons have difficulty in making fine discriminations at distances within arm's length. Not often is the farsighted individual handicapped in giving testimony because of his defect, because most events contested in court take place at distances greater than arm's length.

Color blindness, occurring in about 4 percent of the male population and in only about one fourth as many women, is a condition that may distort some testimony without the witness being aware of his limitation. Some people with moderate degrees of color blindness, in which the reds and greens are distinguished imperfectly, do not discover the fact until adulthood, even though presumably the defect has been present since birth. It is relatively easy to discover even a color weakness by means of the Ishahara test, which consists of a number of cards covered with colored dots. Within the dotted field a pattern of similarly colored dots forms a numeral ordinarily perceptible. The color-blind person either does not see the numeral or does see a pattern, but different from the one normally perceived.

The effect of illumination on visual acuity and also on color vision is an important consideration in evaluating testimony. It is well known that low degrees of illumination decrease visibility, but it is not so well known that the relative brightness of colors changes as illumination decreases. The brightest colors under ordinary daylight are the yellows.

As illumination decreases at nightfall or in darkened rooms, the reds and yellows rapidly decrease in brilliance, and the greens and blues become brighter relative to other colors of the spectrum. It is therefore quite possible for a witness in all sincerity to testify apart from all other distorting influences that the accused was wearing a bluish-green jacket and a black skirt when actually the skirt was dark red. 'False' testimony on one color under low degrees of illumination is no reason for striking out testimony concerning other colors.

The problem of illumination entered into a controversy between two taxi companies. The cabs of one company were painted white and the rival cabs were orange. The taxis could readily be distinguished during the day and under ordinary street illumination at night, but in areas flooded with illumination from reddish-orange neon signs the cabs appeared to be the same color. Consequently not only must the degree of illumination be considered but also the quality of colors at night.

It is a well-known fact that we can see better in a darkened room after being in dim light for some time than we can when we step directly from a brightly lighted area. This increase in night vision takes place very rapidly in the first three or four minutes and then more slowly for the next half hour. The red end of the spectrum shows the least improvement in visibility and the violet or blue end shows the greatest improvement. This suggests that testimony concerning dim red lights at night or in darkened areas is open to more doubt than testimony concerning equally bright (in physical measurements) blue or violet lights. One could also legitimately raise questions about a person's testimony concerning what he saw when he stepped from a brightly lighted room into a darkened street.

Among the illusions that may from time to time distort testimony is the tendency to overestimate vertical and underestimate horizontal distances. Similarly an unbroken line, such as a wire or taut rope, is usually judged shorter than an equal length of rope broken by vertical lines. An empty clothes line would appear shorter than one of equal length with clothes pins on it. 'Unfilled' space (an open lot) is judged smaller than 'filled' space (the same lot with a house on it). Long, perfectly straight lines that intersect with a series of short lines all set at the same oblique angle will appear curved rather than straight.

The visual estimation of speed is often a matter of controversy in cases involving automobile accidents and elsewhere. It has been recognized both by psychologists and the courts that estimation of speed is more inaccurate when motion is directly toward or away from the observer than when it is across his line of vision. This fact is particularly noticeable if one observes an approaching train and compares its apparent speed some distance down the track with the speed as it passes by. An incomplete and unpublished study by some Colgate students, however, found that if the observers were 100 yards to one side of a straight and level road auto speeds were estimated with greater error than if stationed at the roadside. This study also supported the courts' general recognition that practice or experience in estimating speeds improves a witness's competency in giving such testimony.

Still other factors influence estimation of speed. In one study, 29 subjects were asked to judge the rate at which automobiles passed a given point. The cars differed widely, varying from a small four-cylinder car to a large deluxe model. It was clear that the judgments of the observers depended upon the noise the car made, its size: and the rate of the car just preceding (Richardson, 1916).

Distance Judgements. When dealing with small distances within reach, people generally overestimate lengths of one to three inches and underestimate distances of four to 40 inches (Brown, Knauft, and Rosenbaum, 1948). For greater distances measured in feet or hundreds of feet no comparable data are available. However, distance judgments of this magnitude depend upon a host of stimulus conditions too numerous to describe at this point. At middle distances—10 to 100 feet-judgments depend heavily upon cues that come from both eyes. The fact that the eyes are separated by about two and one half inches makes it impossible for both eyes to receive exactly the same image. These slight discrepancies in the images are still detectable by special means when viewing objects as far away as a mile. From these disparate-images we get cues that aid in estimating distance. Moreover, as objects move from in front of our nose to greater distances, both eyes turn outward, converging less and less. The convergence of the eyes controlled by the extraocular muscles also provides a source of cues for distance judgments.

Auditory Sensation. The chief difficulty with testimony involving auditory sensations lies in determining the direction from which sound comes. The ability to localize the source of sounds is very easily disturbed by echoes or large reflecting surfaces. For example, a witness was approaching a street intersection surrounding by buildings four to six stories high. As he was walking on the right sidewalk going south, some sixty yards from the intersection he heard a loud report, which appeared to come from the intersecting street to the east. Upon investigation, he found the sound source was actually on the west. The false localization was attributed to the sound being reflected from the building on the opposite side of the street from the witness. It is possible to conceive of numerous situations in which testimony may be confused by such false localization.

In the absence of reflecting and echoing surfaces, location of sound source is ordinarily reasonably accurate except for sound originating in the median plane of the body. By 'median plane' is meant any point, which is equidistant from each ear. The confusion in such cases is not in regard to its location to the right or left but rather as to whether the sound Came from in front of or behind, above, or below the observer. Gross inaccuracies of this magnitude are rare but do occur, particularly when the sound is unexpected and momentary.

The range of vibrations and frequencies an individual can hear is occasionally of importance in testimony. Generally speaking, as people increase in age they become insensitive to the higher frequencies. From time to time, also, one may meet a witness with a 'tonal island.' Such an individual is insensitive to a range of frequencies, but can hear tones that are higher and some that are lower. Ordinary speech makes use of a great variety of vibration frequencies, so that an individual might have a tonal island and be as unaware of it as most people are unaware of the blind spot in each eye. It is conceivable also that a given warning tone might produce just those frequencies to which the individual is deaf.

Background noises also mask sounds that could otherwise be heard. This effect is such that low-frequency noises even at moderately low intensities can blot out enough speech sounds to make a public speaker unintelligible in an open space without a public address system. On the other hand, some people who work in places where the noise is high in pitch and high in intensity learn to talk 'under the noise' and make themselves understood. High-pitched noise masks principa1ly the high frequencies, but low-pitched noise has a more widespread effect on the total range of sounds (Chapanis, Garner, and Morgan, 1949).

The Cutaneous Senses. The cutaneous senses include touch, pain, heat, and cold. Ordinarily these play a minor part in testimony. In passing, it may be noted that the effects of contrast and adaptation are also found in other sense impressions that are of somewhat more importance in the cutaneous senses.

Contrast refers to the apparent enhancement of differences in experiences in the same sense field that occur either in rapid succession or simultaneously. Thus a warm object may feel very hot to the hand if the individual has just previously handled something cold. Adaptation refers to the temporary decrease in sensitivity that comes about either through a gradual change in the stimulating circumstances or through a prolonged exposure to a constant stimulus. For example, one is not ordinarily aware of the pressure of his clothing except when it is first put on. The tub of water may feel hot at first, but as the skin senses become adapted, it becomes just pleasantly warm. Testimony about such experiences ought to be prefaced by statements concerning prior stimulating conditions.

Test and Smell. Occasionally testimony concerning taste is of legal importance, especially in regard to accusations of poisoning. The principal inaccuracies in this area concern confusion of taste and smell. In reality there are, of course, only four primary tastes: sweet, sour, salt, and bitter. Foods that seem to be primarily fruity or burnt or something other than sweet, sour, salty, or bitter are really smelled rather than tasted. Prior tastes may also distort gustatory observations. Hence it is important when assertions are made about given tastes to know what was eaten or drunk previously."

Expectation. It is a well-documented fact that we perceive what we expect to perceive. The student interested in a particular sports car reports that he sees several such cars around the college campus every day. When other students are questioned, they have never seen such an automobile on the campus. The person who is looking for the particular automobile "sees it." In the same manner, testimony based upon events that have been observed by humans is subjected to the difficulties of expectation on the part of the individual.

The expectation works not only in perceiving what one expects to see but also in remembering and interpreting stimulation from the external environment in terms of expectation. If we expect to see an individual performing a particular function, we are more likely to take semi-ambiguous stimuli and interpret it as evidence that the person is performing the behavior that we expected. Numerous classroom exercises have demonstrated the influence of attention and expectation on recall. Berrien (1952) reported an experiment in which a student walked into the class late and interrupted the lecture by declaring he had lost some white rats. The student walked slowly across the front of the room, turned around, and went out while carrying on a previously rehearsed conversation with the instructor concerning the loss and the search for the rats. In spite of the fact that the student-actor was well known to the class, the estimate of his weight ranged from 145 to 210 pounds (actual weight 190). Eight of the 43 students in the class said that he wore a maroon-colored sweater (he actually wore a tan double-breasted coat), and the majority declared vehemently that he searched in the corners for rats (he made only one furtive glance toward one of the corners). These reports were based on expectations, because most of the students on the campus at the time did wear maroon sweaters and the searching was expected since he had indicated he was looking for lost rats.

Studies in perception clearly show that perception is strongly influenced by past experience and expectation. When people are shown visual illusions, even though knowing they are not looking at a particular object, they identify the illusion as the object. For example, a trapezoidal-shaped piece of metal painted with various shadings of gray when rotated before American subjects appears to be a window frame oscillating. Even when the group sees the trapezoidal-shaped metal at rest and is given an explanation of the illusion, many members still perceive the object as an oscillating window.

On the other hand, when rural Zulu boys were tested with the same illusion, only 45 percent of the group saw the trapezoidal shape as an oscillating window. They had grown up in an environment of huts and enclosures that were round and did not have rectangular windows (Allport and Pettigrew, 1957). Past experience and expectation is so strong that the stimuli received by the receptor cells is always interpreted in light of this expectation.

Emotion. We again emphasize that the jury system allows for biasing of verdicts in terms of emotion rather than fact. Testimony is accepted from people who present themselves well under such stress situations. Unfortunately evidence, such as the new but well-proven scientific methods of identification as discussed by Kirk (1963), are not admissible as evidence. For example, hair samples can be individualized, positive proof of having fired a gun can be obtained, techniques of biologists show individuality of blood, but such scientific evidence can be introduced only as testimony of experts. The ability of the expert as a witness may overshadow the importance of the scientific fact he is presenting. Thus it is appropriate for all those who will ever serve as jurors to understand the problems of witnesses and to recognize the shortcomings of testimony presented by them.

The hearsay rule in testimony requires that if you do not hear, see, smell, or touch it yourself you cannot testify about it. This rule may encourage the use of witnesses who are poorly prepared to testify. Such witnesses are often emotionalized at the time of the occurrence and are likely to have confused perceptions. For example, customers in a store may have seen part of an armed robbery and might better remember the physical characteristics of a "robber" than would the victim of the robbery.

The entire problem of collecting testimony, sorting through it, and then coming to a decision needs further investigation. Fishman (1957) suggested many areas where research was needed in the psychology of testimony and concluded with some comments concerning the usefulness of any such research findings. He suggested that lawyers, judges, and jurors are reluctant to utilize and credit the findings of psychological studies. However, he stated: "Over the past half century there have been appreciable changes in the workings of our courts, and we are currently in a period of far more rapid change than is frequently appreciated. Almost all of these changes have been in agreement with the recommendations and findings of psychologists, psychiatrists, social workers, and others. Lawyers prefer to say that these changes have come about due to the common sense or the empirical experience of law practitioners and theorists. The student of sociology of knowledge knows, however, that one generation's common sense often relies quite heavily on the findings and theories of a previous generation of scientists and theorists." There is hope that the future will show more use of scientific evidence concerning testimony and other aspects of psychology applied in the courtroom.

Judgment of the Jury. Just how a jury comes to a conclusion is not known, but there have been forces at work seeking to abolish or change some aspects of the jury system. It is not in the province of this text to discuss possible reforms in the jury procedures, but it is interesting and important to know some of the obvious prejudices and biases that will influence jury decisions. It has been estimated, for example, that the jury system as practiced today is right in 99 percent of the cases, even though it is right for the wrong reason many of the times. By and large, there is a feeling among law enforcement officers and jurists that the use of juries is more reliable in criminal than in civil proceedings, but again there is little supporting scientific evidence.

After remembering that there are prejudices and shortcomings in the selection of jurors, we must also recognize many of the other problems. Generally attorneys use their challenges to select juries that will be most useful for their side of the proceedings. Whether these attempts are successful or not is questionable, but it does appear that a jury can be induced to identify with a particular lawyer's client (Belli, 1956). When juries are actually listening to testimony, there are a variety of obvious flaws in the situation. One of the most obvious is that humans do not have large enough attention spans to attend to all of the details presented during a long trial. Legal language is often filled with redundant terminology at a level that even confuses trained lawyers. Often lawyers seek to impress the jury and end up boring them. Consequently there must be periods of inattention on the part of the jury. There is no known way at this time to handle such inattention.

Recesses in trials play havoc with jurors' understanding of complicated cases. Time for eating and resting is essential, but courts sometimes recess for other reasons, including well-planned "emergencies" of the opposing attorneys. Each time that evidence is presented and a time lag is introduced before new or conflicting evidence is presented, the less-than-perfect memory plagues even the most conscientious jurors. It is unrealistic to expect jurors to keep in mind all of the facts of a case from one day to another, over several days, or even over a few hours.

Bias on the part of individual members of the jury is also a well-known problem. Many television and movie film melodramas have emphasized this topic. The biases of humans are often not recognized even by the person himself and are thus insidious but important in bringing about decisions. For example, in many sections of the United States, there are deep-seated race prejudices that exist in spite of widespread knowledge about equality of races. In some areas cases are decided not in terms of the evidence presented, but in terms of the jury's dominant prejudice in favor of one group or another.

Although evidence concerning such prejudices and influences in the actual courtroom situation is not available, there is data that indicates that people tend to value traits in others that would resemble their own traits (Fensterheim and Tresselt, 1953). Consequently a juror could be expected to side with the plaintiff or defendant who is more nearly like himself. We expect people to behave in a certain manner, and when we see them behave in a manner that is similar to the one that we feel is acceptable, we are more inclined to want to believe what they say. Jurors, witnesses, judges, and prosecuting and defending attorneys all have biases that are important in the courtroom.

Research has also shown that an individual will eventually conform to a group even when he originally thinks it is wrong, if the other members of his group persist in their belief (Asch, 1955). Thus a member of a jury will eventually agree with the other members of his jury in opposition to his original perception of facts presented as testimony. Later the same person may believe what he has agreed to rather than his original perception of the fact. Festinger (1957) has demonstrated that a person who says something he does not believe is in a state of dissonance and must reduce the uncomfortable feeling. Because he cannot change what he has said, he changes what he believes. Thus a juror may agree with others in his group even though he is sure they are wrong, and once he has agreed, will change his belief to fit his statement.

●●

4

Psychiatric Research

As with most medical specialties, all physicians can diagnose mental disorders and prescribe treatments utilizing principles of psychiatry. Psychiatrists are physicians who specialize in psychiatry and are certified in treating mental illness using the biomedical approach to mental disorders. Psychiatrists may also go through significant training to conduct psychotherapy, psychoanalysis, and/or cognitive behavioral therapy, but it is their medical training, access to medical laboratories, and ability to prescribe medication that differentiates them from other mental health professionals.

Research

Psychiatric research is, by its very nature, interdisciplinary. From a general perspective it studies and combines social, biological and psychological approaches and how those perspectives cause mental disorders. While practicing psychiatrists and other psychiatric researchers study outcomes from such a wide variety of fields, research institutions and publications exist that are dedicated to the interdisciplinary study of mental disorders within the psychiatric context. Under the supervision of institutional review boards, psychiatric researchers look at a variety of topics such as neuroimaging, genetics, and psychopharmacology, which in turn help enhance diagnostic consistency, discover new treatment methods, and classify new mental disorders. On the basis of Tinbergen's four questions a framework of reference or "periodic table" of all fields of anthropological research and humanities can be established. It helps to structure interdisciplinarity in Psychiatry, *e.g.* how Neurology, Psychiatry and Psychotherapy might be connected with other fields of anthropological research.

CLINICAL APPLICATION

Diagnostic Systems

MRI images such as these may assist in a diagnosis by a psychiatrist.

Psychiatric diagnoses take place in a wide variety of settings and are performed by many different health professionals. Therefore, the diagnostic procedure may vary greatly based upon these factors. Typically, though, a psychiatric diagnosis utilizes a differential diagnosis procedure where a mental status examination and physical examination is conducted, pathological, psychopathological and psychosocial histories obtained, neuroimages or other neurophysiological measurements are taken, and personality tests or cognitive tests may be administered. In addition psychiatrists are beginning to utilize genetics during the diagnostic process. Some endophenotypes being researched may predispose certain individuals to certain conditions.

Diagnostic Manuals

Three main diagnostic manuals used to classify mental health conditions are in use today. The ICD-10 is produced and published by the World Health Organisation, includes a section on psychiatric conditions, and is used worldwide. The Diagnostic and Statistical Manual of Mental Disorders, produced and published by the American Psychiatric Association, is primarily focused on mental health conditions and is the main classification tool in the United States. It is currently in its fourth revised edition and is also used worldwide. The Chinese Society of Psychiatry has also produced a diagnostic manual, the Chinese Classification of Mental Disorders.

The stated intention of diagnostic manuals is typically to develop replicable and clinically useful categories and criteria, to facilitate consensus and agreed upon standards, whilst being atheoretical as regards etiology. However, the categories are nevertheless based on particular psychiatric theories and data; they are broad and often specified by numerous possible combinations of symptoms, and many of the categories overlap in symptomology or typically occur together. While originally intended only as a guide for experienced clinicians trained in its use, the nomenclature is now widely used by clinicians, administrators and insurance companies in many countries.

Treatment Settings

This section may need to be rewritten entirely to comply with Wikipedia's quality standards. You can help. The discussion page may contain suggestions.

General Considerations

Individuals with mental health conditions are commonly referred to as patients but may also be called clients, consumers, or service recipients. They may come under the care of a psychiatric physician or other psychiatric practitioners by various paths, the two most common being self-referral or referral by a primary-care physician. Alternatively, a person may be referred by hospital medical staff, by court order, involuntary commitment, or, in the UK and Australia, by sectioning under a mental health law.

Whatever the circumstance of a person's referral, a psychiatrist first assesses the person's mental and physical condition. This usually involves interviewing the person and often obtaining information from other sources such as other health and social care professionals, relatives, associates, law enforcement and emergency medical personnel and psychiatric rating scales. A mental status examination is carried out, and a physical examination is usually performed to establish or exclude other illnesses, such as thyroid dysfunction or brain tumors, or identify any signs of self-harm; this examination may be done by someone other than the psychiatrist, especially if blood tests and medical imaging are performed.

Like all medications, psychiatric medications can cause adverse effects in patients and hence often involve ongoing therapeutic drug monitoring, for instance full blood counts or, for patients taking lithium salts, serum levels of lithium, renal and thyroid function. Electroconvulsive therapy (ECT) is sometimes administered for serious and disabling conditions, especially those unresponsive to medication. The efficacity and adverse effects of psychiatric drugs have been challenged.

The close relationship between those prescribing psychiatric medication and pharmaceutical companies has become increasingly controversial along with the influence which pharmaceutical companies are exerting on mental health policies.

Also controversial are forced drugging and the "lack of insight" label. According to a report published by the U.S. National Council on Disability,

Involuntary treatment is extremely rare outside the psychiatric system, allowable only in such cases as unconsciousness or the inability to communicate. People with psychiatric disabilities, on the other hand, even when they vigorously protest treatments they do not want, are routinely subjected to them anyway, on the justification that they "lack insight" or are unable to recognize their need for treatment because of their "mental illness." In practice, "lack of insight" becomes disagreement with the treating professional, and people who disagree are labeled "noncompliant" or "uncooperative with treatment."

Inpatient Treatment

Psychiatric Treatments have changed over the past several decades. In the past, psychiatric patients were often hospitalized for six months or more, with some cases involving hospitalization for many years. Today, people receiving psychiatric treatment are more likely to be seen as outpatients. If hospitalization is required, the average hospital stay is around one to two weeks, with only a small number receiving long-term hospitalization.

Psychiatric inpatients are people admitted to a hospital or clinic to receive psychiatric care. Some are admitted involuntarily, perhaps committed to a secure hospital, or in some jurisdictions to a facility within the prison system. In many countries including the USA and Canada, the criteria for involuntary admission vary with local jurisdiction. They may be as broad as having a mental health condition, or as narrow as being an immediate danger to themselves and/or others. Bed availability is often the real determinant of admission decisions to hard pressed public facilities. European Human Rights legislation restricts detention to medically-certified cases of mental disorder, and adds a right to timely judicial review of detention.

Patients may be admitted voluntarily if the treating doctor considers that safety isn't compromised by this less restrictive option. Inpatient psychiatric wards may be secure (for those thought to have a particular risk of violence or self-harm) or unlocked/open. Some wards are mixed-sex whilst same-sex wards are increasingly favored to protect women inpatients. Once in the care of a hospital, people are assessed, monitored, and often given medication and care from a multidisciplinary team, which may include physicians, psychiatric nurse practitioners, psychiatric nurses, clinical psychologists, psychotherapists, psychiatric social workers, occupational therapists and social workers. If a person receiving treatment in a psychiatric hospital is assessed as at particular risk of harming themselves or others, they may be put on constant or intermittent one-to-one supervision, and may be physically restrained or medicated. People on inpatient wards may be allowed leave for periods of time, either accompanied or on their own.

In many developed countries there has been a massive reduction in psychiatric beds since the mid 20th century, with the growth of community care. Standards of inpatient care remain a challenge in some public and private facilities, due to levels of funding, and facilities in developing countries are typically grossly inadequate for the same reason.

Outpatient Treatment

People may receive psychiatric care on an inpatient or outpatient basis. Outpatient treatment involves periodic visits to a clinician for consultation in his or her office, usually for an appointment lasting thirty to sixty minutes. These consultations normally involve the psychiatric practitioner interviewing the person to update their assessment of the person's condition, and to provide psychotherapy or review medication. The frequency with which a psychiatric practitioner sees people in treatment varies widely, from days to months, depending on the type, severity and stability of each person's condition, and depending on what the clinician and client decide would be best. Increasingly, psychiatrists are limiting their practices to psychopharmacology (prescribing medications) with less time devoted to psychotherapy or "talk" therapies, or behavior modification. The role of psychiatrists is changing in community psychiatry, with many assuming more leadership roles, coordinating and supervising teams of allied health professionals and junior doctors in delivery of health services.

1. General: The Spiritual Equipment of Man

As in the case of good health, normal spiritual equipment is also a blessing. When defects occur, a crime may be committed. The spiritual equipment of man consists of:

(a) The Natural Urges or Instincts. Man is born with a variety of urges, and they exist to ensure the preservation and survival of himself, and of his species.

These urges occur in different strength or intensity in respect of different people. Even in one person, some urge may be more acute than another, or certain combinations of strong and weak urges may be present in a person.

With most people these urges are satisfied in a natural way; *e.g.* when a person is hungry, he eats, and when he is thirsty, he drinks. Sometimes an urge may be extraordinarily strong, or a person may be unable to satisfy the urge. This may give rise to crime.

The most important urges which are found in all people are the following:

(i) *The Nutritive Urge (Hunger).* This urge determines whether you are hungry or thirsty. If it is over-developed or not satisfied, it may lead to theft.

(ii) *The Sexual Urge.* That is the urge to procreate, and have a family. Deviations may lead to rape, prostitution, homosexuality, etc.

(iii) *The Herd Instinct (Gregarious).* That is the urge to be together in groups, to be a part of a family or a nation. If a child is rejected in a family, he may become a member of a gang or a "hippy" colony, in order to satisfy this urge.

(iv) *The Activity Urge.* The human being must always be busy. This finds expression in labour and active

leisure. When he is inactive, he becomes bored and may think about something to do, which may eventually be to his detriment.

(v) ***The Self-assertion Urge.*** Everyone cherishes a feeling of appreciation for one's self and keenly wants to attain success and fame. When no one takes notice, he will try to attract attention, *e.g.* by playing truant, running away from home, stealing a car, etc.

Although we can distinguish among these basic urges they can never be separated. There is a powerful mutual interaction and that determines an individual's personality and affects his behavior to a considerable degree.

(b) Temperament. Temperament concerns the manner in which an individual's spiritual energy takes its course, and is noticeable in his conduct. It can also be called an individual's personality. Thus we find that some people are surly, while others are friendly; some welcome conversation and easily make friends, while others are reserved; some are impulsive, while others are calm. One's way of conducting oneself reveals one's temperament. Temperamental instability is often found among delinquents. Temperament is closely aligned to attitude.

(c) Feeling or Emotion. An emotion usually originates as a result of something you see, hear or think about. This feeling amy be pleasant (*e.g.* love, gladness) or unpleasant (hate, jealousy, rage). The result of this feeling is a certain action, like assault or murder. Man's life is thus affected to a large extent by his feelings or emotions, and therefore it is accorded a distinct place in the causation of anti-social behavior.

(d) The Will. Throughout one's life, one is faced with choices. One must decide, *e.g.* on a study course, a job, a life companion, etc. often one must choose between two conflicting aims, *e.g.* a student has to write a test. He has to choose between staying at home and studying or going to the theatre or swimming pool. The choice he makes will reveal what he considers the most important. If he chooses to study, and abides by his decision, he has a strong will.

Delinquents often have weak will-power. They are easily led astray by friends who persuade them to do something wrong. They protest, but cannot stick to a choice. One can, of course, also choose to do the wrong and the bad.

(e) The Mind or Intellect. Mani is distinguished from the animal by his mental faculties, or the talents of thinking, reasoning, observation, considering, meditation and planning. He is able to do this only because he has a superior mind, or intellect, which controls his acts or omissions.

People who are intellectually super-normal are sometimes apt to become bored and frustrated on the level of the common normal life, and then they sometimes apply their superior mental power to criminality. In these cases, the crime generally is well planned and the crime techniques so refined and perfected, that many are never discovered or brought to account.

However, investigation has proved that about 60% of persons who commit crimes have a reasonably low intelligence, and have failed a year of school once or more.

This type of person has difficulty in obtaining work, and to stay employed. This results in unemployment, and in order to obtain money, he commits a crime. The crime pattern is usually characterized by clumsiness without refined planning. This type of criminal is caught more easily than the more intelligent criminal.

Some people suffer from other mental abnormalities such as psychoneurosis and psychosis. Their behavior, as well as that of the psychopath, generally is characteristic of their psychic aberrations and their crimes are typical of their mental ailment.

(f) Character. Character is the moral part of the personality that regulates daily behavior. If a person has defects in their character such as aggressiveness, cunning, intolerance or brutality, he will find it difficult to rationalize between right and wrong in moments of emotional upset and will not be able to exercise self-control.

2. Self Concept

The self-concept has been identified as a very important aspect in human life: a person must be able to have respect for himself; to be "his own best friend". This is how a person sees himself. If a person believes that he is worthless, and that society does not care what happens to him, this attitude (self-perception) may well lead to crime.

3. Stress

Stress can lead to irrational conduct, even to crime. If a person labors under severe emotional distress, that person may feel compelled to act in socially unacceptable manners. Stress has become a major problem in modern life, leading to broken families and deviant behavior.

4. Aggression

Aggression and violence often go together. Aggression can be defined as any form of behavior aimed at the partial or total, literal or figurative, destruction of an object or person. The word "violence" is used to describe acts of aggression.

5. Depression

Depression can be a psychosis and also a neurosis. A psychosis is a severe mental illness in which insight was lost. Persons with psychotic depression might believe that the sins of the world are upon them, and that they are a burden to society.

In the case of a neurotic depression, insight will be retained.

A person suffering from depression may believe that life is pointless, so that he might as well "escape" to criminality.

6. Mental Aberrations

The most important mental aberrations are the psychoses, which are severe mental illnesses; notably paranoia and schizophrenia. There are also the neuroses; anxiety states, obsessional compulsive states, hysterical neuroses, dissociative states and neurotic depressions.

There are also organic psychoses; where the mental illness flows from an organic defect in the body of the patient.

It is not difficult to see that any of these conditions could lead to deviant behavior.

7. Personality Disorders

Psychopathy, addictions and deviances can be listed under personality disorders.

Once there is a disintegration of personality, deviant behavior can be expected.

Many serious crimes are committed by persons whose personalities do not conform with the norms accepted by society.

●●

5

Treatment for Offenders

"The generally professed goal of correction is to protect society by preparing men as rapidly and economically as possible to become useful, law-abiding, self-supporting, self-sufficient, independent citizens-men who obey the law because they want to and not because they are afraid not to" (Schnur, 1961). Dr. Schnur hastened to add that although the professed goals of correction are as just stated, these objectives are not being attained. Correction is handicapped by society that does not provide sufficient resources necessary to rehabilitate criminals. In general, members of society simply do not know what they want done with violators of rules and regulations. Treatment procedures are very frequently unrelated to the objective of rehabilitation. The legal processes in many segments of society, the past experience of the law enforcement agents and the prison personnel, the general attitudes of the members of society, all work together-to make it difficult if not impossible to rehabilitate criminals. Dr. Schnur (1961) concluded: "Consequently, confusion and inconsistency, lack of tested knowledge, and vacillation in implementing objectives are all factors which characterize the management of convicted law violators while they are subject to the correctional processes."

Psychological Factors in Rehabilitation. Ideally the treatment of convicted offenders should be such that they will be better qualified as law-abiding citizens after incarceration than before. This means that the eye-for-an-eye or vengeance theory concerning treatment of prisoners simply can no longer be tolerated. Historically convicted criminals have been treated on the theory that they should suffer vengeance for their wrongdoing. In addition, punishment has been provided as a deterrent for criminal behavior on the assumption that punishment of convicted criminals provides examples for others and thus prevents crime. In this book, a discussion of learning theory indicated that available evidence generally dispels the belief that punishment can increase desired behavior of an organism. Even so, many law enforcement systems use punishment, even in the form of a death sentence, as just retribution to the lawbreaker and as a deterrent for other potential lawbreakers. A high rate of recidivism persists despite the use of punishment. The techniques of punishment so frequently used have been shown to be ineffective. Isn't it time to emphasize rehabilitation, not punishment?

When to Treat Offenders. To understand the possibilities for rehabilitation we must examine the areas where society provides treatment facilities for convicted offenders. Three commonly used treatment times in the United States are during probation, incarceration, and parole.

Probation. Some men convicted of a crime are deemed safe to live in their regular community. They are generally first offenders and those who have a good record before the conviction. It is believed that living at home, under close supervision, with rather stringent requirements concerning activities, will be more advantageous to them than incarceration. In most instances, such men are placed on probation only after the court has secured a presentence investigation and when there is a good prognosis for positive correctional influences.

Although there are great variations from one legal system to another concerning the use of probation, the concept certainly has merit the probation officer assigned responsibility for the convicted offender should be well qualified and in charge of a relatively light case load. Ideally probation should be a period during which the probationer is observed closely and guided into good behavior. In such a way, a person continues as a participating member of society and the ideal of rehabilitation is attained.

Unfortunately the full possibilities of probation are not always achieved. The case loads of probation officers are often very heavy, so that guidance of probationers is minimal. Often the rules and regulations set up for probationers are so stringent and rigid that life becomes very uncomfortable for the probationer, and his attitudes toward the system become very negative. And some probation officers are not well trained in the field of human behavior. Thus the full impact of the probation system is not often realized.

Incarceration. When an individual is convicted of breaking a rule or regulation of society and is deemed unfit to remain in society on probation, he is confined in a correctional institution. The type of confinement is dependent upon a variety of factors, but is usually related to the crime committed and the age and sex of the convicted violator. All too often, factors in the background of the violator are ignored in terms of the kind of incarceration or length of confinement assigned to him by the court. Frequently only the past record of parole and previous conviction is considered. Ideally men should be incarcerated in correctional institutions that can provide a training program that will enhance the possibility of the offender's being a better citizen after his incarceration than before. Unfortunately this is not the situation in most institutions.

Entering a prison is often a traumatic event. Most prisons present massive walls that will confine the prisoner for a segment of his life. When he first enters "the walls" he is searched for concealed contraband, fingerprinted, often photographed and assigned a number, required to complete one or two forms often signing away privileges of communication without censorship, and so on. He is given institutional clothing; his own possessions are filed away. He may then be given a friendly pat on the back with a comment or two concerning his preparation for prison life. All too frequently, the preparation is only a few words by the warden or his deputy suggesting that they are here to help the prisoner, that it is not their fault that he is committed to the institution, and that he should keep his nose clean, his mouth shut, work when asked to, and that cooperation is by far the best policy.

Relatively few institutions have admission or reception centers; some have some diagnostic activity; but such programs usually require considerable time. When diagnostic activity does take place, placement in particular functions or training and rehabilitation programs within the prison takes place at a refined level. It is unfortunate that such programs are in effect in only some federal and state institutions and very rarely in county or local prisons or jails.

In most institutions a prisoner is assigned a living place, often in a cell by himself, at least during the first few days or weeks while he is being evaluated. If the prisoner is fortunate enough to be incarcerated in a correctional institution that can provide some sort of treatment, he will be assigned to a particular function. Usually some religious counseling is available, some education is provided, and a type of work activity or training program is conducted. Again these functions take place in the larger prisons and those operated at federal and state levels far more often than at county or local level.

Rehabilitation programs are usually managed by the person primarily concerned with training or rehabilitation. This often results in friction within the prison staff since the custodial staff, including the warden and his deputies, are primarily responsible for maintaining discipline and order within the institution. Sometimes the treatment or rehabilitation programs seem detrimental to the custodial staff, because extra duties and time may be required of them. Treatment personnel thus may work in an atmosphere that is not especially conducive to their function. The prisoners soon recognize the tensions between treatment and custodial personnel and are prone to show disinterest in rehabilitation programs or to be very cautious concerning such programs, because they do not want to alienate the custodial staff or their fellow prisoners.

When we recall how difficult it is to produce changes in behavior under relatively good conditions in schools and homes we can readily understand that rehabilitation in prisons is necessarily difficult if not impossible. The average penal institution is a well-established system. If a man becomes less prone to criminal behavior after his prison stay, it is frequently a result of his own doing rather than particular treatment obtained while incarcerated. In many institutions the officials and keepers are political appointees, often of questionable caliber. Many prisons provide practically no activity except some physical play each day. Thus prisoners have much time to sit and talk to others and think and read. During this time, the younger prisoners learn from the old "pros" and often devise many rather fantastic illusions of what the outside world is really like.

The author has been repeatedly amazed at the concepts of prisoners concerning what they will be able to do when they leave prison. Even those who seem to be benefiting by educational programs and are model prisoners sometimes have erroneous concepts of the "outside world." Some believe that when they leave prison with one or two high school courses completed, but no high school diploma, they will be able to get good jobs at above-average income in their community. It is difficult for them to understand that working in a normal fashion takes a good deal of effort, but provides a feeling of self-satisfaction and not just a monetary return.

In some states, particularly in New York and California, there have been some new attempts at rehabilitation in special prisons. In these prisons the emphasis is placed on rehabilitation and psychiatric treatment rather than detention. After sentencing, the patient is sent to a treatment area. He is assigned to a psychiatrist, and various therapeutic techniques are administered. As improvement is noted, he is transferred to a dormitory style section, with visiting permitted and a more "normal" environmental situation. Thus he is prepared for life in the outside world.

Techniques of treating prisoners are available. Behavioral science knows more than is presently being applied. Unfortunately many institutions pay only lip service to more modern-day concepts concerning rehabilitation. Thus it is not uncommon to hear or read about the great new rehabilitation program in a particular prison or the effectiveness of a new system of handling prisoners. Sometimes such reports are not based on evidence, and very little actual rehabilitation or training is in progress. In such situations the public at large expects that rehabilitation is being accomplished. In other places, the officials in charge are prone to discuss techniques rather than to try them in their own institutions.

For some prisoners a third technique of rehabilitation is used. This technique is parole and is somewhat similar to probation, except that the parolee has already served time in an institution.

Parole. At the time a convicted offender is sentenced, the court ordinarily has the right to order the length of the sentence within limits set by rules and regulations of the state and the crime committed. In some states, a very rigid time schedule is designated for most crimes. Thus the court must adhere to the schedule and assign a man to prison for a particular length of time. In others, the court is allowed to order prisoners to treatment for a variable period of time. In such situations a sentence may be for incarceration for a period not to exceed a maximum nor to be less than a minimum duration. For example, a sentence may be for two to four years. Under such a sentence the prisoner might be eligible for discharge at the end of two years following the specialized conditions for parole. He would be discharged at the end of the maximum sentence of four years with no strings attached.

Parole allows a prisoner to be released into society under special supervised conditions. Each parolee is assigned to a parole officer who is to see that the released violator obeys the rules and regulations of society and the special additional rules enforced upon him by the parole board. In general, the restrictions of the parolee's activity are considerably greater even than for the person on probation. He may be returned to confinement in an institution if he violates any of the parole regulations, and depending upon the state, he may be assigned to a longer sentence than previously, he may be given time off his sentence for the parole time, or he may be restricted from ever having parole again if he is reconvicted. There is no general rule concerning what might happen if a person breaks parole regulations under one jurisdiction as compared to another. However, the general idea of parole is to rehabilitate a person who has been incarcerated by getting him back into society under controlled conditions.

If we consider criminal behavior as similar to mental illness, the individual being treated in a particular specialized situation such as the prison needs special help to adjust to "outside" society. The parole process can provide such an experience. Unfortunately parole officers are frequently overburdened and cannot adequately complete their work.

In some jurisdictions the parole regulations are so strict that it is very difficult if not impossible for prisoners to serve out their parole without violations. In most society a person who has served in prison is looked down upon and not treated as a normal citizen. Consequently, although parole is a good technique, it is difficult to use adequately in typical United States society. As more members of society become enlightened concerning prisoners and the purposes of parole, and as there is increased use of indeterminate sentences providing parole as long as the parole officer feels it is needed, parole will gain more value in rehabilitation of criminal behavior.

It is rather interesting to note that some prisoners do not want to go out on parole when eligible. Particularly prisoners who have been given sentences where there is a relatively short time between the minimum and maximum sentences may rather serve the maximum in prison than to go out on parole at the end of the minimum sentence. They feel that their chances of conforming to all of the strict 'rules and regulations of parole are very slim. Thus they reason that they will be recommitted as parole violators and have even longer incarceration ahead of them. They also feel that if they serve out their complete sentence, they have "paid their debt" to society. Consequently, they may want to complete their maximum sentence so that when they are released they are, in their own view, at least as good as regular citizens or maybe a little better since they have paid society and therefore deserve something in return. Unfortunately there is usually not enough competent personnel on the prison staff to change these attitudes of prisoners.

Treatment of Drug Addicts. Specialized treatment for drug addiction has received a great deal of publicity. Although return to the use of drugs is very high, at least one author (Lindesmith, 1957) indicated that contrary to popular beliefs, most drug addicts do want to escape from the habit. He stated that he had never met a person addicted for a year or more who had not tried to kick the habit.

The techniques of getting rid of drug addiction vary, but there are two major concepts of treatment. One consists of completely eliminating the use of the drug by keeping all drugs away from the drug addict even though he may have a physiological dependency. Thus the drug addict is forced to go through withdrawal symptoms as rapidly as possible. A second concept involves the provision of a substitute for the drug or a gradual reduction in the dosage of the drug over a period of time.

Specialized hospitals or wards within hospitals are available for the treatment of drug addiction. Unfortunately the relapse rate is extremely high, and a person once addicted is practically never cured. The ex-drug addict always remembers the experience of the drug and when faced with severe problems may return to the use of the drug.

Treatment of drug addicts is receiving additional publicity and more understanding and sympathy from society at large. Naturally this will help to reduce the numbers of individuals dependent upon drugs for a "normal" feeling in life. As more and more people understand the effect of drugs, the chances of curing drug addiction will greatly improve.

Treatment of Juvenile Delinquents. In general a juvenile delinquent is treated the same as an adult criminal in that parole, probation, and incarceration are all available as techniques. However, specialized institutions and perhaps more liberal views toward behavioral nonconformities are accepted by the courts. Chances for probation are better for a juvenile than for an adult, and more attempts are being made by society to set up treatment and prevention techniques for juvenile delinquents. Admittedly this is a proper direction for reducing crime, since the juvenile delinquents of today are often the criminals of tomorrow.

Most of the treatment or rehabilitation programs for all prisoners, adult or juvenile, have been established in the state and federal institutions for prisoners with relatively long-term sentences. This has actually been a detriment to maximum crime prevention, because the younger criminal is often incarcerated for short sentences. Thus he tends to get little by way of treatment or rehabilitation. Some studies have been completed (London and Myers, 1961) in an attempt to provide information concerning adequate treatment for short-term offenders. After considerable research, the authors concluded that a treatment center for chronic offenders was considerably less promising than treatment of the relatively healthy person and for the first offender. These results bear further consideration. Perhaps clinics might be set up in local jails to provide proper treatment for first offenders and relatively healthy people before they become hardened criminals. London and Myers suggested that although most first offenders are healthy, they are in need of guidance and support in their regular environment.

Recently treatment and prevention have been combined. "Predelinquent" groups have been isolated by some researchers. Attempts have thus been made to prevent delinquent behavior by treating these "predelinquents." Kvaraceus (1959) reported that the public schools can become exceptionally valuable as agencies where personnel can spot the potential delinquent and give him a helping hand in his regular cultural milieu. Kvaraceus believes that the delinquent can be prevented somewhat by providing a good community. Such a community is primarily the school and home environment so that programs must be available in these environments. This article emphasized the importance of training techniques to provide "predelinquents" with adequate rather than antisocial adjustment techniques.

Essentially the same position is maintained by a well-known authority in the field of juvenile delinquency, Dr. E. T. Glueck. Glueck (1960) indicated that the common denominator of delinquency seems to be aggressive antisocial behavior and that the task of society is to reeducate families of children found to be vulnerable to delinquency so that the antisocial behavior would not develop into severe enough form to become criminal behavior. Unfortunately the procedures for doing this are not well established. The amount of energy and resources necessary to do such training might at first seem exorbitantly expensive, and consequently society generally is not ready to support preventive treatment.

Although it may seem obvious that treatment must be in terms of the person rather than the crime committed, society at large still doesn't accept such a concept. Most judges, reflecting popular opinion, do not suit the punishment entirely to the criminal. In fact because of the laws, judges often assign punishment according to the crime, tempered with their own "educated guess" of the criminal. Cooper (1961) cited one judge as stating that there is a very definite need to suit the punishment to the offender, not the crime. He stated, "A presentence investigation of high order ought to be a routine aspect of treatment for every first offender before the court...." Many other farsighted judges are considering the same concept and perhaps will lead the way for society to accept the idea of gearing treatment to the person rather than to the crime committed.

New Concepts of Sentencing. In some legal jurisdictions, new laws and interpretations have brought about changes in sentencing. The indeterminate-length sentence, as suggested earlier, has merit for certain areas. If the proper agencies are available, a convicted criminal can be treated until rehabilitated rather than incarcerated or paroled for a certain number of days, weeks, or months without regard to rehabilitation.

A relatively new concept involves the sentencing to a minimum and maximum sentence to be served during nonworking hours or weekends. Such a sentence of 60 to 90 days, for example, might be ordered served from 7:00 A.M. Saturday to 7:00 A.M. Monday for 30 to 45 weeks.

There are many difficulties and problems in implementing a "weekend" incarceration program. The regular routine of the prison is obviously disrupted, prisoners can communicate outside more easily than usual, more checking in and out of sentenced prisoners involves staff personnel in time consuming activity, more records are necessary, and of course there is a possibility that the sentenced man may not return for his weekend in prison. On the other hand, there are several important advantages. Primarily a home and family may be saved. If a man has a suitable job and is providing support for his family, such a sentence will allow him to continue to do so. The obvious advantage of keeping a family together is supplemented by the saving to the citizens of the community in not having to provide public relief support for a wife and children, and so on, as well as having one more member of the community continue to provide a share of the costs through his taxes. In addition the "weekend prisoner" can lead a more nearly normal life. As he becomes aware of the prison life as well as the "outside" life, he will likely learn that he does not want to spend any additional time in prison. He also will tell others of this and thus will provide a detriment to criminal behavior while still not being as completely biased as a person incarcerated for two or three months at a time. The "weekend prisoner" will also encourage some of the regular prisoners in "going straight" after finishing their sentences.

There are attempts being made to try new methods of handling criminal behavior. As additional techniques are tried and evidence is accumulated, it seems likely that some of the systems will prove to be valuable in reducing crime rate.

Applying Psychological Principles to Correction. At this point we must review some of the comments concerning treatment of criminals in light of the psychological principles of learning discussed of this book. Criminal behavior, like any other behavior, has been learned. Changing criminal behavior should be accomplished by applying the same principles useful in changing any other behavior. Rehabilitation programs, probation, parole, and all other attempts at converting undesirable behavior to more desirable behavior must involve learning.

When we recall the current high rate of recidivism, we realize that the present rehabilitation attempts must not be as adequate as desired. What are some of the characteristics that may lead to the high rate of recidivism? As expressed earlier, except for some new approaches in incarceration procedures, the typical prison provides prisoners with long periods of time with relatively little activity. A great deal of idleness is not only condoned but actually enforced. Keepers and deputies generally do not want to be bothered all the time. Thus prisoners learn to do as little as possible, for the keepers provide reinforcement for such behavior. Any activity that causes additional work for the keepers and deputies is not reinforced and becomes extinguished.

Such an analysis reflects too on the caliber of the keepers, guards, and deputies in many prisons. Unfortunately these positions are often filled for reasons other than the competence of the person to carry out a rehabilitation program for criminals. Even in prisons where a rehabilitation program is in effect, there are several difficulties in effecting behavior changes of value to prisoners. First, there is a difficult transfer problem from the learning situation in a prison to the situation in the outside world. Society is not ready to establish prisons that are similar to the environment outside of prison. (Perhaps quite legitimately so, since the deterrent effect of the possible incarceration would not be nearly as effective if prison living conditions were the same as living conditions outside of prison.) Thus the stimulus situation in prison is different than the stimulus situation in the outside world. If a prisoner learns to handle a particular type of job or interpersonal relationship with others while in a prison situation, little, if any, of the learned response can be expected to transfer to the situation outside the prison.

Second, it is extremely expensive to provide training facilities and freedom necessary for effective learning in a prison environment. For example, one keeper is usually in charge of many prisoners, and to assure their incarceration, the prisoners must be restricted in their movement and interaction with others.

Third, the length of sentences imposed upon individuals are usually set only as a result of the crime. Individual differences in the ability to 'learn from a situation are overlooked. Sentences must be more flexible so that individuals who profit from their rehabilitation or learning program may be released or brought back into normal society as rapidly as possible. It is no better to release a man after two years of incarceration if he is not rehabilitated than to keep a man two years if he has been rehabilitated properly in 18 months. Some individuals learn more rapidly than others and this fact must be considered in prison sentences.

Whether or not there is a formal rehabilitation program, the prison environment is certainly not the same as that outside. In the United States, all prisons require segregation of male and female prisoners. Consequently estimates of homosexuality in prison ranging from 30 to 85 percent of the inmates are probably not exaggerated. However, even the lower figure is considerably above the average for the outside world. It seems quite likely that the homosexual behavior is the result of the special environment, which forces release of sexual motivation in a homosexual manner. Thus the very nature of the prison environment creates undesirable behavior that is difficult to transfer to the outside.

The problem of homosexual behavior is not very adequately handled in most prisons. Most countries throughout the world do not favor conjugal visits within the prisons. Mexico is the only country making a general exception to this policy.

Conjugal visitations have generally been considered detrimental to the running of prisons for several reasons: *(1)* the visits seem to emphasize only the physical aspects of sex, *(2)* married inmates who could enjoy conjugal visits are thought to be the best-adjusted prisoners without such relations, and homosexuals and sex deviates are the ones least likely to benefit from conjugal visits, and *(3)* wives outside of prison may become pregnant and further increase the problems of the state and the prisoners.

It is somewhat surprising to find that one large facility in the United States allows conjugal visitation as part of its formal rules and regulations. The Parchman Institution of the Mississippi State Penitentiary system has developed an informal conjugal visitation program into official policy that is quite likely to endure. Hopper (1962) stated that the program apparently provides advantages to the entire prison complex. Parchman Institution is set up as a complex of small, community type camps. According to Hopper, this arrangement facilitates conjugal visits in that it affords more freedom of visitation in general. Each camp is somewhat isolated, and visitors go directly to the camp where they wish to visit. There are relatively few inmates in each camp and less than half of them are married, so relatively few wives visit anyone camp at one time. The visitation program at Parchman allows a wife to visit her husband every weekend for a short period of time. Hopper stated that the homosexuality problem is only minor at Parchman and that the conjugal visiting has the approval and praise of the staff and inmates of the institution. He concluded that, "the experience at Parchman seems to warrant the conclusion that conjugal visiting should be studied not only in comparison with, but in conjunction with, the types of marital relationships and in a variety of institutions. Parchman's experience does not prove that the objections to conjugal visiting are invalid; it suggests, however, that conjugal visiting, at least in some penal situations, cannot be ruled out as a possible adaptation."

It is also important to recognize that society may have other objections to rehabilitation programs. Many writers have suggested that society at large really enjoys having some members incarcerated. It provides the non-criminals with a method of releasing, their own feelings of inadequacy or frustration. Even ignoring these hypotheses, we know that society wants crime punished by unpleasant living. Consequently prisons cannot be set up as model societies but must continue to be environments that are less desirable than the normal outside world. Today emphasis is still not upon rehabilitation but on protecting society from the criminal and punishing the criminal for his behavior while providing an example of what might happen to someone else committing the same act.

The use of psychotherapists in prisons has been tried and given a good deal of publicity in many rather isolated situations. By and large, psychotherapy is probably a learning situation, and the principles of learning as discussed earlier. However, psychotherapy is a more advanced technique and often can accomplish a great deal with some individual criminals. The psychotherapist recognize that offenders frequently do not want to be patients; thus psychotherapy is by no means the answer to all problems. As previously stated, psychotherapeutic techniques are probably advantageous, particularly for first offenders. Such techniques may be extremely valuable for many juvenile delinquents before they get too seriously in trouble with the law.

Our discussions have concerned treatment of offenders. We must remember that the term offender refers to a person who has been convicted of a crime. As long as society accepts criminal behavior by some individuals and does not call it crime, we must expect that individuals convicted for the same type of behavior will often feel that rehabilitation programs are ridiculous.

An illustration of special rules for special segments of society was shown in a series of news and editorial articles beginning September 1963. At a private house party in Southampton, Long Island, following a debutante ball, 125 young men from wealthy homes created several thousand dollars' worth of property damage. At first, the owner of the home and the debutante's stepfather who leased the home as a dormitory for overflow guests refused to prosecute the guilty youths. The youths were released the day after the event on their promises to make good the damages. Many newspaper writers were incensed by the apparent double standards of society that allowed these youths to go without trial or proper penalty for their actions. One writer (Robb, 1963) stated: "When is a delinquent not a delinquent? When is the wanton destruction of property by a gang of young men not a crime?" Robb answered these questions—that it depends upon the individual. Even though $3,000-10,000 worth of damages were inflicted on a home by offenders over 18 years of age and the owner of the house called the police to stop the rioting, there was apparently to be no prosecution. Robb stated, "How can a judge in good conscience, sentence to jail or a correctional institution, an undereducated slum youth who has done $35 worth of damage to a house when he has the Southampton precedent before him?"

Even though the aggrieved parties would not or could not press charges against the youths, the state could prosecute, because damages exceeded $250. Thus in this particular instance, public furor forced the governing bodies to take action. A grand jury invited 27 of the youths to testify. Very few of the youths appeared for the hearing. Later hearings required some of the youths to attend.

Reviewing the follow-up news reports, the whole sequence seems ludicrous. The investigation and trial dragged on through 1964, with charges against one youth dropped at one hearing, several youths acquitted on grounds of insufficient evidence at another trial, charges against others dropped for lack of evidence, and so on. Finally, a little more than one year following the event, the Suffolk County Court dismissed the charges against the last of the youths for insufficient evidence. The case was finally closed. In essence no one was proven guilty of property destruction. Of course, the original rioting and destruction of property had occurred, but no one was legally to blame.

Rehabilitation is difficult enough at any time. Men are incarcerated for crimes that seem as innocent to them as the Southampton event seemed to the youths involved. When such incarcerated men hear how some youths are treated, they lose faith in the entire legal system. Many prisoners feel they were given a bad break in their sentencing. Rehabilitation is even more difficult than usual under such circumstances.

In the United States, as well as most of the civilized world, treatment while incarcerated depends on who you are, what educational and socioeconomic background you come from, and so on. This does not mean to imply that prisons give wealthy prisoners better breaks because they are wealthy. Certainly there are some prison officials, keepers, judges, jurors, and other humans who can be bribed. However, by and large, prison officials try to do a conscientious job.

The fact is that doing a good job often results in giving the better-educated prisoner a better situation in prison. The jobs on the prison newspaper, in the library, commissary, and so on, go to those who can best handle them. The person with little or no education gets jobs requiring little ability and learns little from the job or doesn't get a job at all.

We must also be aware that people from better socioeconomic backgrounds and with more education, wealth, and contacts know or learn how to keep from going to prison for some acts that might result in incarceration for another person. By and large, it is the duty of society to provide good rehabilitation programs for the prisoners who have come from lower socioeconomic and educational backgrounds. This emphasis must not be overlooked in designing rehabilitation programs.

Prevention

Certainly the topic of prevention of criminal behavior deserves a thorough analysis. Unfortunately only very little good experimental evidence indicating the best method of achieving crime reduction is available. Many of the techniques of treating mental illness discussed in of this book are valuable for treating criminals. We will not repeat a discussion of these points. Thus we will discuss crime prevention in light of available evidence and with an emphasis on suggesting steps toward improved techniques. We will cover two aspects: *(1)* the prevention of repetition of criminal behavior by known offenders (we will extend our previous discussions of treatment to cover some additional data concerning developments in correctional procedures), and *(2)* the prevention of the original criminal behavior (we will reexamine causes of criminal behavior).

Prevention of crime, whether it be the: stopping of criminal behavior of a previously. convicted offender or a previously law abiding person, depends on the person and society. Thus it is appropriate to consider changing the views of society.

Changing Society. Society's views toward criminals may be thought of as a prejudice. The problems of prejudices toward minority groups have been given a great deal of attention. We can draw from this material to suggest means for changing the prejudices of society toward criminals.

We considered criminal behavior as breaking rules or regulations of society. We further suggested that unintentional violations or inappropriate habitual transgressions are not normally called criminal behavior. Thus we followed Lindner's (1955) point of view that real criminals are satisfying their own internal needs or motivations. Society must gain some understanding of this type of behavior. The general public considers a criminal as an undesirable person who cannot become more desirable. In short, most members of society have a stereotype or exaggerated belief associated with the word criminal. They believe that anyone branded with the word criminal must be expected to have certain traits even though there may be contradictory evidence available.

Since stereotypes aid people in simplifying their thinking and justifying their hostilities about others, they are difficult to modify. But stereotypes do change in time, and there is reason to believe that the common stereotype of a criminal is changing. Thus there is more hope for prevention and rehabilitation programs as the members of society change their views of criminals. Particularly the concepts that criminals are "born bad" and that they are "tough," "unchangeable," and "animals" are giving way.

Social scientists have pointed out tentative laws that are of some use in changing prejudices. The application of such laws to the problem of changing society's view toward criminals opens up new possibilities for prevention of crime.

Allport (1954) suggested laws that can influence prejudice and that merit consideration in this discussion. *(1)* Pyramiding stimulation is an important principle. "While single programs—a film perhaps—show slight effects, several related programs produce effects apparently even greater than could be accounted for in terms of simple summation." *(2)* Specificity of effect is a principle of importance. What is learned in one context is not necessarily carried over to another as would be expected by generalization effect. *(3)* People who are not firmly committed to one view or another are easier swayed by mass media and other techniques. *(4)* Propaganda or other mass media information is more effective when it has no counterpropaganda. This, of course, suggests that pro-tolerance propaganda is needed not just for its positive value, but also to counter the opposite views that might be presented. *(5)* Messages of mass communication can better effect changes in people if they are geared into the person's existing security systems rather than causing a person anxiety. *(6)* The prestigeful symbol is well known as an aid in creating changes in beliefs of large numbers of people. Thus an important member of society can speak out in favor of a prison rehabilitation program and have an effect on the beliefs of other members of society.

There are many sources of information about how to change beliefs of people. Advertisers, propagandists, therapists, teachers, and many more use techniques to modify the beliefs of others. The important point is not to argue whether such changes can be accomplished, but to decide on what beliefs concerning criminals are generally in error and then try to change the erroneous beliefs. If society at large will believe that criminals can be rehabilitated, then there will be a greatly improved chance of accomplishing rehabilitation.

Assuming that steps are underway, and will be continued, to educate the public concerning criminal behavior, it becomes feasible to study possible methods of preventing crime.

Rehabilitation and Reducing Recidivism. The question of whether correctional processes in general use are a success or failure deserves comment. Certainly when a program reduces the repetition rate of known criminals it would seem that the program was more of a success than a failure. On the other hand, just because some individuals are not influenced in the desired manner by a program or process is not proof that the program is necessarily a failure. The high rate of recidivism has often been cited as an indication of the inadequacy of rehabilitation programs. This may be unjustified criticism. The 60-to-70-percent rate of recidivism often reported may well be an artifact of the data collection and reporting techniques.

Rubin (1958) suggested that a rate as high as 60 percent is impossible. He assumed that the average sentence of a prisoner incarcerated for his second or subsequent prison term is for at least four years and that each prisoner could serve several four-year terms before death. If this is so, then the number confined in the United States in state and federal prisons cannot be composed of two thirds of men who have been released previously and reincarcerated. If 60 percent of the men released each year were returned to prison for an average period of four years, the number of men confined at anyone time on their second or subsequent prison term alone would be over two and a half times the total number of prisoners released each year. Current statistics show that the number confined in state and federal prisons in the United States is less than two and one half times the number of prisoners released each year.

Simply computing the proportion of inmates in a prison who have served previous terms certainly isn't an indication of the return rate. Most prisoners serve relatively short sentences on the first offense and longer sentences after the first offense. Thus criminals serving their second or third sentence accumulate in prisons to a larger degree than do first offenders.

It is also quite possible that the data often cited simply represents information from some particular prisons. It is fairly well established that some prisons within a system have a higher proportion of two and three time losers than do other prisons in the same system. Considering the available data and the arguments by Rubin, it seems logical to assume that as many as two thirds of prisoners do not return after once being released. Glaser (1964) cited data from one study done by the United States Bureau of Prisons. After five years only 32.6 percent of the prisoners released earlier were sentenced to new terms of imprisonment or returned to prison as parole violators. He also cited data that showed only 51.2 percent of 149,617 inmates of state prisons had compiled prior criminal records.

A study of differential recidivism rates by type of offense was reported by Metuzner and Weil (1963). Two and one half years after release from Massachusetts State Prison, 56 percent of the releases were returned to prison. Half of the releases were returned on technical parole violation and half for new offenses. Of the men involved in this study 61 percent had been released on parole, 24 percent on certificate of discharge for finishing sentence, and 15 percent paroled and subsequently discharged from parole during the follow-up period.

Analysis of the returnees showed that the greatest difference in return rate was between sex offenders and all other offenders. The authors prepared a probability-of-return table for inmates classified into six categories. Return rates for prisoners in the various categories were *(1)* no prior commitments or no prior arrests—22 percent, (2) some prior commitments and either sex offenders or parole violators whose age at last commitment was more than 24-30 percent, *(3)* no prior commitments but some prior arrests—37 percent,

(4) sex offenders or prior violators with prior commitments, age 24 or less at last commitment-61 percent, *(5)* some prior commitments, offense against person, except sex, or against property or combination of both offenses, white—69 percent, *(6)* some prior commitments, offense against person, except sex, and offense against property or a combination of both offenses, other than white—86 percent.

In another study using follow-up records Minnesota State Reformatory inmates were checked five years after release. Twenty-one percent of the released inmates had received new felony convictions in the five-year follow-up period. Another 17 percent had been returned to prison for other reasons such as parole violation. Thus a total of 38 percent had returned to prison during the five-year follow-up period (Zuckerman, Barron, and Whittiar, 1953).

A well-done study by Glaser (1964) used 1,015 cases randomly drawn from the population of adult male prisoners released from federal prisons in 1956. This study found that 31 percent of the prisoners released in 1956 were reimprisoned within five years. Glaser also investigated the "failure rate." Thus everyone returned to prison or convicted of a felony type of offense was placed in the failure group. The total failure group was about 35 percent of the releases, since 4 percent of the released prisoners received non-prison sentences for felony like offenses. Of the remaining 65 percent of releases who were classified as successes, 52 percent had no further criminal record whatsoever; the others had been charged with minor offenses or had been charged but not convicted of more major offenses. Glaser concluded, "In the first two to five years after their release, only about one-third of all the men released from an entire prison system are returned to prison."

Apparently there is not as high a rate of recidivism as has been cited in the past. Perhaps the system of incarceration does decrease the criminal behavior of the once convicted offenders. We shall examine this concept in more detail in the following sections.

The Effects of Incarceration. As previously cited, incarceration is often a system for punishing criminal behavior and providing examples for potential criminals. Thus there is little reason to expect that much rehabilitation can be accomplished. On the other hand, there have been attempts in various parts of the United States to improve incarceration as a means of rehabilitating criminals. Notably work in the states of New York, California, Maryland, and Michigan has attempted new techniques and the introduction of more understanding of human behavior to the problem of modifying criminals while they are serving a prison term.

In several special facilities emphasis has been placed on rehabilitation and psychiatric treatment rather than detention and punishment. If a convicted and sentenced criminal seems able to benefit from treatment after testing and introduction into the prison setup, he may be taken to a special treatment wing for the remainder of his sentence. The treatment then is somewhat similar to that given in a mental hospital, with therapeutic techniques being administered under the supervision of a psychiatrist. As marked improvement is noted the prisoner may receive more visitors, live in the dormitory, and be placed in a more comfortable environment rather than one of reprisals and negative reinforcements.

As with prevention of first offenses, it is obvious that there are advantages in expending the greatest rehabilitative efforts on younger convicted criminals. In general they have less strongly entrenched criminal tendencies, are more amenable to changes in behavior, and have a longer life ahead of them as potentially useful citizens. There have been many attempts to improve convicted juveniles and adults. We will discuss a few of the studies concerning each group.

Rehabilitating-Juveniles. As early as 1940 legislation was passed in some states of the United States to provide special methods of treating youthful offenders. The general provisions of the legislative acts created boards, committees, or authorities to handle a juvenile after a court decided guilt. They also established reception centers with diagnostic facilities and special treatment centers. The special legislation for juvenile offenders restricted the court to the judgment of guilt or innocence; then a special authority or committee diagnosed the particular individual and tried to create a program that would best suit his needs. Scott (1961) described some of the program from Michigan when he stated the purposes of the reception-diagnostic center as follows: "*1.* To provide a thorough evaluation of the offender's personality, background, and experience, and of the nature of the problem behavior *2.* To determine which cases require institutional treatment *3.* To release other cases directly to the community on probation *4.* If an institution is indicated, to select the best one adapted to the offender's possibilities and needs, including the degree of security required *5.* To develop a range and variety of institutions and programs sufficiently flexible to provide, insofar as feasible, for the varying needs of offenders *6.* To determine the probable date of readiness to return to the community without the limitation of a minimum sentence *7.* To separate the younger, less-hardened offender from the older, more-hardened of fender. (Obviously calendar age is not the only criterion.)"

The idea of a committee or authority disposing of the guilty offender by setting his sentence has not been agreed upon by most state legislatures. But the concept has been generally accepted under a program whereby the court allows a diagnostic center to recommend a program, and then the court usually imposes the suggested program.

The traditional treatment or rehabilitation for youthful offenders is the same as for the adult offender. Essentially reformatories are by and large the same as regular prisons except for the age of the incarcerated offenders. In some newer attempts at rehabilitation programs, specialized reformatories or technical schools have been established. Such schools are minimum security facilities in which there is an attempt to group together 8 to 10 prisoners or relatively small groups with a leader. One such program is the Michigan Youth Camps.

The camp program in Michigan as described by Scott (1961) involved a group leader working with small groups of 6-8 members in a very free environment. Individuals were allowed to talk as they wished, but were led through training programs to help rehabilitate them to be members of society. The members of the groups were allowed to participate in group therapy sessions, with a good deal of counselor time available for individual consultation. Scott suggested that his personal experience with the program showed that a great many of the problems involved were of an interpersonal nature. What really went on in terms of rehabilitation was the building up of rapport between the counselor and the offender so that attitudes, concepts, and behavior could be changed. Most of the changes that took place were not direct or specified, but instead were indirectly the result of the program. For example, he noticed changes in, behavior such as offenders talking about "Mr." instead of "Hey, Teach!" when addressing an instructor.

Scott went on to describe the difficulty of establishing such programs in terms of community relations. It became apparent very early in the programs that the communities where the camps were to be located were not favorably impressed toward such an activity in their immediate environment. With knowledge gained by time and experience, camp programs were set up in such a manner as to directly involve the communities. Thus the individual communities were not just told that the program was going to be there, but members of the community were brought in to work with the personnel in the camps and slowly but surely, volunteer services, lay leaders, interested citizens, and so on, established relationships with the offenders. The camp members were brought into the communities on passes and furloughs so that they were able to more adequately adjust to a real life normal environment when it carne time for their release from custody.

Scott emphasized the great importance of the community in the role of crime prevention. He emphasized that future efforts toward lowering crime rate need to be directed toward coordinating all possible services to create proper environments, so that juvenile delinquency will decrease and so that rehabilitated prisoners will be returned to an environment that will be conducive to proper adjustments.

Shelley and Johnson (1961) reported a study of the effectiveness of the counseling service for youthful offenders in the Michigan work camps. Two matched groups of youthful offenders living in minimum security facilities were compared for changes in antisocial scores as measured by the Thematic Apperception Test. The major difference between the two camps was that one had an organized counseling program whereas the other did not, during the period of the study. The data showed a significant difference between the groups in change of antisocial scores. The tests were first administered to prisoners during their first weeks in camp. The second administration was after the prisoners had served six months in camp. The group with the organized counseling program made significantly larger reductions in antisocial scores than did the group in the camp that had no organized counseling program. Follow-up records showed that individuals with the greatest reduction in the antisocial scores had a significantly higher rate of parole success than did those showing little change. Apparently counseling in a correctional camp may have some positive values in reducing antisocial tendencies and improving chances for successful parole.

Work with juveniles has produced positive effects on recidivism. In six years of operation the Pilot Intensive Counseling Organization in California classified over 1,600 youths as amenable or non-amenable to treatment by individual counseling. Half of the youths classified as amenable were given no special counseling (control group), and the other half received individual psychotherapy. Thirty-three months after release, those who received intensive counseling averaged 2¾ months' less time back in prison than did those in the control group.

Even though there have been effective rehabilitation programs in some institutions or work camps, there is a very pessimistic view held by many social workers involved with youthful delinquents. Burks (1964) reported on a two-day workshop concerning Youth Week held in New York City. He reported that the conference in general was optimistic in referring to rehabilitation, training, and anti-delinquency programs, yet social workers repeatedly discussed "unreachables."

Burks stated, 'The unreachables' are those, usually of racial minority groups, who show no interest in reforming their ways or in any kind of training. Although there were reports of excellent rehabilitation programs, there was also the shadowy feeling expressed by some that the problem might be outgrowing present remedies.

Some of the participating social workers said that a number of existing programs failed for lack of proper emphasis and knowledge. Many 'unreachable families,' it was noted, cannot identify with, or actively resent, rehabilitation programs that they feel are based on middleclass concepts. More than once Negro social workers pointed out to their white colleagues that 'understanding' and 'respect' are frequently not enough in dealing with delinquents of the lowest rungs of the social order."

Apparently the social workers attending the conference recognized that their colleagues currently being trained are poorly prepared to handle hard-core slum problems. There are thousands of youths brought up in deprived families, clinging to a language and culture that the social workers simply cannot contact. In addition, there are many youths developing in the large population areas of the country that will not be prepared to adequately handle even simple or low-level jobs. Proper attitudes and work habits have to be instilled- in the toughest classes, but how to accomplish this is still unknown.

The major effort in rehabilitation of criminals, whether they be juveniles or adults, has been after they are convicted and sentenced for relatively major crimes. There is very little work done with rehabilitation of prisoners in county jails, local jails, or the smaller institutions. Thus it is usually the long-term prisoner convicted for a relatively serious offense that receives some rehabilitative efforts. However, this is not always the case. London and Myers (1961) told of a psychiatric clinic established for youthful offenders confined to a county jail in Connecticut. The experimental clinic was established under a grant from the United States Public Health Service to develop a treatment program, which would be effective and could be established in other jails. Significant relationships between the extent and type of psychiatric problems of youthful offenders and their social class, race, and record of recidivism were discovered. The researchers concluded that, "the clinic seems more promising to offer definitive treatment for the relatively healthy person and for the first offender. Because these are usually acute cases, they lend themselves to goal-limited therapeutic measures. Most first offenders are healthy but even those who display a mental disorder have a high incidence of stress at the time of arrest, regardless of diagnosis. This would tend to support a hypothesis that the first offenders deserve the most careful diagnostic assessment in order to find cases suitable for treatment." The researchers stated that, "The jail clinic seems less promising as a treatment center for chronic offenders, especially those with antisocial reactions because they are confined for relatively short sentences. However, careful diagnostic evaluation and planning for treatment after release may be carried out in the clinic for this group."

Apparently this one study indicated that there was hope of working with youthful offenders (age 16-25) at the county or local jail level even though the normal sentence to such jails is for short rather than long-term incarceration. Unfortunately the type of treatment to use for such youthful offenders is not well established.

Adult Rehabilitation. The effectiveness of incarceration as a means of reducing criminal behavior has been competently studied and reported by Glaser (1964). An extensive research project supported by the Ford Foundation was specifically designed to study the failure rates of different types of offenders released from prisons. The purpose was to determine the amount of reversion or non-reversion to crime and to determine insofar as possible what practical measures could be used to reduce recidivism. Glaser found from interviews with 250 successful releasees that 52 percent said that they changed from a life of crime during imprisonment. In other words, they were reformed while serving their prison sentence. How the reformation took place was then investigated in some detail by Glaser and his associates.

It was found that in terms of the total rehabilitative effect of the prison when considered in terms of successful post prison life, inmate-inmate relationships were of less importance than inmate-staff relationships. About half of the released prisoners who reported that they changed during imprisonment credited a staff member with being most influential in their reformation. The prison staff members cited most frequently as important in the reformation were the work supervisors. Chaplains, caseworkers, volunteer religious workers, and so on, were cited by only a small proportion of the total ex-prisoners who felt that they were reformed while in prison. Glaser concluded "The prison employee who has the greatest reformative influence on an offender is the one who is able to demonstrate sincere and sustained concern for and confidence in the offender's rehabilitation. The prison employee's concern is most effectively manifested by gestures of interest and acts of assistance for the offender which exceed the minimal requirements of the employee's job in the prison." Glaser thought that the minimal impact of caseworkers in the prisons was probably not of importance in the overall view of rehabilitation on prisoners. He found that grouping or isolating prisoners while in prison has an effect on rehabilitation. He suggested that "Promoting the isolation of inmates from each other fosters rehabilitation where the techniques for promoting isolation consists of: *(a)* providing physical arrangements of inmate housing which facilitate an inmate's achievement of privacy when he desires it; *(b)* separating inmates considered criminogenic influences on each other; *(c)* encouraging staff-desired patterns of inmate discrimination in choice of prisoner associates." He further indicated that promoting isolation in inmates is not always good and if the technique is employed to promote the "do your own time" ideology of the prison subculture, isolation becomes a disadvantage rather than an advantage.

Why caseworkers have apparently not been as successful with adult prisoners as with juveniles was also investigated by Glaser. He suggested that "the advancement of treatment goals requires centralization of more authority in the officials who are spokesmen for treatment interests...."

Work in prison has been thought of as a valuable asset for rehabilitation. Certainly lack of things to do in prison would be expected to decrease the probability of successful rehabilitation. Training in specific activities would seem to help a prisoner adjust better when he is released. Glaser (1964) investigated the work situation in federal prisons in some detail. He concluded that "...during about the first four months out of prison, prison work experience is used in post-release employment by only about a quarter of those releases who by then have some post-release jobs of one week or more. . . ." He further suggested "that in about one-tenth of inmate post-release jobs there are benefits from new learning acquired in prison work, in about three or four percent of these jobs there are benefits from the preservation of old skills through practice in prison, and in about five or six percent of the post-release jobs the prison provided useful physicalor psychological conditioning."

Some of the data collected by Glaser and his associates showing the comparison of failures and successes of released prisoners compared to the type of prison training or work experience and use of that training on post release jobs. There are small but significant differences between success and failure rates outside of prison for releases using prison training or experience on their first post release job. Glaser's data is presented showing that the failure rates for releases of federal prisons varies according to the type of work assignment while in prison. Obviously the unskilled or semiskilled jobs in prison are no more closely related to failure outside of prison than are the more complicated or higher level jobs in prison. Apparently there is little relationship between type of work in prison and recidivism rate, but the prison jobs with highest influence in the prison (orderly, officer's clerk, and so on) seem to be held by prisoners who have highest "failure rate" after release.

The effect of incarceration is governed not only by the factors just discussed but also by the institution's feeling about what it should do. In most prisons, treatment programs are considered secondary to the running of a smooth organization with as little upheaval and effort as possible. What limited treatment resources are available are often provided only after other institutional assignments have been completed. As indicated in earlier sections of this and the preceding chapter, there is a strong feeling among many prison personnel that the rehabilitation efforts place additional load on the custodial personnel and that it is unfair and unfortunate for them that such programs are in effect. The rehabilitative effort is frequently carried out by people of the same status as the custodial staff or is forgotten completely in many institutions.

Some evidence that the attitudes of custodial and treatment personnel differ and that it influences prisoners' attitudes was collected by Rabin and Hess (1965). They administered a questionnaire covering origins of criminality, prison politics, treatment methods, and other aspects of penal philosophy to prison personnel and inmates and compared the returned forms. Custodial and administrative personnel had no differences in attitudes as measured by their questionnaires. However, there were some differences of opinion between custodial or administrative staff *vs.* treatment personnel and marked differences between inmates and custodial or administrative personnel. There were relatively few differences between inmates and treatment personnel opinions, yet both groups differed considerably from the custodial and administrative personnel.

Even when some rehabilitative effort is carried out in the prison there is only a slim hope that this effort will have lasting effects on releases. Schnur (1961) emphasized this point of view when he asked, "Just how much can society expect from the correctional processes?" He went on to suggest that the correctional processes can often be held accountable for the lack of rehabilitation of prisoners, but that other factors are also important. He stated: "It would not be realistic to blame them for all the failures even if the correctional processes were perfectly implemented. After all, the releases from such a perfect program re-enter an imperfect society that made criminals out of them originally. These influences are still in vicious operation. Part of the price for the freedom of the strong to enjoy their vices is paid by the crimes committed by the weak. A man released who is highly resistant to crime can often be expected only to resist so much of the crime-inciting conditions. His success or failure is affected by the weakness and strengths of the social conditions into which he is released. A less resistant man released into conditions with more strengths than weaknesses may be more successful than the strongly resistant released into very weakening conditions. The fact is that success or failure of correctional clients is to be explained by both the correctional process and the experiences in the release situation.

Post-prison Environment. As has been repeatedly emphasized, the prisoner incarcerated for a criminal act serves his term because he violated a rule or regulation of society. He violated this rule or regulation because something within him interacted with his environment. One well-accepted concept concerning effective rehabilitation is to train a person to handle himself adequately in the world at large. Unfortunately most prisoners return to the same environment from which they originally entered prison. In other words, they go right back to the environment in which it was easy for them to commit a crime, but society expects them to have learned something in prison that will make them law-abiding citizens.

It seems obvious that society must attempt to change the environment as well as the individual, so that the interaction will result in acceptable behavior instead of criminal behavior.

What does the prisoner find upon release from his incarceration? Can he be expected to go to a non-prison environment and find wonderful economic opportunities and possibilities for a good life? The question, of course, must be answered almost categorically, no. Very few prisoners leave their period of incarceration to return to a rosy, economic future. Most will have more difficulty in finding positions, adequate compensation, and a decent standard of living than they had before they entered prison in the first place.

Previously we pointed out that prisoners often gain unrealistic views of the outside world while they are serving their term in prison. Often they believe that they will be able to earn a far better income and maintain a higher standard of living than can be realistically achieved. The reasons for these have been discussed earlier, but the fact remains that this is going to make things more difficult for them when they do reenter society. Glaser (1964) in his study found what kind of jobs prisoners expect upon release from prison. Table 16.4 shows the results of a survey of prisoners and releases from federal prisons. The expectations are quite unrealistic. Forty two percent of new prisoners and 54 percent of releases, four months out, expect to have professional or business positions five years after release from prison. Other studies have shown the same unrealistic view to be common in prisoners.

On the other hand, when most prisoners are released they have little resources available at the time of release and find that the post-release jobs are generally low-level, with relatively small income. Many do not find any employment. Glaser found that only one half of the releases of federal prisons work from 80 to 100 percent of the time during the second month out of prison, and that this proportion only rises to two thirds in the third month out of prison.

Releases upon leaving prison generally have low economic income capability. They have expenditure expectations that are quite high. This combination leads to an easy return to criminal behavior. A valuable type of educational program within a prison might well be directed toward helping prisoners understand their possibilities in the "outside world" and helping them to achieve more realistic expectations of the future.

Successfulness of obtaining and staying on a post-release job is directly related to successfulness in staying out of prison. The type of post-release employment obtained is most often not just the result of a prison record, but rather a lack of extensive or skilled work experience or ability. Thus it is imperative while in prison to get some training of value immediately after release or to gain experience as soon after release as possible.

Glaser (1964) also studied the social world of the ex-prisoner and indicated that: "Over 90% of the men released from prison returned to communities in which they previously resided. This means that they generally returned to an area where their criminal reputation is known, that it also generally means that they returned ,to the area where they can receive assistance from kin." Glaser showed, somewhat contrary to general expectations concerning environmental influences on criminal behavior, that there is a higher than average post-release failure rate for ex-prisoners who go to a community other than their preincarceration residence. He does show, however, that the most unfavorable post-release environment is one in which the ex-prisoner lives alone.

There is no doubt that post-prison environment has an influence upon the release. Remedies for post-release problems must include action in the communities as well as work with the release both before and after release. Glaser suggested some remedies for post release problems as follows:

(1) Major advances in the contribution of prisons to the solution of inmate post-release problems, with a relatively small percentage increase in total prison costs, could be achieved merely by systematic extension of programs already successfully initiated. Notable among these expandable programs are:

(a) compulsory inmate savings of some prison earnings to meet-post-release expenses, supplemented by gratuities or loans where necessary;

(b) facilitation of inmate communication with law-abiding outside persons, through reduction of censorship of correspondence and of impediments to visiting;

(c) graduation of the disbursement of such funds, through parole supervision offices;

(d) communication of parole supervision staff with inmates prior to the inmate's release (in correspondence, in prerelease classes, and in initial parole interviews at the prisons);

(e) involvement of outside organizations in inmate organizations, and vice versa, through service and hobby clubs, personal development and mutual therapy groups, churches, and other types of voluntary organizations;

(f) operation of loan funds as flexible financial aid effective for some releases, administered through parole supervision agencies in a manner based on the experience of the states that have operated these funds for decades.

(2) Routinization of these programs, so they will be more consistently operated and developed, requires their administration by persons who continually receive feedback indicating the consequences of these programs; this means that their operation at the prisons should be, at least in part, a regular responsibility of parole supervision staff.

(3) Selective employment of parolees and of prison discharges by government agencies, and augmen-

tation of their eligibility for unemployment insurance, can reduce the net social and economic costs to the public from recidivism and reimprisonment.

(4) This half-century's most promising correctional development for alleviating post-release problems of prisoners consists of the counseling centers in metropolitan areas to which prisoners scheduled for release are transferred some months before their release date, and from which they regularly go forth to enter the job market and to develop correctionally acceptable post-prison social relationships, before they are released on a regular parole or on any other traditional types of release from prison.

Residential centers for the community guidance and graduated release of convicted persons are a logical extension of a changing conception of the state's responsibility in dealing with felons. This is a change from the classic objective of completely depriving a man of his freedom for a period which ends abruptly when he has "paid for his crime," to the objective of both removing and restoring freedom on a gradual basis in a manner which will most facilitate the felon's achievement of a non-criminal life. Parole and probation were earlier steps in this direction, but they were handicapped through the inability of staff to be in contact with their clients' lives in the free community as much as occurs with the new types of institution. However, we have found that parole and probation vary tremendously in these and other respects, both in actual administration and in the standards that officials seek to attain.

Preventing New Crime. Although it has been pointed out in this and the preceding chapter of this book that the prevention of new crime is difficult if not impossible there is some hope that preventive techniques can lessen crime rate. We concluded that, by and large, individual characteristics were not related to criminal versus non-criminal behavior but were related to specific types of criminal behavior. There was considerably more evidence available to indicate that environmental factors are related to criminal versus non-criminal behavior. Thus in the following discussions we will consider characteristics of the environment which might be controlled to lower the amount of criminal behavior.

Preventing new crime may be approached from two directions. *(1)* The global approach is concerned with improving the entire social milieu and environmental conditions. *(2)* The individual approach attempts to isolate potential criminals before they become criminals. We will discuss characteristics of the environment under the above two mentioned categories as well as the feasibility of selecting predelinquents.

Global Approach. In the earlier parts of this chapter and we reviewed many characteristics of the environment that seemed to be related to criminal versus non-criminal behavior. It appears that more criminals are developed in certain environments than in others. However, we must constantly bear in mind that even in the delinquency or criminally prone environments only a very small proportion of the total population resort to criminal activity.

In the early 1920's several investigators found that a tendency for crime and delinquency was unevenly distributed throughout the various geographic areas they studied. Extensive research in Chicago showed that certain areas produced a larger number of criminal cast than did other areas of the city. This led to the conclusion that social environment had something to do with the development of delinquency and criminal behavior. This thinking has been expanded into the concept of a "delinquent subculture." The concept of a subculture related to deviant behavior leads to consideration of a global approach as a means of lowering overall crime rate. However, there are people who challenge the general theory. Many experts suggest that delinquency rates vary because of the treatment by police and the courts and that the environment doesn't create the situation as much as the individuals who might be involved in criminal behavior gravitate to a particular environment. It is also conceivable that many delinquent or criminal activities will go unnoted from some subcultures of society, whereas the same activities will be recorded in police records if they take place in other societies. Of course, the more serious offenses are generally reported regardless of the subcultures in which they take place.

Forman (1963) was concerned with the problem of whether a general subsection of society may be largely involved in criminal behavior. If so, he wondered how such an environment could affect some of its members but not all. Forman suggested that it is possible that there simply aren't enough people from one subculture in a particular neighborhood to make a global approach to crime prevention reasonable. Some experts have previously suggested that only 10 to 15 percent of a culture might be involved in crime. Forman obtained data to show that in some high-rate-delinquency areas more than 33 percent of all the boys in the area within the age range which might logically be considered juveniles, were delinquent. In other words, the high rate areas may contain a subculture making up one third of the total population.

If we can assume that there is some retardation of delinquents in schools, Forman showed that in a room of 30 students of a high-delinquency-rate area, about six of the students would be delinquents. If these six delinquents were evenly distributed throughout the room, every student in the room would be within arm reach of a delinquent. Forman thus concluded that within this context the delinquent subculture theory seems quite tenable. He stated, "A concentration of this magnitude of delinquents would seem to provide a sufficient number of individuals in close contact with each other to maintain and pass on the attitudes, knowledge, skills, etc., making up a delinquent sub-culture and a large enough group so that it could offer substantial rewards to those who conformed to it and punish those who did not."

The concept of a global approach has been popular for many years. Dudycha (1957) expressed generally accepted views that social factors are important in the development of criminal behavior. Particular areas of the country such as transition areas on the fringes of commercial and industrial sections of the cities are conducive areas for the development of delinquency. He suggested that displacement of residential areas by commerce or by population movements are important. Even so, Dudycha emphasized that there is no real prevention program that can work by handling an entire area or environment because such an approach must by necessity include so many non-delinquents that it becomes unwieldy as a program. He suggested the best technique seems to be a psychological approach where particular individual problems are studied and courses of action are tailored to an individual's needs.

Even though it is difficult to consider treating an entire environment following the global approach, there have been attempts to do so. How successful these programs have been was reviewed by Witmer and Tufts (1954). They concluded that the effectiveness of most environmental measures directed specifically to reduction of delinquency had not been adequately determined. For example, curfew laws, laws forbidding the sale of liquor to minors, particular plans of school curricular or changes of school environment, have been tried but good studies of the effectiveness of these were not known to the authors. Witmer and Tufts concluded that there was no definite evidence of the value of local self-help enterprises in the high-delinquency-rate areas. Although many people working on such projects feel that there was a definite decline in delinquency rates as the lower socioeconomic or slum areas were improved, objective data to support such feelings was not reported.

Witmer and Tufts also evaluated the increased use of recreational programs in delinquent areas. By and large, there was a reduction in delinquency rate, but such a reduction might have been the result of a selection process. The children who obtained supervised recreation might have been less prone to delinquency anyhow. In summary, we must conclude that theoretically the global approach has some merit. However, most data concerning the success of delinquency prevention programs does not favor the global approach.

Individual Approach. The available objective evidence concerning prevention of crime indicates that the best procedure is identification of the potential delinquent or criminal followed by intensive care or treatment. We discussed some aspects of identifying criminals. We considered modifying behavior and some of the problems of mental health. We will not repeat these points at this time, but we will consider some of the recent information concerning diagnosis or prognosis of delinquents' or criminals' behavior.

Two researchers, Sheldon and Eleanor Glueck, are well known for their work in predicting delinquent behavior. After intensive study of many delinquents and non-delinquents, the Gluecks developed a table for predicting delinquency. We will consider this prediction technique in some detail.

Before considering prediction techniques or the use of interviews or scales, it is important to heed a point brought out by Kvaraceus (1959a). One of the best, if not the best, single indicator of possible future delinquency is past behavior. Kvaraceus pointed out that in the United States it usually takes at least five or six delinquent acts before the community begins to take a delinquent seriously. He stated: "Few youngsters turn delinquent overnight. Most of them take about ten years to develop into a full-fledged delinquent. During this incubation period, they give off many signs and signals of their future difficulties—if we would only catch the cue or take the hint." Many cases of delinquent behavior are not disposed of officially by petition or formal hearings in the courts. If these cases are watched more carefully in the future, there is a good possibility that pre-delinquents may be kept from becoming delinquents or criminals.

The Glueck Social Prediction Table. The Gluecks studied many juveniles and found that five social factors reflecting parent-child relationships differentiated the true juvenile delinquents from the non-delinquents with whom the delinquents had been matched case by case for age, ethnic derivation, general intelligence, and residence in underprivileged urban areas. The five factors that differentiated delinquents from non-delinquents were *(1)* discipline of boy by father, *(2)* supervision of boy by mother, *(3)* affection of father for boy, *(4)* affection of mother for boy, and *(5)* family cohesiveness. Other factors were investigated, but these five worked best in discriminating true juvenile delinquents from non-juvenile delinquents before entering school. These factors were used for a prediction table, although they were selected by studying juveniles who were known to be delinquents or non-delinquents. This method of estimating validity of the scale may not provide predictive validity. However, the scale did have concurrent validity.

Eleanor Glueck (1962) recognized that the five factor prediction table was constructed retrospectively on one group of persistent juvenile offenders and their matched non-offenders. She had hoped that it would predict delinquency of young children before overt symptoms of delinquent like behavior were shown. Dr. Glueck hoped that the scale could be improved and sharpened to identify delinquents before the onset of evidences of delinquent like behavior. She suggested that three factors, supervision of boy by mother, discipline of boy by mother, and rearing by affectionless parent substitutes could be used instead of the original five-factor table. She reported an analysis of data with these three factors showing that a fair or suitable supervision of boy by mother resulted in a delinquency score of 29.7; unsuitable supervision of boy by mother, a delinquency score of 83.2. On the factor of discipline of boy by mother, firm but kindly, gave a delinquency score of 6.1; lax, overstrict, or erratic, a delinquency score of 73.7. Children reared by a parent substitute had a delinquency score of 79.3; those reared by parents, a score of 38.0. Dr. Glueck concluded that the Social Prediction Table was valuable and had concurrent validity. She also recognized that other factors related to personality make-up and primary associations must be investigated. She suggested that additional data was being gathered by others concerning this topic.

Prigmore (1963) reported a study concerning the Social Prediction Table. Using different judges or raters, he obtained various ratings of the same individuals to the extent that he questioned the reliability of the scale. Prigmore used southern-educated Negroes, northern-educated Negroes, southern-educated white and northern educated-white social workers to rate 60 cases. The education and experience for an raters were somewhat the same, because they were all social workers. Prigmore concluded that the Glueck scale might have to be restricted to a particular reference group, or else a clear-cut system of categories must be established. He said, "The Glueck scale cannot be used by raters from different cultural backgrounds if reliable ratings are to be obtained." Prigmore further investigated the reliability of the Glueck factors themselves and thought that they were open to question. He said: "The Glueck factors are complex, highly inferential variables for which adequate external criteria are only partially available. It is to be noted from the findings that corporal punishment by father or lack of it is such a clear-cut external criterion for parental discipline that the factor showed less variability. But the other factors, particularly the extremely complex factors on affection, lack such clear-cut criterion." He went on to explain that a predictive instrument that is unreliable cannot be valid. Therefore, because of the lack of reliability, the validity of the Glueck scale for prediction of delinquency is dubious. (Prigmore's work was carried out before the previously mentioned article by Eleanor Glueck had been reported. In effect, Eleanor Glueck had conceded the lack of reliability of ratings on some of the factors and had suggested the three new factors mentioned in the preceding paragraphs.)

Eleanor Glueck (1963) reported a further analysis of the Glueck Social Prediction Table to allow for the problem of raters having difficulty with some of the original five factors. In many homes, discipline of the boy by the father is not very likely because the father is not a part of the family. She showed that a second three-factor table consisting of *(1)* supervision of boy by the mother, *(2)* discipline of boy by mother, and *(3)* rearing by parent substitute, was a valuable means of estimating pre-delinquents. Further, she indicated that by dropping the rearing-by-parent-substitutes factor and substituting a family-cohesiveness factor, the identification of delinquents was improved. Dr. Glueck defined cohesiveness of a family as a "we" feeling among members of the immediate family as evident by group interests, and so on.

At this writing complete data on the use of the Glueck Table as a predictor of delinquency has not become available. The New York City Youth Board and the Commissioners Youth Council of Washington, D.C. are making experimental use of the new three-factor prediction table. Dr. Glueck indicated that the results are more than promising and "it looks very much as if the newest three-factor table can now be recommended for general use." The three-factor table she refers to include *(1)* supervision of boy by mother, with suitable supervision giving a delinquency score of 9.9, fair supervision, 57.5, unsuitable supervision, 83.2; *(2)* discipline of the boy by the mother, firmly but kindly yielding a delinquency score of 6.1, erratically, 52.3, over strictly, 73.3, and laxly, 82.9; *(3)* cohesiveness of family, with marked cohesiveness of the family yielding a 20.6 delinquency score, some cohesiveness, 61.3, and none, 96.9.

Many people have pointed out that the dialogue concerning the Glueck scale will continue until long-range validation studies have either proven or disproven its value. However, Voss (1963) reported some data on predictive validity of the scale. He indicated that retrospective investigations did not establish validity for the Glueck Social Prediction Table. Voss stated: "The table was constructed on the basis of equal numbers of delinquents and non-delinquents, and is inefficient as a prognostic device when only a small percentage become delinquent. A reasonable approximation of the actual delinquency rate must be used in the construction of a prediction table. Otherwise, the labeling of every boy in the sample as a non-delinquent delivers a higher degree of predictive accuracy;" He concluded his statement of his work in analysis of validation studies completed so far as follows: "The validity of the Glueck's Prediction Instrument is still in doubt, and only an amazing reversal of the current results in the Youth Board investigation will validate the Glueck Social Prediction Table."

Other scales have been devised. In general we do not now have the ability to predict delinquency accurately. Several studies have shown specific factors related to delinquent behavior. By and large these studies show concurrent validity rather than an ability to predict future delinquency.

●●

6

Developmental Psychology

'Developmental psychology', also known as human development, is the scientific study of systematic psychological changes that occur in human beings over the course of the life span. Originally concerned with infants and children, the field has expanded to include adolescence and adult development, aging, and the entire life span. This field examines change across a broad range of topics including motor skills and other psycho-physiological processes; cognitive development involving areas such as problem solving, moral understanding, and conceptual understanding; language acquisition; social, personality, and emotional development; and self-concept and identity formation.

Developmental psychology includes issues such as the extent to which development occurs through the gradual accumulation of knowledge versus stage-like development, or the extent to which children are born with innate mental structures versus learning through experience. Many researchers are interested in the interaction between personal characteristics, the individual's behavior, and environmental factors including social context, and their impact on development; others take a more narrowly focused approach.

Developmental psychology informs several applied fields, including: educational psychology, child psychopathology, and forensic developmental psychology. Developmental psychology complements several other basic research fields in psychology including social psychology, cognitive psychology, ecological psychology, and comparative psychology.

Approaches

Many theoretical perspectives attempt to explain development; among the most prominent are: Jean Piaget's Stage Theory, Lev Vygotsky's Social Contextualism (and its heirs, the Cultural Theory of Development of Michael Cole, and the Ecological Systems Theory of Urie Bronfenbrenner), Albert Bandura's Social learning theory, and the information processing framework employed by cognitive psychology.

To a lesser extent, historical theories continue to provide a basis for additional research. Among them are Erik Erikson's eight stages of psychosocial development and John B. Watson's and B. F. Skinner's behaviorism (for more on behaviorism's role see Behavior analysis of child development).

Many other theories are prominent for their contributions to particular aspects of development. For example, attachment theory describes kinds of interpersonal relationships and Lawrence Kohlberg describes stages in moral reasoning.

Folklore also describes a good method to the growth of child psychology.

Theorists and Theories

- John Bowlby, Harry Harlow, Mary Ainsworth: Attachment theory
- Urie Bronfenbrenner: the social ecology of human development
- Jerome Bruner: Cognitive (constructivist); learning theory / Narrative construction of reality
- Erik Erikson: Erikson's stages of psychosocial development

- Sigmund Freud: Psychosexual development
- Jerome Kagan: A pioneer of developmental psychology
- Lawrence Kohlberg: Kohlberg's stages of moral development
- Jean Piaget: Theory of cognitive development, Genetic epistemology
- Lev Vygotsky: Social contextualism; Zone of proximal development
- Judith Rich Harris: Modular theory of social development

Piagetian Stages of Cognitive Development

Piaget was a French speaking Swiss theorist who posited that children learn through actively constructing knowledge through hands-on experience. He suggested that the adult's role in helping the child learn was to provide appropriate materials for the child to interact and construct. He would use Socratic questioning to get the children to reflect on what they were doing. He would try to get them to see contradictions in their explanations. He also developed stages of development. His approach can be seen in how the curriculum is sequenced in schools, and in the pedagogy of preschool centers across the United States.

Vygotsky's Cultural-historical Theory

Vygotsky was a theorist from the Soviet era, who posited that children learn through hands-on experience, as Piaget suggested. However, unlike Piaget, he claimed that timely and sensitive intervention by adults when a child is on the edge of learning a new task (called the "zone of proximal development") could help children learn new tasks. This technique is called "scaffolding," because it builds upon knowledge children already have with new knowledge that adults can help the child learn. Vygotsky was strongly focused on the role of culture in determining the child's pattern of development, arguing that development moves from the social level to the individual level.

Ecological Systems Theory

Also called "Development in Context" or "Human Ecology" theory, Ecological Systems Theory, originally formulated by Urie Bronfenbrenner specifies four types of nested environmental systems, with bi-directional influences within and between the systems. The four systems are Microsystem, Mesosystem, Exosystem, and Macrosystem. Each system contains roles, norms and rules that can powerfully shape development. Since its publication in 1979, Bronfenbrenner's major statement of this theory, The Ecology of Human Development has had widespread influence on the way psychologists and others approach the study of human beings and their environments. As a result of this conceptualization of development, these environments— from the family to economic and political structures—have come to be viewed as part of the life course from childhood through adulthood.

Attachment Theory

Attachment theory, originally developed by John Bowlby, focuses on close, intimate, emotionally meaningful relationships. Attachment is described as a biological system that evolved to ensure the survival of the infant. A child who is threatened or stressed will move toward caregivers who create a sense of physical, emotional and psychological safety for the individual. Later Mary Ainsworth developed the Strange Situation Protocol and the concept of the secure base. See also the critique by developmental psychology pioneer Jerome Kagan.

Nature/Nurture

A significant question in developmental psychology is the relationship between innateness and environmental influence in regard to any particular aspect of development. This is often referred to as "nature versus nurture" or nativism versus empiricism. A nativist account of development would argue that the processes in question are innate, that is, they are specified by the organism's genes. An empiricist perspective would argue that those processes are acquired in interaction with the environment. Today developmental psychologists rarely take such extreme positions with regard to most aspects of development; rather they investigate, among many other things, the relationship between innate and environmental influences. One of the ways in which this relationship has been explored in recent years is through the emerging field of evolutionary developmental psychology.

One area where this innateness debate has been prominently portrayed is in research on language acquisition. A major question in this area is whether or not certain properties of human language are specified genetically or can be acquired through learning. The empiricist position on the issue of language acquisition suggests that the language input provides the necessary information required for learning the structure of language and that infants acquire language through a process of statistical learning. From this perspective, language can be acquired via general learning methods that also apply to other aspects of development, such as perceptual learning. The nativist position argues that the input from language is too impoverished for infants and children to acquire the structure of language. Linguist Noam Chomsky asserts that, evidenced by the lack of sufficient information in the language input, there is a universal grammar that applies to all human languages and is pre-specified. This has led to the idea that there is a special cognitive module suited for learning language, often called the language acquisition device.

Chomsky's critique of the behaviorist model of language acquisition is regarded by many as a key turning point in the decline in the prominence of the theory of behaviorism generally. But Skinner's conception of "Verbal Behavior" has not died, perhaps in part because it has generated successful practical applications.

Mechanisms of Development

Developmental psychology is concerned not only with describing the characteristics of psychological change over time, but also seeks to explain the principles and internal workings underlying these changes. Psychologists have attempted to better understand these factors by using models. Developmental models are sometimes computational, but they do not need to be. A model must simply account for the means by which a process takes place. This is sometimes done in reference to changes in the brain that may correspond to changes in behavior over the course of the development. Computational accounts of development often use either symbolic, connectionist (neural network), or dynamical systems models to explain the mechanisms of development.

RESEARCH AREAS

Cognitive Development

Cognitive development is primarily concerned with the ways in which infants and children acquire, develop, and use internal mental capabilities such as problem solving, memory, and language. Major topics in cognitive development are the study of language acquisition and the development of perceptual and motor skills. Piaget was one of the influential early psychologists to study the development of cognitive abilities. His theory suggests that development proceeds through a set of stages from infancy to adulthood and that there is an end point or goal. Other accounts, such as that of Lev Vygotsky, have suggested that development does not progress through stages, but rather that the developmental process that begins at birth and continues until death is too complex for such structure and finality. Rather, from this viewpoint, developmental processes proceed more continuously, thus development should be analyzed, instead of treated as a product to be obtained.

Modern cognitive development has largely moved away from Piagetian stage theories, and is influenced by accounts of domain-specific information processing, which posit that development is guided by innate evolutionarily specified and content-specific information processing mechanisms.

Social and Emotional Development

Developmental psychologists who are interested in social development examine how individuals develop social and emotional competencies. For example, they study how children form friendships, how they understand and deal with emotions, and how identity develops. Research in this area may involve study of the relationship between cognition or cognitive development and social behavior.

Research Methods

Developmental psychology employs many of the research methods used in other areas of psychology. However, infants and children cannot always be tested in the same ways as adults, so different methods are often used to study their development.

Research Design

Developmental psychologists have a number of methods to study changes in individuals over time. In a longitudinal study, a researcher observes many individuals born at or around the same time (a cohort) and carries out new observations as members of the cohort age. This method can be used to draw conclusions about which types of development are universal (or normative) and occur in most members of a cohort. Researchers may also observe ways in which development varies between individuals and hypothesize about the causes of variation observed in their data. Longitudinal studies often require large amounts of time and funding, making them unfeasible in some situations. Also, because members of a cohort all experience historical events unique to their generation, apparently normative developmental trends may in fact be universal only to their cohort.

In a cross-sectional study, a researcher observes differences between individuals of different ages at the same time. This generally requires less resources than the longitudinal method, and because the individuals come from different cohorts, shared historical events are not so much of a confounding factor. By the same token, however, cross-sectional research may not be the most effective way to study differences between participants, as these differences may result not from their different ages but from their exposure to different historical events.

An accelerated longitudinal design or cross-sequential study or cohort-sequential design combines both methodologies. Here, a researcher observes members of different birth cohorts at the same time, and then tracks all participants over time, charting changes in the groups. By comparing differences and similarities in development, one can more easily determine what changes can be attributed to individual or historical environment, and which are truly universal. Clearly such a study can be even more resource-consuming than a longitudinal study.

Additionally, these are all correlational, not experimental, designs, and so one cannot readily infer causation from the data they yield. Nonetheless, correlational research methods are common in the study of development, in part due to ethical concerns. In a study of the effects of poverty on development, for instance, one cannot easily randomly assign certain families to a poverty condition and others to an affluent one, and so observation alone has to suffice.

Stages of Development

The prenatal development of human beings is viewed in three separate stages, which are not the same as the trimesters of a woman's pregnancy:

1. Germinal (conception through week 2)
2. Embryonic (weeks 3 through 8)
3. Fetal (week 9 through birth)

The germinal stage begins when a sperm penetrates an egg in the act of conception (normally the result of sexual intercourse between a man and a woman). At this point a zygote is formed. Through the process of mitosis, the cells divide and double.

The embryonic stage occurs once the zygote has firmly implanted itself in the uterine wall. It is in this stage that the vital organs are formed, and while the external body is still extremely dissimilar from an adult human, some features such as eyes and arms, and eventually ears and feet, become recognizable.

The fetal period is the pre-natal period when the brain has its greatest development, becoming more and more complex over the last few months.

During pregnancy there is a risk to the developing child from drugs and other teratogens, spousal abuse and other stress on the mother, nutrition and the age of the mother. Genetic testing prior to pregnancy is also increasingly available. Three methods of determining fetal defects and health include the ultrasound, amniocentesis, and chorionic villus sampling. Although difficult, some methods of treating fetal disorders have been developed, both surgical and drug based.

Infancy

From birth until the onset of speech, the child is referred to as an infant. Developmental psychologists vary widely in their assessment of infant psychology, and the influence the outside world has upon it, but certain aspects are relatively clear.

While no agreement has yet been reached regarding the level of stimulation an infant requires, a normal level of stimulation is very important, and a lack of stimulation and affection can result in learning difficulties and a host of other developmental and social disorders. Some feel that classical music, particularly Mozart is good for an infant's mind. While some tentative research has shown it to be helpful to older children, no conclusive evidence is available involving infants.

The majority of a newborn infant's time is spent in sleep. At first this sleep is evenly spread throughout the day and night, but after a couple of months, infants generally become diurnal.

Infants can be seen to have 6 states, grouped into pairs:

- quiet sleep and active sleep (dreaming, when REM occurs)
- quiet waking, and active waking
- fussing and crying

Infants respond to stimuli differently in these different states. Habituation is frequently used in testing psychological phenomenon. Both infants and adults attend less as a result of consistent exposure to a particular stimulus. The amount of time spent attending to an alternate stimulus (after habituation to the initial stimulus) is indicative of the strength of the remembered percept of the previous stimulus, or dis-habituation.

Habituation is used to discover the resolution of perceptual systems, for example, by habituating a subject to one stimulus, and then observing responses to similar ones, one can detect the smallest degree of difference that is detectable by the subject.

Infants have a wide variety of reflexes, some of which are permanent (blinking, gagging), and others transient in nature. Some have obvious purposes, some are clearly vestigial, and some do not have obvious purposes. Primitive reflexes reappear in adults under certain conditions, such as neurological conditions like dementia or traumatic lesions. A partial list of infantile reflexes includes:

- Moro reflex or startle reflex:
    1. Startle
    2. spreading out the arms (adduction)
    3. unspreading the arms (abduction)
    4. Crying (usually)
- Tonic neck reflex or fencer's reflex
- Rooting reflex, sucking reflex, suckling reflex: can be initiated by scratching the infant's cheek; the reaction is pursing of the lips for sucking.
- Stepping reflex, step-up reflex: can be initiated if you support the infant upright from its armpits below a given surface so the baby lifts its foot and steps up on the surface (like climbing a stair).
- Grasp reflex: can be initiated by scratching the infant's palm.

- Parachute reflex: the infant is suspended by the trunk and suddenly lowered as if falling for an instant. The child spontaneously throws out the arms as a protective mechanism. The parachute reflex appears before the onset of walking.

- Plantar reflex or Babinski reflex: a finger is stroked firmly down the outer edge of the baby's sole; the toes spread and extend out.

Infants have significantly worse vision than older children. Infant sight, blurry in early stages, improves over time. Infants less than 2 months old are thought to be color blind.

Hearing is well-developed prior to birth, however, and a preference for the mother's heartbeat is well established. Infants are fairly good at detecting the direction from which a sound comes, and by 18 months their hearing ability is approximately equal to that of adults.

Smell and taste are present, with infants having been shown to prefer the smell and taste of a banana, while rejecting the taste of shrimp. There is good evidence for infants preferring the smell of their mother to that of others.

Infants have a fully developed sense of touch at birth, and the myth believed by some doctors even today that infants feel no pain is inaccurate. Doctors are slowly becoming aware of the need for pain prevention for newborns.

Piaget asserted that there were several sensorimotor stages within his broader Theory of cognitive development.

- The first sub-stage occurs from birth to six weeks and is associated primarily with the development of reflexes. Three primary reflexes are described by Piaget: sucking of objects in the mouth, following moving or interesting objects with the eyes, and closing of the hand when an object makes contact with the palm (palmar grasp). Over these first six weeks of life, these reflexes begin to become voluntary actions; for example, the palmar reflex becomes intentional grasping. (Gruber and Vaneche, 1977).

- The second sub-stage occurs from six weeks to four months and is associated primarily with the development of habits. Primary circular reactions or repeating of an action involving only ones own body begin. An example of this type of reaction would involve something like an infant repeating the motion of passing their hand before their face. Also at this phase, passive reactions, caused by classical or operant conditioning, can begin (Gruber et al., 1977).
- The third sub-stage occurs from four to nine months and is associated primarily with the development of coordination between vision and prehension. Three new abilities occur at this stage: intentional grasping for a desired object, secondary circular reactions, and differentiations between ends and means. At this stage, infants will intentionally grasp the air in the direction of a desired object, often to the amusement of friends and family. Secondary circular reactions, or the repetition of an action involving an external object occur begin; for example, moving a switch to turn on a light repeatedly. The differentiation between means also occurs. This is perhaps one of the most important stages of a child's growth as it signifies the dawn of logic (Gruber et al., 1977). Towards the late part of this sub-stage infants begin to have a sense of object permanence, passing the A-not-B error test.

- The fourth sub-stage occurs from nine to twelve months and is associated primarily with the development of logic and the coordination between means and ends. This is an extremely important stage of development, holding what Piaget calls the "first proper intelligence." Also, this stage marks the beginning of goal orientation, the deliberate planning of steps to meet an objective (Gruber et al. 1977).

- The fifth sub-stage occurs from twelve to eighteen months and is associated primarily with the discovery of new means to meet goals. Piaget describes the child at this juncture as the "young scientist," conducting pseudo-experiments to discover new methods of meeting challenges (Gruber et al. 1977).

- The sixth sub-stage is associated primarily with the beginnings of insight, or true creativity. This marks the passage into the preoperational stage.

When studying infants, the habituation methodology is an example of a method often used to assess their performance. This method allows researchers to obtain information about what types of stimuli an infant is able to discriminate. In this paradigm, infants are habituated to a particular stimulus and are then tested using different stimuli to evaluate discrimination. The critical measure in habituation is the infants' level of interest. Typically, infants prefer stimuli that are novel relative to those they have encountered previously. Several methods are used to measure infants' preference. These include the high-amplitude sucking procedure, in which infants suck on a pacifier more or less depending on their level of interest, the conditioned foot-kick procedure, in which infants move their legs to indicate preference, and the head-turn preference procedure, in which the infant's level of interest is measured by the amount of time spent looking in a particular direction. A key feature of all these methods is that, in each situation, the infant controls the stimuli being presented. This gives researchers a means of measuring discrimination. If an infant is able to discriminate between the habituated stimulus and a novel stimulus, they will show a preference for the novel stimulus. If, however, the infant cannot discriminate between the two stimuli, they will not show a preference for one over the other.

Object permanence is an important stage of cognitive development for infants. Numerous tests regarding it have been done, usually involving a toy, and a crude barrier which is placed in front of the toy, and then removed, repeatedly. In sensorimotor stages 1 and 2, the infant is completely unable to comprehend object permanence. Jean Piaget conducted experiments with infants which led him to conclude that this awareness was typically achieved at eight to nine months of age. Infants before this age are too young to understand object permanence, which explains why infants at this age do not cry when their mothers are gone. "Out of sight, out of mind." A lack of Object Permanence can lead to A-not-B errors, where children reach for a thing at a place where it should not be. (see also: Infant metaphysics)

Toddler

Intelligence is demonstrated through the use of symbols, language use matures, and memory and imagination are developed. Thinking is done in a nonlogical, nonreversible manner. Egocentric thinking predominates.

Socially, toddlers are little people attempting to become independent at this stage, which they are commonly called the " terrible twos". They walk, talk, use the toilet, and get food for themselves. Self-control begins to develop. If taking the initiative to explore, experiment, risk mistakes in trying new things, and test their limits is encouraged by the caretaker(s) the child will become autonomous, self-reliant, and confident. If the caretaker is overprotective or disapproving of independent actions, the toddler may begin to doubt their abilities and feel ashamed for the desire for independence. The child's autonomic development will be inhibited, and be less prepared to successfully deal with the world in the future.

Early Childhood

When children attend preschool, they broaden their social horizons and become more engaged with those around them. Impulses are channeled into fantasies, which leaves the task of the caretaker to balance eagerness for pursuing adventure, creativity and self expression with the development of responsibility. If caretakers are properly encouraging and consistently disciplinary, children are more likely to develop positive self-esteem while becoming more responsible, and will follow through on assigned activities. If not allowed to decide which activities to perform, children may begin to feel guilt upon contemplating taking initiative. This negative association with independence will lead them to let others make decisions in place of them.

Childhood

In middle childhood, intelligence is demonstrated through logical and systematic manipulation of symbols related to concrete objects. Operational thinking develops, which means actions are reversible, and egocentric thought diminishes.

Children go through the transition from the world at home to that of school and peers. Children learn to make things, use tools, and acquire the skills to be a worker and a potential provider. Children can now receive feedback from outsiders about their accomplishments. If children can discover pleasure in intellectual stimulation, being productive, seeking success, they will develop a sense of competence. If they are not successful or cannot discover pleasure in the process, they may develop a sense of inferiority and feelings of inadequacy that may haunt them throughout life. This is when children think of them selves as industrious or as inferior

Adolescence

Adolescence is the period of life between the onset of puberty and the full commitment to an adult social role, such as worker, parent, and/or citizen. It is the period known for the formation of personal and social identity (see Erik Erikson) and the discovery of moral purpose (see William Damon). Intelligence is demonstrated through the logical use of symbols related to abstract concepts and formal reasoning. A return to egocentric thought often occurs early in the period. Only 35% develop the capacity to reason formally during adolescence or adulthood. (Huitt, W. and Hummel, J. January 1998)

The adolescent asks "Who am I? Who do I want to be?" Like toddlers, adolescents must explore, test limits, become autonomous, and commit to an identity, or sense of self. Different roles, behaviors and ideologies must be tried out to select an identity. Role confusion and inability to choose vocation can result from a failure to achieve a sense of identity.

Early Adulthood

The person must learn how to form intimate relationships, both in friendship and love. The development of this skill relies on the resolution of other stages. It may be hard to establish intimacy if one has not developed trust or a sense of identity. If this skill is not learned the alternative is alienation, isolation, a fear of commitment, and the inability to depend on others.

A related framework for studying this part of the life span is that of Emerging adulthood, introduced in 2000 by

Jeffrey Arnett. Scholars of emerging adulthood are interested not only in relationship development (focusing on the role of dating in helping individuals settle on a long-term spouse/ partner), but also the development of sociopolitical views and occupational choice.

Middle age

Middle adulthood generally refers to the period between ages 40 to 65. During this period, the middle-aged experience a conflict between generativity and stagnation. They may either feel a sense of contributing to the next generation and their community or a sense of purposelessness.

Physically, the middle-aged experience a decline in muscular strength, reaction time, sensory keenness, and cardiac output. Also, women experience menopause and a sharp drop in the hormone estrogen. Men do not have an equivalent to menopause, but they do experience a decline in sperm count and speed of ejaculation and erection. Most men and women remain capable of sexual satisfaction after middle age.

Old age

This stage generally refers to those over 75 years. During old age, people experience a conflict between integrity vs. despair. When reflecting on their life, they either feel a sense of accomplishment or failure.

Physically, older people experience a decline in muscular strength, reaction time, stamina, hearing, distance perception, and the sense of smell. They also are more susceptible to severe diseases such as cancer and pneumonia due to a weakened immune system. Mental disintegration may also occur, leading to Dementia or Alzheimer's Disease. However, partially due to a lifetime's accumulation of antibodies, the elderly are less likely to suffer from common diseases such as the cold or flu.

Whether or not intellectual powers increase or decrease with age remains controversial. Longitudinal studies have suggested that intellect declines, while cross-sectional studies suggest that intellect is stable. It is generally believed that crystallized intelligence increases up to old age, while fluid intelligence decreases with age.

Parenting

In Western developed societies, mothers (and women generally) were emphasized to the exclusion of other caregivers, particularly as the traditional role of the father was more the breadwinner, and less the direct caregiver of an infant, he has been traditionally viewed as impacting an infant indirectly through interactions with the mother of the child.

The emphasis of study has shifted to the primary caregiver (regardless of gender or biological relation), as well as all persons directly or indirectly influencing the child (the family system). The roles of the mother and father are more significant than first thought as we moved into the concept of primary caregiver.

Affirming a role for fathers, studies have shown that children as young as 15 months benefit significantly from substantial engagement with their father. In particular, a study in the U.S.A. and New Zealand found the presence of the natural father was the most significant factor in reducing rates of early sexual activity and rates of teenage pregnancy in girls. Covariate factors used included early conduct problems, maternal age at first childbirth, race, maternal education, father's occupational status, family living standards, family life stress, early mother-child interaction, measures of psychosocial adjustment and educational achievement, school qualifications, mood disorder, anxiety disorder, suicide attempts, violent offending, and conduct disorder. Further research has found fathers have an impact on child academic performance, including involved nonresident fathers. However, father absence is associated with a range of negative outcomes for children, including child and later criminal behavior.

Historical Antecedents

The modern form of developmental psychology has its roots in the rich psychological tradition represented by Aristotle, Tabari, Rhazes, Alhazen, and Descartes. William Shakespeare had his melancholy character Jacques (in As You Like It) articulate the seven ages of man: these included three stages of childhood and four of adulthood. In the mid-eighteenth century Jean Jacques Rousseau described three stages of childhood: infans (infancy), puer (childhood) and adolescence in Emile: Or, On Education. Rousseau's ideas were taken up strongly by educators at the time.

In the late nineteenth century, psychologists familiar with the evolutionary theory of Darwin began seeking an evolutionary description of psychological development; prominent here was G. Stanley Hall, who attempted to correlate ages of childhood with previous ages of mankind.

●●

7

Developmental Psychobiology

Developmental psychobiology is an interdisciplinary field, encompassing developmental psychology, biological psychology, neuroscience and many other areas of biology. The field covers all phases of organismic ontogeny, with particular emphasis on prenatal, perinatal and early childhood development. Developmental psychobiologists employ and integrate both biological and psychological concepts and methods (cf. Michel & Moore, 1995) and have historically been highly concerned with the interrelation between ontogeny and phylogeny (or individual development and evolutionary processes; see, *e.g.*, Blumberg, 2002, 2005; Gottlieb, 1991). Developmental psychobiologists also tend to be systems thinkers, avoiding the reification of artificial dichotomies (*e.g.*, "nature" vs. "nurture") and the arguments they tend to engender.

Science

In its broadest sense, science (from the Latin scientia, meaning "knowledge") refers to any systematic knowledge or practice. In its more usual restricted sense, science refers to a system of acquiring knowledge based on scientific method, as well as to the organized body of knowledge gained through such research. This article focuses on the more restricted use of the word. Science as discussed in this article is sometimes termed experimental science to differentiate it from applied science, which is the application of scientific research to specific human needs, though the two are often interconnected.

Science is the effort to discover and increase human understanding of how reality works. Its purview is the portion of reality which is independent of religious, political, cultural, or philosophical outlook. Using controlled methods, scientists collect data in the form of observations, record observable physical evidence of natural phenomena, and analyze this information to construct theoretical explanations of how things work. Knowledge in science is gained through research. The methods of scientific research include the generation of hypotheses about how phenomena work, and experimentation that tests these hypotheses under controlled conditions. The outcome or product of this empirical scientific process is the formulation of theory that describes human understanding of physical processes and facilitates prediction.

Lavoisier says, "... the impossibility of separating the nomenclature of a science from the science itself is owing to this, that every branch of physical science must consist of three things: the series of facts which are the objects of the science, the ideas which represent these facts and the words by which these ideas are expressed."

A broader modern definition of science may include the natural sciences along with the social and behavioral sciences, as the main subdivisions of science, defining it as the observation, identification, description, experimental investigation, and theoretical explanation of phenomena. However, other contemporary definitions still place the natural sciences, which are closely related with the physical world's phenomena, as the only true vehicles of science.

History of Science

While empirical investigations of the natural world have been described since antiquity (for example, by Aristotle, Theophrastus and Pliny the Elder), and scientific methods have been employed since the Middle Ages (for example, by Ibn al-Haytham, Abu Rayhan Biruni and Roger Bacon), the dawn of modern science is generally traced back to the early modern period, during what is known as the Scientific Revolution of the 16th and 17th centuries.

Well into the eighteenth century, science and natural philosophy were not quite synonymous, but only became so later with the direct use of what would become known formally as the scientific method, which was earlier developed during the Middle Ages and early modern period in Europe and the Middle East (see History of scientific method). Prior to the 18th century, however, the preferred term for the study of nature was natural philosophy, while English speakers most typically referred to the study of the human mind as moral philosophy. By contrast, the word "science" in English was still used in the 17th century to refer to the Aristotelian concept of knowledge which was secure enough to be used as a sure prescription for exactly how to do something. In this differing sense of the two words, the philosopher John Locke in An Essay Concerning Human Understanding wrote that "natural philosophy [the study of nature] is not capable of being made a science".

By the early 1800s, natural philosophy had begun to separate from philosophy, though it often retained a very broad meaning. In many cases, science continued to stand for reliable knowledge about any topic, in the same way it is still used in the broad sense (see the introduction to this article) in modern terms such as library science, political science, and computer science. In the more narrow sense of science, as natural philosophy became linked to an expanding set of well-defined laws (beginning with Galileo's laws, Kepler's laws, and Newton's laws for motion), it became more popular to refer to natural philosophy as natural science. Over the course of the nineteenth century, moreover, there was an increased tendency to associate science with study of the natural world (that is, the non-human world). This move sometimes left the study of human thought and society (what would come to be called social science) in a linguistic limbo by the end of the century and into the next.

Through the 19th century, many English speakers were increasingly differentiating science (meaning a combination of what we now term natural and biological sciences) from all other forms of knowledge in a variety of ways. The now-familiar expression "scientific method," which refers to the prescriptive part of how to make discoveries in natural philosophy, was almost unused during the early part of the 19th century, but became widespread after the 1870s, though there was rarely total agreement about just what it entailed. The word "scientist," meant to refer to a systematically-working natural philosopher, (as opposed to an intuitive or empirically-minded one) was coined in 1833 by William Whewell. Discussion of scientists as a special group of people who did science, even if their attributes were up for debate, grew in the last half of the 19th century. Whatever people actually meant by these terms at first, they ultimately depicted science, in the narrow sense of the habitual use of the scientific method and the knowledge derived from it, as something deeply distinguished from all other realms of human endeavor.

By the twentieth century, the modern notion of science as a special brand of information about the world, practiced by a distinct group and pursued through a unique method, was essentially in place. It was used to give legitimacy to a variety of fields through such titles as "scientific" medicine, engineering, advertising, or motherhood. Over the 1900s, links between science and technology also grew increasingly strong.

Distinguished from Technology

By the end of the century, it is arguable that technology had even begun to eclipse science as a term of public attention and praise. Scholarly studies of science have begun to refer to "technoscience" rather than science or technology separately.

Meanwhile, such fields as biotechnology and nanotechnology are capturing the headlines. One author has suggested that, in the coming century, "science" may fall out of use, to be replaced by technoscience or even by some more exotic label such as "techknowledgy."

Scientific Method

A scientific method seeks to explain the events of nature in a reproducible way, and to use these reproductions to make useful predictions. It is done through observation of natural phenomena, and/or through experimentation that tries to simulate natural events under controlled conditions. It provides an objective process to find solutions to problems in a number of scientific and technological fields.

Based on observations of a phenomenon, a scientist may generate a model. This is an attempt to describe or depict the phenomenon in terms of a logical physical or mathematical representation. As empirical evidence is gathered, a scientist can suggest a hypothesis to explain the phenomenon. This description can be used to make predictions that are testable by experiment or observation using scientific method. When a hypothesis proves unsatisfactory, it is either modified or discarded.

While performing experiments, scientists may have a preference for one outcome over another, and it is important that this tendency not bias their interpretation. A strict following of a scientific method attempts to minimize the influence of a scientist's bias on the outcome of an experiment. This can be achieved by correct experimental design, and a thorough peer review of the experimental results as well as conclusions of a study. Once the experiment results are announced or published, an important cross-check can be the need to validate the results by an independent party.

Once a hypothesis has survived testing, it may become adopted into the framework of a scientific theory. This is a logically reasoned, self-consistent model or framework for describing the behavior of certain natural phenomena. A theory typically describes the behavior of much broader sets of phenomena than a hypothesis—commonly, a large number of hypotheses can be logically bound together by a single theory. These broader theories may be formulated using principles such as parsimony (*e.g.*, "Occam's Razor"). They are then repeatedly tested by analyzing how the collected evidence (facts) compares to the theory. When a theory survives a sufficiently large number of empirical observations, it then becomes a scientific generalization that can be taken as fully verified.

Despite the existence of well-tested theories, science cannot claim absolute knowledge of nature or the behavior of the subject or of the field of study due to epistemological problems that are unavoidable and preclude the discovery or establishment of absolute truth. Unlike a mathematical proof, a scientific theory is empirical, and is always open to falsification, if new evidence is presented. Even the most basic and fundamental theories may turn out to be imperfect if new observations are inconsistent with them. Critical to this process is making every relevant aspect of research publicly available, which allows ongoing review and repeating of experiments and observations by multiple researchers operating independently of one another. Only by fulfilling these expectations can it be determined how reliable the experimental results are for potential use by others.

Isaac Newton's law of gravitation is a famous example of an established law that was later found not to be universal—it does not hold in experiments involving motion at speeds close to the speed of light or in close proximity of strong gravitational fields; outside these conditions, Newtonian mechanics remains an excellent model of motion and gravity, while general relativity accounts for the same phenomena that Newton's Laws do, and more. General relativity is now regarded as a more comprehensive theory, reducing to Newtonian mechanics at lower speeds. Newtonian mechanics remains in use worldwide, due to its computational simplicity.

One position in the philosophy of science, initially advanced by Paul Feyerabend in Against Method, is that there really is no such thing as the scientific method. Rather, philosophers of science say that there are scientific methods. For example, controlled experiments are commonly performed in physics, chemistry, medicine, etc.. While controlled experiments are impossible in climatology, geology or astrophysics, in these sciences, observations for posited predictions serve to corroborate hypotheses.

Mathematics

Mathematics is essential to many sciences. One important function of mathematics in science is the role it plays in the expression of scientific models. Observing and collecting measurements, as well as hypothesizing and predicting, often require extensive use of mathematics and mathematical models. Calculus may be the branch of mathematics most often used in science, but virtually every branch of mathematics has applications in science, including "pure" areas such as number theory and topology. Mathematics is fundamental to the understanding of the natural sciences and the social sciences, many of which also rely heavily on statistics.

Statistical methods, comprised of mathematical techniques for summarizing and exploring data, allow scientists to assess the level of reliability and the range of variation in experimental results. Statistical thinking also plays a fundamental role in many areas of science.

Computational science applies computing power to simulate real-world situations, enabling a better understanding of scientific problems than formal mathematics alone can achieve. According to the Society for Industrial and Applied Mathematics, computation is now as important as theory and experiment in advancing scientific knowledge.

Whether mathematics itself is properly classified as science has been a matter of some debate. Some thinkers see mathematicians as scientists, regarding physical experiments as inessential or mathematical proofs as equivalent to experiments. Others do not see mathematics as a science, since it does not require an experimental test of its theories and hypotheses. Mathematical theorems and formulas are obtained by logical derivations which presume axiomatic systems, rather than the combination of empirical observation and logical reasoning that has come to be known as scientific method. In general, mathematics is classified as formal science, while natural and social sciences are classified as empirical sciences.

Philosophy of Science

The philosophy of science seeks to understand the nature and justification of scientific knowledge. It has proven difficult to provide a definitive account of scientific method that can decisively serve to distinguish science from non-science. Thus there are legitimate arguments about exactly where the borders are, leading to the problem of demarcation. There is nonetheless a set of core precepts that have broad consensus among published philosophers of science and within the scientific community at large.

Science is reasoned-based analysis of sensation upon our awareness. As such, a scientific method cannot deduce anything about the realm of reality that is beyond what is observable by existing or theoretical means. When a manifestation of our reality previously considered supernatural is understood in the terms of causes and consequences, it acquires a scientific explanation.

Some of the findings of science can be very counter-intuitive. Atomic theory, for example, implies that a granite boulder which appears a heavy, hard, solid, grey object is actually a combination of subatomic particles with none of these properties, moving very rapidly in space where the mass is concentrated in a very small fraction of the total volume. Many of humanity's preconceived notions about the workings of the universe have been challenged by new scientific discoveries. Quantum mechanics, particularly, examines phenomena that seem to defy our most basic postulates about causality and fundamental understanding of the world around us.

There are different schools of thought in the philosophy of scientific method. Methodological naturalism maintains that scientific investigation must adhere to empirical study and independent verification as a process for properly developing and evaluating natural explanations for observable phenomena. Methodological naturalism, therefore, rejects supernatural explanations, arguments from authority and biased observational studies. Critical rationalism instead holds that unbiased observation is not possible and a demarcation between natural and supernatural explanations is arbitrary; it instead proposes falsifiability as the landmark of empirical theories and falsification as the universal empirical method. Critical rationalism argues for the ability of science to increase the scope of testable knowledge, but at the same time against its authority, by emphasizing its inherent fallibility. It proposes that science should be content with the rational elimination of errors in its theories, not in seeking for their verification (such as claiming certain or probable proof or disproof; both the proposal and falsification of a theory are only of methodological, conjectural, and tentative character in critical rationalism). Instrumentalism rejects the concept of truth and emphasizes merely the utility of theories as instruments for explaining and predicting phenomena.

Science, Pseudoscience and Nonscience

Any established body of knowledge which masquerades as science in an attempt to claim a legitimacy which it would not otherwise be able to achieve on its own terms is not science; it is often known as fringe- or alternative science. The most important of its defects is usually the lack of the carefully controlled and thoughtfully interpreted experiments which provide the foundation of the natural sciences and which contribute to their advancement. Another term, junk science, is often used to describe scientific theories or data which, while perhaps legitimate in themselves, are believed to be mistakenly used to support an opposing position. There is usually an element of political or ideological bias in the use of the term. Thus the arguments in favor of limiting the use of fossil fuels in order to reduce global warming are often characterized as junk science by those who do not wish to see such restrictions imposed, and who claim that other factors may well be the cause of global warming. A wide variety of commercial advertising (ranging from hype to outright fraud) would also fall into this category. Finally, there is just plain bad science, which is commonly used to describe well-intentioned but incorrect, obsolete, incomplete, or over-simplified expositions of scientific ideas.

The status of many bodies of knowledge as true sciences, has been a matter of debate. Discussion and debate abound in this topic with some fields like the social and behavioural sciences accused by critics of being unscientific. Many groups of people from academicians like Nobel Prize physicist Percy W. Bridgman, or Dick Richardson, Ph.D.—Professor of Integrative Biology at the University of Texas at Austin, to politicians like U.S. Senator Kay Bailey Hutchison and other co-sponsors, oppose giving their support or agreeing with the use of the label "science" in some fields of study and knowledge they consider non-scientific, ambiguous, or scientifically irrelevant compared with other fields. Karl Popper denied the existence of evidence and of scientific method. Popper holds that there is only one universal method, the negative method of trial and error. It covers not only all products of the human mind, including science, mathematics, philosophy, art and so on, but also the evolution of life. He also contributed to the Positivism dispute, a philosophical dispute between Critical rationalism (Popper, Albert) and the Frankfurt School (Adorno, Habermas) about the methodology of the social sciences.

Philosophical Focus

Historian Jacques Barzun termed science "a faith as fanatical as any in history" and warned against the use of scientific thought to suppress considerations of meaning as integral to human existence. Many recent thinkers, such as Carolyn Merchant, Theodor Adorno and E. F. Schumacher considered that the 17th century scientific revolution shifted science from a focus on understanding nature, or wisdom, to a focus on manipulating nature, *i.e.* power, and that science's emphasis on manipulating nature leads it inevitably to manipulate people, as well. Science's focus on quantitative measures has led to critiques that it is unable to recognize important qualitative aspects of the world. It is not clear, however, if this kind of criticism is adequate to a vast number of non-experimental scientifics fields like astronomy, cosmology, evolutionary biology, complexity theory, paleontology, paleoanthropology, archeology, earth sciences, climatology, ecology and other sciences, like statistical physics of irreversible non-linear systems, that emphasize systemic and historically contingent frozen accidents. Considerations about the philosophical impact of science to the discussion of the meaning (or lack thereof) in human existence are not suppressed but strongly discussed in the literature of science divulgation, a movement sometimes called The Third Culture.

The implications of the ideological denial of ethics for the practice of science itself in terms of fraud, plagiarism, and data falsification, has been criticized by several academics. In "Science and Ethics", the philosopher Bernard Rollin examines the ideology that denies the relevance of ethics to science, and argues in favor of making education in ethics part and parcel of scientific training.

Media and the Scientific Debate

The mass media face a number of pressures that can prevent them from accurately depicting competing scientific claims in terms of their credibility within the scientific community as a whole. Determining how much weight to give different sides in a scientific debate requires considerable expertise on the issue at hand. Few journalists have real scientific knowledge, and even beat reporters who know a great deal about certain scientific issues may know little about other ones they are suddenly asked to cover.

Politics and Science

Many of the same issues that dog the relationship of science with the media also colour the use of science and scientific arguments by politicians. As a broad generalisations, many politicians seek certainties and facts whilst scientists typically offer probabilities and caveats. However, politicians ability to be heard in the mass media frequently distorts the scientific understanding by the public. Recent example in Britain include the controversy over the MMR inoculation and in the distant past the sacking of a Government Minister, Ms Edwina Curry for revealing (correctly) the high probability that battery eggs were contaminated with Salmonella.

Epistemological Issues

Psychologist Carl Jung believed that though science attempted to understand all of nature, the experimental method used would pose artificial, conditional questions that evoke only partial answers. Robert Anton Wilson criticized science for using instruments to ask questions that produce answers only meaningful in terms of the instrument, and that there was no such thing as a completely objective vantage point from which to view the results of science. Parkin suggests that, compared to other ways of knowing (ex. divination), the epistemological stance of science is on the same spectrum as any other approach; it is simply in a different area of the range in terms of its specific techniques and processes. In this sense, to the degree that divination is an epistemologically specific means of gaining insight into a given question, Parkin suggests that science itself can be considered a form of divination that is framed from a Western view of the nature (and thus possible applications) of knowledge (*i.e.* a Western epistemology).

Scientific Community

The scientific community consists of the total body of scientists, its relationships and interactions. It is normally divided into "sub-communities" each working on a particular field within science.

Fields of Science

Fields of science are commonly classified along two major lines: natural sciences, which study natural phenomena (including biological life), and social sciences, which study human behavior and societies. These groupings are empirical sciences, which means the knowledge must be based on observable phenomena and capable of being experimented for its validity by other researchers working under the same conditions. There are also related disciplines that are grouped into interdisciplinary and applied sciences, such as engineering and health science. Within these categories are specialized scientific fields that can include elements of other scientific disciplines but often possess their own terminology and body of expertise.

Mathematics, which is sometimes classified within a third group of science called formal science, has both similarities and differences with the natural and social sciences. It is similar to empirical sciences in that it involves an objective, careful and systematic study of an area of knowledge; it is different because of its method of verifying its knowledge, using a priori rather than empirical methods. Formal science, which also includes statistics and logic, is vital to the empirical sciences. Major advances in formal science have often led to major advances in the physical and biological sciences. The formal sciences are essential in the formation of hypotheses, theories, and laws, both in discovering and describing how things work (natural sciences) and how people think and act (social sciences).

Institutions

Learned societies for the communication and promotion of scientific thought and experimentation have existed since the Renaissance period. The oldest surviving institution is the Accademia dei Lincei in Italy. National Academy of Sciences are distinguished institutions that exist in a number of countries, beginning with the British Royal Society in 1660 and the French Academic des Sciences in 1666.

International scientific organizations, such as the International Council for Science, have since been formed to promote cooperation between the scientific communities of different nations. More recently, influential government agencies have been created to support scientific research, including the National Science Foundation in the U.S.

Other prominent organizations include the academies of science of many nations, CSIRO in Australia, Centre national de la recherche scientifique in France, Max Planck Society and Deutsche Forschungsgemeinschaft in Germany, and in Spain, CSIC.

Literature

An enormous range of scientific literature is published. Scientific journals communicate and document the results of research carried out in universities and various other research institutions, serving as an archival record of science. The first scientific journals, Journal des Sçavans followed by the Philosophical Transactions, began publication in 1665. Since that time the total number of active periodicals has steadily increased. As of 1981, one estimate for the number of scientific and technical journals in publication was 11,500. Today Pubmed lists almost 40,000, related to the medical sciences only.

Most scientific journals cover a single scientific field and publish the research within that field; the research is normally expressed in the form of a scientific paper. Science has become so pervasive in modern societies that it is generally considered necessary to communicate the achievements, news, and ambitions of scientists to a wider populace.

Science magazines such as New Scientist, Science & Vie and Scientific American cater to the needs of a much wider readership and provide a non-technical summary of popular areas of research, including notable discoveries and advances in certain fields of research. Science books engage the interest of many more people. Tangentially, the science fiction genre, primarily fantastic in nature, engages the public imagination and transmits the ideas, if not the methods, of science.

●●

8

Psychology and Research Methods

Psychology is an academic and applied discipline involving the scientific study of human mental functions and behavior. Occasionally, in addition or opposition to employing the scientific method, it also relies on symbolic interpretation and critical analysis, although these traditions have tended to be less pronounced than in other social sciences such as sociology. Psychologists study such phenomena as perception, cognition, emotion, personality, behavior and interpersonal relationships. Some, especially depth psychologists, also study the unconscious mind.

Psychological knowledge is applied to various spheres of human activity, including issues related to everyday life—such as family, education and employment—and to the treatment of mental health problems. Psychologists attempt to understand the role of mental functions in individual and social behavior, while also exploring the underlying physiological and neurological processes. Psychology includes many sub-fields of study and applications concerned with such areas as human development, sports, health, industry, media and law. Psychology incorporates research from the natural sciences, social sciences and humanities. A person who studies or practices psychology is called a psychologist.

Philosophical and Scientific Toots

The study of psychology in philosophical context dates

back to the ancient civilizations of Egypt, Greece, China and India. Psychology began adopting a more clinical and experimental approach under medieval Muslim psychologists and physicians, who built psychiatric hospitals for such purposes.

In 1802, French physiologist Pierre Cabanis helped to pioneer biological psychology with his essay Rapports du physique et du moral de l'homme (On the relations between the physical and moral aspects of man). Cabanis interpreted the mind in light of his previous studies of biology,arguing that sensibility and soul are properties of the nervous system.

Though the use of psychological experimentation dates back to Alhazen's Book of Optics in 1021, psychology as an independent experimental field of study began in 1879, when Wilhelm Wundt founded the first laboratory dedicated exclusively to psychological research at Leipzig University in Germany, for which Wundt is known as the "father of psychology". The year 1879 is thus sometimes regarded as the "birthdate" of psychology. The American philosopher William James published his seminal book, Principles of Psychology in 1890, laying the foundations for many of the questions that psychologists would focus on for years to come. Other important early contributors to the field include Hermann Ebbinghaus (1850–1909), a pioneer in the experimental study of memory at the University of Berlin; and the Russian physiologist Ivan Pavlov (1849-1936) who investigated the learning process now referred to as classical conditioning.

Psychoanalysis

From the 1890s until his death in 1939, the Austrian physician Sigmund Freud developed a method of psychotherapy known as psychoanalysis. Freud's understanding of the mind was largely based on interpretive methods, introspection and clinical observations, and was focused in particular on resolving unconscious conflict, mental distress and psychopathology. Freud's theories became very well-known, largely because they tackled subjects such as sexuality, repression, and the unconscious mind as general aspects of psychological development. These were largely considered taboo subjects at the time, and Freud provided a catalyst for them to be openly discussed in polite society. While Freud is perhaps best known for his tripartite model of the mind, consisting of the id, ego, and superego, and his theories about the Oedipus complex, his most lasting legacy may be not the content of his theories but his clinical innovations, such as the method of free association and a clinical interest in dreams.

Freud had a significant influence on Swiss psychiatrist Carl Jung, whose analytical psychology became an alternative form of depth psychology. Other well-known psychoanalytic thinkers of the mid-twentieth century included Sigmund Freud's daughter, psychoanalyst Anna Freud; German-American psychologist Erik Erickson, Austrian-British psychoanalyst Melanie Klein, English psychoanalyst and physician D. W. Winnicott, German psychologist Karen Horney, German-born psychologist and philosopher Erich Fromm, and English psychiatrist John Bowlby. Contemporary psychoanalysis comprises diverse schools of thought, including ego psychology, object relations, interpersonal, Lacanian, and relational psychoanalysis. Modification of Jung's theories has led to the archetypal and process-oriented schools of psychological thought.

Austrian-British philosopher Karl Popper argued that Freud's psychoanalytic theories were presented in untestable form. Psychology departments in American universities today are scientifically oriented, and Freudian theory has been marginalized, being regarded instead as a "desiccated and dead" historical artifact, according to a recent APA study. Recently, however, South African neuroscientist Mark Solms and other researchers in the emerging field of neuro-psychoanalysis have argued for Freud's theories, pointing out brain structures relating to Freudian concepts such as libido, drives, the unconscious, and repression.

Behaviorism

Behaviorism arose partly due to the popularity of laboratory-based animal experimentation and partly in reaction to Freudian psychodynamics, which was difficult to test empirically because, among other reasons, it tended to rely on case studies and clinical experience, and dealt largely with intra-psychic phenomena that were difficult to quantify or to define operationally. Moreover, in contrast with early psychologists Wilhelm Wundt and William James, who studied the mind via introspection, the behaviorists argued that the contents of the mind were not open to scientific scrutiny and that scientific psychology should only be concerned with the study of observable behavior. There was no consideration of internal representation or the mind. Founded in the early 20th century by American psychologist John B. Watson, behaviorism was embraced and extended by Americans Edward Thorndike, Clark L. Hull, Edward C. Tolman, and later B.F. Skinner.

Behaviorism differs from other perspectives in a number of ways. Behaviorists focus on behavior-environment relations and analyze overt and covert (*i.e.*, private) behavior as a function of the organism interacting with its environment. Behaviorists do not reject the study of covert or private events (*e.g.*, dreaming), but rather reject the proposition that an autonomous causal entity inside the organism causes overt (*e.g.*, walking, talking) or covert (*e.g.*, dreaming, imagining) behavior. Concepts such as "mind" or "consciousness" are not used by behaviorists because such terms do not describe actual psychological events (such as imagining) but are used as explanatory entities hidden somewhere in the organism.

By contrast, behaviorism treats private events as behavior, and analyzes them in the same way as overt behavior. Behavior refers to the concrete events of the organism, overt or private.

American linguist Noam Chomsky's critique of the behaviorist model of language acquisition is regarded by many as a key turning point in the decline of behaviorism's general prominence. But Skinner's behaviorism has not died, perhaps in part because it has generated successful practical applications. The ascendancy of behaviorism as an overarching model in psychology, however, gave way to a new dominant paradigm: cognitive approaches.

Humanism and Existentialism

Humanistic psychology was developed in the 1950s in reaction to both behaviorism and psychoanalysis. By using phenomenology, intersubjectivity and first-person categories, the humanistic approach seeks to glimpse the whole person—not just the fragmented parts of the personality or cognitive functioning. Humanism focuses on uniquely human issues and fundamental issues of life, such as self-identity, death, aloneness, freedom, and meaning. There are several factors which distinguish the humanistic approach from other approaches within psychology. These include the emphasis on subjective meaning, a rejection of determinism, and a concern for positive growth rather than pathology. Some of the founding theorists behind this school of thought were American psychologists Abraham Maslow, who formulated a hierarchy of human needs, and Carl Rogers, who created and developed client-centered therapy; and German-American psychiatrist Fritz Perls, who helped create and develop Gestalt therapy. It became so influential as to be called the "third force" within psychology, along with behaviorism and psychoanalysis.

Influenced largely by the work of German philosopher Martin Heidegger and Danish philosopher Soren Kierkegaard, psychoanalytically-trained American psychologist Rollo May developed an existential breed of psychology in the 1950s and 1960s. Existential psychologists argued that people must come to terms with their mortality and that, in so doing, people will be obligated to accept that they are free—that they possess free will and are at liberty to defy expectations and conventions in order to forge their own, meaningful paths through life. May believed that an important element of the meaning-making process is the search for myths, or narrative patterns into which the individual may fit.

From the existential perspective, not only does the quest for meaning follow from an acceptance of mortality, but the attainment of meaning can overshadow the prospect of death. As Austrian existential psychiatrist and Holocaust survivor Viktor Frankl observed, "We who lived in concentration camps can remember the men who walked through the huts comforting others, giving away their last piece of bread. They may have been few in number, but they offer sufficient proof that everything can be taken from a man but one thing: the last of the human freedoms—to choose one's attitude in any given set of circumstances, to choose one's own way".

May helped to pioneer the development of existential therapy, and Frankl created a variety of it called logotherapy. In addition to May and Frankl, Swiss psychoanalyst Ludwig Binswanger and American psychologist George Kelly may be said to belong to the existential school. Both existential and humanistic psychologists argue that people should strive to reach their full potential, but only humanistic psychologists believe that this striving is innate. For existential psychologists, the striving only follows an anxiety-producing contemplation of mortality, freedom, and responsibility.

Cognitivism

Behaviorism was the dominant paradigm in American psychology throughout the first half of the 20th century. However, the modern field of psychology largely came to be dominated by cognitive psychology. Noam Chomsky's 1959 review of B. F. Skinner's Verbal Behavior challenged the behaviorist approaches to studies of behavior and language dominant at the time and contributed to the cognitive revolution in psychology. Chomsky was highly critical of what he considered arbitrary notions of 'stimulus', 'response' and 'reinforcement' which Skinner borrowed from animal experiments in the laboratory. Chomsky argued that Skinner's notions could only be applied to complex human behavior, such as language acquisition, in a vague and superficial manner. Chomsky emphasized that research and analysis must not ignore the contribution of the child in the acquisition of language and proposed that humans are born with a natural ability to acquire language. Work most associated with psychologist Albert Bandura, who initiated and studied social learning theory, showed that children could learn aggression from a role model through observational learning, without any change in overt behavior, and so must be accounted for by internal processes.

With the rise of computer science and artificial intelligence, analogies were drawn between information processing by humans and information processing by machines. This, combined with the assumptions that mental representations exist and that mental states and operations could be inferred through scientific experimentation in the laboratory, led to the rise of cognitivism as a popular model of the mind. Research in cognition was also backed by the aim to gain a better understanding of weapons operation since World War II.

Cognitive psychology differs from other psychological perspectives in two key ways. First, it accepts the use of the scientific method, and generally rejects introspection as a method of investigation, unlike symbol-driven approaches such as Freudian psychodynamics. Second, it explicitly acknowledges the existence of internal mental states—such as belief, desire and motivation—whereas behaviorism does not. In fact, like Freud and depth psychologists, cognitive psychologists are even interested in unconscious phenomena, including repression; but cognitive psychologists prefer to explore these phenomena in terms of operationally-defined components, such as subliminal processing and implicit memory, that are amenable to experimental investigation. Moreover, cognitive psychologists have questioned the very existence of some of these components. For example, American psychologist Elizabeth Loftus has used empirical methods to demonstrate ways in which apparent memories can be brought to light via fabrication rather than through the elimination of repression.

Preceding the cognitive revolution by several decades, Hermann Ebbinghaus had pioneered the experimental study of memory, arguing that higher mental processes are not hidden from view, but instead could be studied using experimentation. Links between psychological activity and brain and nervous system function also became understood, partly due to the experimental work of people such as English neuroscientist Charles Sherrington and Canadian psychologist Donald Hebb, and partly due to studies of people with brain injury. These mind-body links are explored at length by cognitive neuropsychologists. With the development of technologies for measuring brain function, neuropsychology and cognitive neuroscience have become increasingly active areas of contemporary psychology. Cognitive psychology has been subsumed along with other disciplines, such as philosophy of mind, computer science, and neuroscience, under the umbrella discipline of cognitive science.

Schools of Thought

Various schools of thought have argued for a particular model to be used as a guiding theory by which all, or the majority, of human behavior can be explained. The popularity of these has waxed and waned over time. Some psychologists may think of themselves as adherents to a particular school of thought and reject the others, although most consider each as an approach to understanding the mind, and not necessarily as mutually exclusive theories. On the basis of Tinbergen's four questions a framework of reference of all fields of psychological research can be established (including anthropological research and humanities).

In modern times, psychology has adopted an integrated perspective towards understanding consciousness, behavior, and social interaction. This perspective is commonly referred to as the biopsychosocial approach. The basic tenet of the biopsychosocial model is that any given behavior or mental process affects and is affected by dynamically interrelated biological, psychological, and social factors. The psychological aspect refers to the role that cognition and emotions play in any given psychological phenomenon—for example, the effect of mood or beliefs and expectations on an individual's reactions to an event. The biological aspect refers to the role of biological factors in psychological phenomena—for example, the effect of the prenatal environment on brain development and cognitive abilities, or the influence of genes on individual dispositions. The socio-cultural aspect refers to the role that social and cultural environments play in a given psychological phenomenon—for example, the role of parental or peer influence in the behaviors or characteristics of an individual.

Subfields

Psychology encompasses a vast domain, and includes many different approaches to the study of mental processes and behavior. Below are the major areas of inquiry that comprise psychology. A comprehensive list of the sub-fields and areas within psychology can be found at the list of psychology topics and list of psychology disciplines.

Abnormal Psychology

Abnormal psychology is the study of abnormal behavior in order to describe, predict, explain, and change abnormal patterns of functioning. Abnormal psychology studies the nature of psychopathology and its causes, and this knowledge is applied in clinical psychology to treat patients with psychological disorders.

It can be difficult to draw the line between normal and abnormal behaviors. In general, abnormal behaviors must be maladaptive and cause an individual significant discomfort in order to be of clinical and research interest. According to the DSM-IV-TR, behaviors may be considered abnormal if they are associated with disability, personal distress, the violation of social norms, or dysfunction.

Biological Psychology

Biological psychology is the scientific study of the biological substrates of behavior and mental states. Seeing all behavior as intertwined with the nervous system, biological psychologists feel it is sensible to study how the brain functions in order to understand behavior. This is the approach taken in behavioral neuroscience, cognitive neuroscience, and neuropsychology. Neuropsychology is the branch of psychology that aims to understand how the structure and function of the brain relate to specific behavioral and psychological processes. Neuropsychology is particularly concerned with the understanding of brain injury in an attempt to work out normal psychological function. The approach of cognitive neuroscience to studying the link between brain and behavior is to use neuroimaging tools, such as to observe which areas of the brain are active during a particular task.

Cognitive Psychology

Cognitive psychology studies cognition, the mental processes underlying behavior. Perception, learning, problem solving, memory, attention, language and emotion are all well-researched areas. Cognitive psychology is associated with a school of thought known as cognitivism, whose adherents argue for an information processing model of mental function, informed by positivism and experimental psychology.

On a broader level, cognitive science is a conjoined enterprise of cognitive psychologists, neurobiologists, researchers in artificial intelligence, logicians, linguists, and social scientists, and places a slightly greater emphasis on computational theory and formalization. Both areas can use computational models to simulate phenomena of interest. Because mental events cannot directly be observed, computational models provide a tool for studying the functional organization of the mind. Such models give cognitive psychologists a way to study the "software" of mental processes independent of the "hardware" it runs on, be it the brain or a computer.

Comparative Psychology

Comparative psychology refers to the study of the behavior and mental life of animals other than human beings. It is related to disciplines outside of psychology that study animal behavior such as ethology. Although the field of psychology is primarily concerned with humans the behavior and mental processes of animals is also an important part of psychological research. This being either as a subject in its own right (*e.g.*, animal cognition and ethology) or with strong emphasis about evolutionary links, and somewhat more controversially, as a way of gaining an insight into human psychology. This is achieved by means of comparison or via animal models of emotional and behavior systems as seen in neuroscience of psychology (*e.g.*, affective neuroscience and social neuroscience).

Counseling Psychology

Counseling psychology seeks to facilitate personal and interpersonal functioning across the lifespan with a focus on emotional, social, vocational, educational, health-related, developmental, and organizational concerns. Counselors are primarily clinicians, using psychotherapy and other interventions in order to treat clients. Traditionally, counseling psychology has focused more on normal developmental issues and everyday stress rather than psychopathology, but this distinction has softened over time. Counseling psychologists are employed in a variety of settings, including universities, hospitals, schools, governmental organizations, businesses, private practice, and community mental health centers.

Clinical Psychology

Clinical psychology includes the study and application of psychology for the purpose of understanding, preventing, and relieving psychologically-based distress or dysfunction and to promote subjective well-being and personal development. Central to its practice are psychological assessment and psychotherapy, although clinical psychologists may also engage in research, teaching, consultation, forensic testimony, and program development and administration. Some clinical psychologists may focus on the clinical management of patients with brain injury—this area is known as clinical neuropsychology. In many countries clinical psychology is a regulated mental health profession.

The work performed by clinical psychologists tends to be done inside various therapy models, all of which involve a formal relationship between professional and client—usually an individual, couple, family, or small group—that employs a set of procedures intended to form a therapeutic alliance, explore the nature of psychological problems, and encourage new ways of thinking, feeling, or behaving. The four major perspectives are Psychodynamic, Cognitive Behavioral, Existential-Humanistic, and Systems or Family therapy. There has been a growing movement to integrate these various therapeutic approaches, especially with an increased understanding of issues regarding culture, gender, spirituality, and sexual-orientation. With the advent of more robust research findings regarding psychotherapy, there is growing evidence that most of the major therapies are about of equal effectiveness, with the key common element being a strong therapeutic alliance. Because of this, more training programs and psychologists are now adopting an eclectic therapeutic orientation.

Critical Psychology

Critical psychology applies the methodology of critical theory to psychology. As such, it critiques not only the psychic substrates of the status quo, but also the elements of mainstream psychology that are, themselves, seen as contributors to oppressive ideologies. Critical psychology operates on the belief "that mainstream psychology has institutionalized a narrow view of the field's ethical mandate to promote human welfare" by promoting individual remedies to social ills, encouraging trivial and inconsequential research, and engaging in other practices that its positivistic methods fail to place under critical scrutiny.

A critical psychologist might ask whether a case of "work stress" warrants efforts to change the macro-level systems that control the work, rather than merely to treat the individual who experiences the stress—or, more accurately, who shares the stress with countless other individuals. One might also ask why "mainstream trauma efforts fail to incorporate a focus on human rights and social justice" in war-ravaged communities. In short, critical psychology seeks, where it deems appropriate, to raise psychology's level of analysis from the individual to society, and to render psychology more transformative than ameliorative. Critical psychology has been applied to a wide array of psychology's other subfields, and many of its theorists are employed in mainstream psychological professions.

Developmental Psychology

Mainly focusing on the development of the human mind through the life span, developmental psychology seeks to understand how people come to perceive, understand, and act within the world and how these processes change as they age. This may focus on intellectual, cognitive, neural, social, or moral development. Researchers who study children use a number of unique research methods to make observations in natural settings or to engage them in experimental tasks. Such tasks often resemble specially designed games and activities that are both enjoyable for the child and scientifically useful, and researchers have even devised clever methods to study the mental processes of small infants. In addition to studying children, developmental psychologists also study aging and processes throughout the life span, especially at other times of rapid change (such as adolescence and old age). Developmental psychologists draw on the full range of theorists in scientific psychology to inform their research.

Educational Psychology

Educational psychology is the study of how humans learn in educational settings, the effectiveness of educational interventions, the psychology of teaching, and the social psychology of schools as organizations. The work of child psychologists such as Lev Vygotsky, Jean Piaget and Jerome Bruner has been influential in creating teaching methods and educational practices. Educational psychology is often included in teacher education programs, at least in North America, Australia, and New Zealand.

Evolutionary Psychology

Evolutionary psychology explores the genetic roots of mental and behavioral patterns, and posits that common patterns may have emerged because they were highly adaptive for humans in the environments of their evolutionary past—even if some of these patterns are maladaptive in today's environments. Fields closely related to evolutionary psychology are animal behavioral ecology, human behavioral ecology, dual inheritance theory, and sociobiology. Memetics, founded by British evolutionary biologist Richard Dawkins, is a related but competing field that proposes that cultural evolution can occur in a Darwinian sense but independently of Mendelian mechanisms; it therefore examines the ways in which thoughts, or memes, may evolve independently of genes.

Forensic Psychology

Forensic psychology covers a broad range of practices including the clinical evaluations of defendants, reports to judges and attorneys, and courtroom testimony on given issues. Forensic psychologists are appointed by the court or hired by attorneys to conduct competency to stand trial evaluations, competency to be executed evaluations, sanity evaluations, involuntary commitment evaluations, provide sentencing recommendations, and sex offender evaluation and treatment evaluations and provide recommendations to the court through written reports and testimony. Many of the questions the court asks the forensic psychologist go ultimately to legal issues, although a psychologist cannot answer legal questions. For example, there is no definition of sanity in psychology. Rather, sanity is a legal definition that varies from place to place throughout the world. Therefore, a prime qualification of a forensic psychologist is an intimate understanding of the law, especially criminal law.

Global Psychology

Global psychology is a subfield of psychology that addresses the issues raised in the global sustainability debate. Like critical psychology, global psychology expands the objective of psychology to macro-level trends; it examines the overwhelming consequences of global warming, economic destabilization and other large-scale phenomena, while recognizing that global sustainability can best be achieved by psychologically sound individuals and cultures. Global psychologists advocate a simple and sensible, yet comprehensive, psychology, whose strength is its focus on the long-term well-being of all of humanity.

Health Psychology

Health psychology is the application of psychological theory and research to health, illness and health care. Whereas clinical psychology focuses on mental health and neurological illness, health psychology is concerned with the psychology of a much wider range of health-related behavior including healthy eating, the doctor-patient relationship, a patient's understanding of health information, and beliefs about illness. Health psychologists may be involved in public health campaigns, examining the impact of illness or health policy on quality of life and in research into the psychological impact of health and social care.

Industrial/Organizational Psychology

Industrial and organizational psychology (I/O) applies psychological concepts and methods to optimize human potential in the workplace. Personnel psychology, a subfield of I/O psychology, applies the methods and principles of psychology in selecting and evaluating workers. I/O psychology's other subfield, organizational psychology, examines the effects of work environments and management styles on worker motivation, job satisfaction, and productivity.

Legal Psychology

Legal psychology is a research-oriented field populated with researchers from several different areas within psychology (although social and cognitive psychologists are typical). Legal psychologists explore such topics as jury decision-making, eyewitness memory, scientific evidence, and legal policy. The term "legal psychology" has only recently come into use, and typically refers to any non-clinical law-related research.

Personality Psychology

Personality psychology studies enduring patterns of behavior, thought, and emotion in individuals, commonly referred to as personality. Theories of personality vary across different psychological schools and orientations. They carry different assumptions about such issues as the role of the unconscious and the importance of childhood experience. According to Freud, personality is based on the dynamic interactions of the ego, superego, and id. Trait theorists, in contrast, attempt to analyze personality in terms of a discrete number of key traits by the statistical method of factor analysis. The number of proposed traits has varied widely. An early model proposed by Hans Eysenck suggested that there are three traits that comprise human personality: extraversion-introversion, neuroticism, and psychoticism. Raymond Cattell proposed a theory of 16 personality factors. The "Big Five" or Five Factor Model, proposed by Lewis Goldberg currently has strong support among trait theorists.

Quantitative Psychology

Quantitative psychology involves the application of mathematical and statistical modeling in psychological research, and the development of statistical methods for analyzing and explaining behavioral data. The term Quantitative psychology is relatively new and little used (only recently have Ph.D. programs in quantitative psychology been formed), and it loosely covers the longer standing subfields psychometrics and mathematical psychology.

Psychometrics is the field of psychology concerned with the theory and technique of psychological measurement, which includes the measurement of knowledge, abilities, attitudes, and personality traits. Measurement of these unobservable phenomena is difficult, and much of the research and accumulated knowledge in this discipline has been developed in an attempt to properly define and quantify such phenomena. Psychometric research typically involves two major research tasks, namely: *(i)* the construction of instruments and procedures for measurement; and *(ii)* the development and refinement of theoretical approaches to measurement.

Whereas psychometrics is mainly concerned with individual differences and population structure, mathematical psychology is concerned with modeling of mental and motor processes of the average individual. Psychometrics is more associated with educational psychology, personality, and clinical psychology. Mathematical psychology is more closely related to psychonomics/experimental and cognitive, and physiological psychology and (cognitive) neuroscience.

Social Psychology

Social psychology is the study of social behavior and mental processes, with an emphasis on how humans think about each other and how they relate to each other. Social psychologists are especially interested in how people react to social situations. They study such topics as the influence of others on an individual's behavior (*e.g.* conformity, persuasion), and the formation of beliefs, attitudes, and stereotypes about other people. Social cognition fuses elements of social and cognitive psychology in order to understand how people process, remember, and distort social information. The study of group dynamics reveals information about the nature and potential optimization of leadership, communication, and other phenomena that emerge at least at the microsocial level. In recent years, many social psychologists have become increasingly interested in implicit measures, mediational models, and the interaction of both person and social variables in accounting for behavior.

School Psychology

School psychology combines principles from educational psychology and clinical psychology to understand and treat students with learning disabilities; to foster the intellectual growth of "gifted" students; to facilitate pro social behaviors in adolescents; and otherwise to promote safe, supportive, and effective learning environments. School psychologists are trained in educational and behavioral assessment, intervention, prevention, and consultation, and many have extensive training in research. Currently, school psychology is the only field in which a professional can be called a "psychologist" without a doctoral degree, with the National Association of School Psychologists (NASP) recognizing the Specialist degree as the entry level. This is a matter of controversy as the APA does not recognize anything below a doctorate as the entry level for a psychologist. Specialist-level school psychologists, who typically receive three years of graduate training, function almost exclusively within school systems, while those at the doctoral-level are found in a number of other settings as well, including universities, hospitals, clinics, and private practice.

RESEARCH METHODS

Research in most areas of psychology is conducted in broad accord with the standards of the scientific method, encompassing both qualitative ethological and quantitative statistical modalities to generate and evaluate explanatory hypotheses with regard to psychological phenomena. Investigation may be pursued by experimental protocols, but alternative methods are sometimes preferred due to research ethics, the state of development in a given research domain, and other reasons.

Psychology tends to be eclectic, drawing on knowledge from other fields to help explain and understand psychological phenomena. For example, evolutionary psychologists may synthesize data from multiple subfields of psychology, biology, and anthropology. Additionally, they make extensive use of two distinctive types of reasoning. While often employing the deductive-nomological reasoning of strict positivism, they also rely on inductive reasoning to generate accounts of hunter-gatherer life that could explain the adaptive value of different thoughts and actions.

Qualitative psychological research utilizes a broad spectrum of observational methods, including action research, ethnography, exploratory statistics, structured interviews, and participant observation, to enable the gathering of rich information unattainable by classical experimentation. Research in humanistic psychology is more typically pursued via ethnographic, historical, and historiographic methods than via science. Psychodynamic research has traditionally entailed interpreting clinical case studies, and subschools ranging from Freudian psychoanalysis to Neo-Jungian archetypal psychology have employed myth as a vehicle of interpretation. Recent developments, particularly in neuro-psychoanalysis, have demanded a relatively high degree of scientific rigor.

A precursor to critical psychology, liberation psychology, cited traditional surveys in its emancipatory quests. There is debate amongst critical psychologists as to whether they should be the ones to apply the research they conduct—as to how action-oriented or awareness-oriented they should be. In general, though, their methods tend to be critical rather than positivistic, and therefore tend not only to avoid the scientific method, but also to identify the ways in which this method is improperly used and downright abused. A key concept in critical-psychological research is reflexivity, or critical self-examination that entails "a conscious exploration of how [psychologists'] own values and assumptions affect [their] theoretical and methodological goals, activities, and interpretations". Taking a reflexive approach, critical psychologists both scrutinize the current state of psychological affairs, and seek defensible positions on the "old questions—such as free will vs. determinism, nature vs. nurture, [and] consciousness vs. unconscious forces".

The testing of different aspects of psychological function is a significant area of mainstream psychology. Psychometric and statistical methods predominate, including various well-known standardized tests as well as those created ad hoc as the situation or experiment requires.

Academic psychologists may focus purely on research and psychological theory, aiming to further psychological understanding in a particular area, while other psychologists may work in applied psychology to deploy such knowledge for immediate and practical benefit. These approaches are not mutually exclusive, and many psychologists will be involved in both researching and applying psychology at some point during their career. Many clinical psychology programs aim to develop in practicing psychologists both knowledge of and experience with research and experimental methods, which they may interpret and employ as they treat individuals with psychological issues.

When an area of interest requires specific training and specialist knowledge, especially in applied areas, psychological associations normally establish a governing body to manage training requirements. Similarly, requirements may be laid down for university degrees in psychology, so that students acquire an adequate knowledge in a number of areas. Additionally, areas of practical psychology, where psychologists offer treatment to others, may require that psychologists be licensed by government regulatory bodies as well.

Controlled Experiments

Experimental psychological research is conducted in a laboratory under controlled conditions. This method of research relies on the application of the scientific method to understand behavior. Experimenters use several types of measurements, including rate of response, reaction time, and various psychometric measurements. Experiments are designed to test specific hypotheses (deductive approach) or evaluate functional relationships (inductive approach). They allow researchers to establish causal relationships between different aspects of behavior and the environment. In an experiment, one or more variables of interest are controlled by the experimenter (independent variable) and another variable is measured in response to different conditions (dependent variable). Experiments are one of the primary research methods in many areas of psychology, particularly cognitive/psychonomics, mathematical psychology, psychophysiology and biological psychology/cognitive neuroscience.

Experiments on humans have been put under some controls, namely informed and voluntary consent. After World War II, the Nuremberg Code was established, because of Nazi abuses of experimental subjects. Later, most countries (and scientific journals) adopted the Declaration of Helsinki. In the US, the National Institutes of Health established the Institutional Review Board in 1966, and in 1974 adopted the National Research Act (HR 7724). All of these measures encouraged researchers to obtain informed consent from human participants in experimental studies. A number of influential studies led to the establishment of this rule; such studies included the MIT and Fernald School radioisotope studies, the Thalidomide tragedy, the Willowbrook hepatitis study, and Stanley Milgram's studies of obedience to authority.

Survey Questionnaires

Statistical surveys are used in psychology for measuring attitudes and traits, monitoring changes in mood, checking the validity of experimental manipulations, and for a wide variety of other psychological topics. Most commonly, psychologists use paper-and-pencil surveys. However, surveys are also conducted over the phone or through e-mail. Increasingly, web-based surveys are being used in research. Similar methodology is also used in applied setting, such as clinical assessment and personnel assessment.

Longitudinal Studies

A longitudinal study is a research method which observes a particular population over time. For example, one might wish to study specific language impairment (SLI) by observing a group of individuals with the condition over a period of time. This method has the advantage of seeing how a condition can affect individuals over long time scales. However, such studies can suffer from attrition due to drop-out or death of subjects. In addition, since individual differences between members of the group are not controlled, it may be difficult to draw conclusions about the populations. Longitudinal study is a developmental research strategy that involves testing an age group repeatedly over many years. Longitudinal studies answer vital questions about how people develop. This developmental research follows people over years and the outcome has been an incredible array of findings, especially relating to psychological problems.

Observation in Natural Settings

In the same way Jane Goodall studied the role of chimpanzee social and family life, psychologists conduct similar observational studies in human social, professional and family lives. Sometimes the participants are aware they are being observed and other times it is covert: the participants do not know they are being observed. Ethical guidelines need to be taken into consideration when covert observation is being carried out.

Qualitative and Descriptive Research

Research designed to answer questions about the current state of affairs such as the thoughts, feelings and behaviors of individuals is known as descriptive research. Descriptive research can be qualitative or quantitative in orientation. Qualitative research is descriptive research that is focused on observing and describing events as they occur, with the goal of capturing all of the richness of everyday behavior and with the hope of discovering and understanding phenomena that might have been missed if only more cursory examinations have been made.

Neuropsychological Methods

Neuropsychology involves the study of both healthy individuals and patients, typically who have suffered either brain injury or mental illness.

Cognitive neuropsychology and cognitive neuropsychiatry study neurological or mental impairment in an attempt to infer theories of normal mind and brain function. This typically involves looking for differences in patterns of remaining ability (known as 'functional disassociations') which can give clues as to whether abilities are comprised of smaller functions, or are controlled by a single cognitive mechanism.

Artificial neural network with two layers, an interconnected group of nodes, akin to the vast network of neurons in the human brain.

In addition, experimental techniques are often used to study the neuropsychology of healthy individuals. These include behavioral experiments, brain-scanning or functional neuroimaging, used to examine the activity of the brain during task performance, and techniques such as transcranial magnetic stimulation, which can safely alter the function of small brain areas to reveal their importance in mental operations.

Computational Modeling

Computational modeling is a tool often used in mathematical psychology and cognitive psychology to simulate a particular behavior using a computer. This method has several advantages. Since modern computers process extremely quickly, many simulations can be run in a short time, allowing for a great deal of statistical power. Modeling also allows psychologists to visualize hypotheses about the functional organization of mental events that couldn't be directly observed in a human.

Several different types of modeling are used to study behavior. Connectionism uses neural networks to simulate the brain. Another method is symbolic modeling, which represents many different mental objects using variables and rules. Other types of modeling include dynamic systems and stochastic modeling.

Animal Studies

Animal learning experiments are important in many aspects of psychology such as investigating the biological basis of learning, memory and behavior. In the 1890s, physiologist Ivan Pavlov famously used dogs to demonstrate classical conditioning. Non-human primates, cats, dogs, rats and other rodents are often used in psychological experiments. Controlled experiments involve introducing only one variable at a time, which is why animals used for experiments are housed in laboratory settings. In contrast, human environments and genetic backgrounds vary widely, which makes it difficult to control important variables for human subjects.

Status as a Science

Criticisms of psychology often come from perceptions that it is a "fuzzy" science. Philosopher Thomas Kuhn's 1962 critique implied psychology overall was in a pre-paradigm state, lacking the agreement on overarching theory found in mature sciences such as chemistry and physics. Psychologists and philosophers have addressed the issue in various ways.

Because some areas of psychology rely on research methods such as surveys and questionnaires, critics have asserted that psychology is not scientific. Other phenomena that psychologists are interested in such as personality, thinking, and emotion cannot be directly measured and are often inferred from subjective self-reports, which may be problematic.

The validity of probability testing as a research tool has been called into question. There is concern that this statistical method may promote trivial findings as meaningful, especially when large samples are used. Some psychologists have responded with an increased use of effect size statistics, rather than sole reliance on the traditional $p<.05$ decision rule in statistical hypothesis testing.

Sometimes the debate comes from within psychology, for example between laboratory-oriented researchers and practitioners such as clinicians. In recent years, and particularly in the U.S., there has been increasing debate about the nature of therapeutic effectiveness and about the relevance of empirically examining psychotherapeutic strategies. One argument states that some therapies are based on discredited theories and are unsupported by empirical evidence. The other side points to recent research suggesting that all mainstream therapies are of about equal effectiveness, while also arguing that controlled studies often do not take into consideration real-world conditions.

Fringe Clinical Practices

There is also concern about a perceived gap between scientific theory and its application, in particular with the application of unproven or unsound clinical practices. Researchers such as Beyerstein (2001) say there has been a large increase in the number of mental health training programs that do not emphasize science training. According to Lilienfeld (2002) "a wide variety of unvalidated and sometimes harmful psychotherapeutic methods, including facilitated communication for infantile autism... suggestive techniques for memory recovery (*e.g.*, hypnotic age-regression, guided imagery, body work), energy therapies (*e.g.*, Thought Field Therapy, Emotional Freedom Technique)... and New Age therapies of seemingly endless stripes (*e.g.*, rebirthing, reparenting, past-life regression, Primal...therapy, neuro-linguistic programming, alien abduction therapy, angel therapy) have either emerged or maintained their popularity in recent decades." Allen Neuringer made a similar point in the field of the experimental analysis of behavior in 1984.

●●

9

Thinking Psychology

As we go higher up in the scale, we observe that new elements begin to appear in the process whereby the organism alters its behaviour. Although animals seem to communicate, they cannot think. Thinking is a cognitive process characterized by the use of symbols as representations of objects and events. A house, for instance, is a symbol because it stands for the object house. Thought can deal with remembered, absent, or even imagined objects or events, as well as with those, which impinge on the sensory system. Thought is symbolic and has a wider content than other kinds of activity. It not merely incorporates present perception and activities but also deals with their meanings in a way that goes beyond the present. Since a symbol is a stimulus representing something, symbols can acquire meaning either in natural relation of events like the thunder which is always a warning of rain, or by learning the meaning that has been given to it by society. For example, a red traffic light, which has no natural relation has come to mean "stop". This meaning has been learned by associating the red light with the word stop. Many different types of symbols have been devised and almost all societies use them. Societies which speak different languages may use gestures as symbols to overcome the language barrier. More highly developed systems of symbols are found in the natural languages in which words are spoken and written in different combinations. A language is more than a set of words. Each word is a stimulus that can by association come to symbolize some event in our experience.

Mediating Processes. The problem before us is what goes on between the stimulus and response. In thinking or problem solving a meaning is a link to something else. Meanings, therefore, serve as intervening links connecting psychological events. When we say that a meaning is a connecting link, we mean that it is a mediating process. Thus then, the meanings are useful as mediating processes because they link other processes Dr responses.

To illustrate the mediation of a response, the following experiment will serve the purpose. Tolman (1939), observed that the hunger-motivated rats were jumping during their learning of a discrimination of a jumping apparatus. The stimuli to be discriminated were a white card and a black card. When a rat jumped to the white card it was rewarded by food, and when it jumped to the black card it was punished. Prior to jumping, it was observed that the rat in its trial-and-error learning turned back and forth, or tried to jump at one card and then at another. Such a behaviour indicates how overt responses made by the rat mediated other responses. In this experiment, each response led to another and each served to mediate other responses. Human beings acquire so many meanings so that meanings and the behaviour mediated by them, are important in understanding higher mental processes in man.

Thinking Process. The word thinking as commonly used denotes a wide range of activities. On the one hand, it means a little more than "remember" or "recall" and on the other hand it refers to the highly rigorous and reflective activity when someone attempts to solve a complex problem. Really speaking, thinking refers to abstract activity of the mind and whether it is simple or complex, it always involves mediating process. When we think, something of the past links with our present responses because the mediating processes act as links between the stimulus situation and the response we make to it. For example, if we were to solve a jigsaw-puzzle, we would waste a lot of time in arranging and rearranging the pieces; instead however, we think how best to fit in the pieces and thus we solve the puzzle quickly and economically. Thinking, therefore, can be said to represent the observable behaviour and the physical rearrangement of stimuli.

Trace Processes. The simplest kind of thinking, as mediating process is a memory trace that lasts for sometime and serves as a useful clue for the solution of a simple problem. This process has been experimentally demonstrated in animals by Hunter (1913), in the delayed reaction test. Such a test has been used with a number of different animals to show the existence of a mediating process. In such experiments, the stimulus is no longer present and the animal must use some process representing it in order to solve the problem. The length of time the animal can delay after the stimulus has ceased, serves as a measure of the rate at which the process—the trace of the previous stimulus—disappears.

The length of time various animals and children can delay in this type of test and are able to solve the problem has been measured. In order to infer from the method that such a process plays the role in the solution of the problem, the test must meet the following requirements: *(1)* there must be some stimulus which is known to produce a characteristic response; *(2)* the stimulus must be presented and withdrawn during the delay interval; and *(3)* no other stimulus outside the body should indicate the correct response.

The Role of Images. It has been demonstrated that visual images are involved in thinking. Although most of us can sometimes retain visual impressions of things, which we have seen, usually such impressions are vague and lack in details. However, there are individuals who are able to retain visual images that are almost photographic in clarity.

They can glance briefly at a picture and when it is removed, they can still see its image located in space before their eyes. They can maintain the image for several minutes and describe it in greater detail than would be possible from memory alone. Such people are said to have a "photographic memory" or, to use the technical term, eidetic imagery. Such eidetic imagery is relatively uncommon and studies with children have shown that only about 5 per cent report visual images that last for more than a half-minute and possess sharp details. Although we cannot observe other persons images objectively, we believe that they exist. In some individuals, visual images predominate; auditory images occur frequently but images of muscular sensations, of pain, hunger and other organic sensations are relatively rare.

The role of visual images in man has been disputed; some say that they are involved in the mediating processes whereas others are of the opinion that thinking process can be carried on without any images and hence the term of imageless thought. Without going into the controversy we may presume that some sort of images exist because a person can be made to recall past experiences or events and asked how these were recalled. For the most part, the answer of these persons has been, that visual images had been used in the process of recalling the experiences or events.

Implicit Muscular Movements. It is conceivable that the nervous system stores up experience through muscular movements and it "thinks" by reactivating muscular patterns of response. John B. Watson (1924), was the first to maintain that thinking involves implicit muscular movements. He believed that these movements are so minute to be visible and yet sufficiently real in the process of thinking. These implicit movements, according to him, mediate between the initial stimulus and the eventual response. Although there is some evidence to show that the higher mental processes involve implicit muscular movements, no psychologist will now support Watson's nation that thinking is nothing but implicit muscular movement. It is believed that implicit responses can serve as mediating processes in thinking; that both images and implicit responses as well as other types of processes play a role in thinking but we cannot conclude as the early behaviourists did that thinking is nothing but a sequence of implicit responses.

Concept Formuation

When a symbol represents a class of objects or events with common properties, we say that it refers to a concept. Boy, money, vegetable etc.; are examples of concepts based on common elements. We use concepts to order and classify our environment. If one set of properties defines the concept, we call it a simple concept; but complex concepts are also possible and, as we shall see three types of complex concepts have been distinguished, namely, conjunctive concepts, disjunctive concepts and relational concepts.

In concept formation the mediating process plays an important role. Concept formation is a process of isolating a common attribute or attributes of objects or events. By common attribute we mean an attribute shared by many objects or events. Concepts are necessary to enable us to classify things into different classes. For example, with the concept of fruit, we can classify things into "fruit" and "non-fruit". The common attribute, therefore, is the basis in making such classifications, that is, in forming our concepts.

Types of Concepts. As noted earlier, the term concept refers to properties, which objects and events have in common. Psychologists have worked on concept formation and have discovered that there are three types of complex concepts.

1. ***Conjunctive Concepts.*** This type of concept is characterized by the presence of several

characteristics given together. For example, if we are given together cards on which are painted green squares along-side with blue squares, we join the colour green or blue with squares which makes up for a conjunctive concept. These types of concepts seem to be fairly easy for people to form.

2. ***Rational Concepts.*** In these concepts, we do not take into account the absolute property of objects or elements like colour but some other common property. In the example given in disjunctive concepts we had squares and triangles both made up of green colour. The common pro)erty, therefore, was the green colour. However, both the objects are geometrical figures and hence we form the relational concept of geometrical figures in spite of the one common and absolute property of the colour green.

3. ***Disjunctive Concepts.*** In the case of disjunctive concepts, we try to separate things into groups. For instance, if we are given a card painted with three green squares and three green triangles, although the common property here is the green colour in both the squares and the triangles, yet these objects differ in shape and hence the case of disjunctive concepts. In this type of concepts a member of a disjunctive concept contains at least one element from a larger group of elements. In our example the concept has three of anything like green, squares and triangles. This type of concepts seem to be rather difficult for people to attain.

Words and Concepts. Actually, there seems to be no need of words or language to form concepts. In fact, many of our concepts are formed without the use of words or language although, words and language are a great help in the formation of concepts. For example, in an experiment, rats were trained to learn the concept of triangularity by rewarding them when they approached the triangle and punishing them when they approached the non-triangle. The results showed that the rats had formed the concept of triangularity without any words or language. In humans, however, language is so closely connected with the formation of concepts that it is impossible to think of concepts without language and vice versa.

In the process of concept formation we learn to do two things: *(1)* to discriminate the property or properties that several objects have in common and this process is called abstraction; and *(2)* to assign to the abstracted property or properties a particular "word label". When the word label is constantly applied to the property or properties abstracted, we learn the concept. If appropriate words are not available, it is easy to attach a word meaning to each class. Thus then, it is obvious that in concept formation, discrimination and abstraction always go together with the naming of classes. In terms of learning theory, concept formation utilizes the psychological processes of generalization and discrimination. For example, a child who learns the concept dog may generalize the term to include all small four-legged animals. However, gradually either because the parents correct him or due to personal observations, the child learns to make finer discriminations till his concept approximates the conventional concept of dog. The child may further refine the concept and distinguish between friendly dogs and unfriendly dogs. Since human beings use language they are able to form all types of concepts, from fairly concrete ones such as dogs, to highly abstract ones such as justice and God.

Factors Meeting Concept Formation. It is of practical and academic interest to know what factors help or hinder the process of concept formation. There are various factors, which operate in concept formation but for our purpose only some will be mentioned.

(1) ***Transfer.*** As we have already seen in the chapter on learning, transfer helps a lot if the concept already learnt is similar to the one being learnt. This type of transfer we have called a positive transfer; but similarity can also be a hindrance, in the sense that, it may produce a negative transfer. For example, in learning a new concept, if this concept appears to be similar to the one already learned but it differ in some important respects, the person will have difficulty in understanding the new concept. It is for this reason, that it is necessary to know both the similarities as well as the differences between the learning of a new concept and the one, which is already learned.

(2) ***Distinctiveness.*** By distinctiveness we mean the degree to which common elements are isolated, grouped, or made obvious in some way or the other. It is common place that anything which makes the common property of the concept stand out prominently will help in concept formation; whereas anything that is obscure or embedded in complex form will not be clear and distinct and hence it will pose a difficulty in forming a concept. In an experiment, when the experimenter used meaningless drawings and outlined in red the property to be extracted, he found that concept formation was much more rapid than it did otherwise.

(3) ***Other Factors.*** The three important factors, which affect concept formation are: *(i)* the ability to manipulate material. For instance, if a person is given the freedom to rearrange, redraw, or reorganize the materials containing common properties, it is possible that he will learn the appropriate concepts. *(ii)* The second factor is the

instruction or general purpose a person has. If a person is told to try to discover a common element, that is, to search for the concept, he will be able to form the concept quicker and, *(iii)* a person will learn faster if he has all the relevant information available at the same time instead of getting information piece by piece at a time.

The Problem Solving Behaviour

It was already stated that thinking consists of mediating processes many of which are words and concepts. However, what starts the trend of thinking, what guides it, or what brings it to a stop is the problem, in other words, the course of thinking has to be investigated. This question has been answered by saying that there are two important factors in the process of thinking, namely, motivation and habit or set. It is true that thinking is usually motivated, it is the desire, the craving to go from unclear to clear which starts the process of thinking. Motivation gives direction to thought processes and each stage in thinking is controlled by motives. We must distinguish between two types of motives that are involved in thinking: *(1)* a motive like love or curiosity or ambition, which precedes the behaviour and *(2)* a motive induced by the problem itself to complete the task or anticipate the solution of the problem.

Besides motivation, thinking is also guided by habit or set. For example, practice to solve a problem in one way leads us to solve a new problem in the same way if the stimuli, of course, are similar in both the problems. Like transfer of training, the set can be positive or negative in its effects. Several experiments have shown that habit strength or set can be much stronger factor in the thinking process.

Sometimes we may be so accustomed to use particular objects in particular ways that we are unable to see new ways of using them when new ways are needed to solve a problem. This effect of set is called functional fixedness, which hinders problem-solving.

Process in Problem-solving. As it was already observed, thinking begins with some kind of felt need or motive which cannot at once be satisfied, but it is guided by some habit or set towards its solution. This process of problem solving involves either mechanical solutions or solution through understanding or through insight. In mechanical solutions, the solutions are arrived at by trial-and-error method as in the case of puzzle solving. In solving problems by understanding, we attempt to solve problems by proceeding from the general principles to specific means. The general principles supply us with the understanding of the problem and the application of these general principles to a specific problem enables us to solve the problems in question. It is possible to trace the steps involved in reaching the solution of the problem concerned in we ask the person as to how he solved the problem. Sometimes, the solution seems to come suddenly and the subject is unable to offer any explanation for it. In such cases, the problem is solved through insight. In insightful solutions, we suddenly hit upon the solution having had a thorough insight into the problem. However, it must be remembered that this insight into the problem may be because of a previous learning.

Creative Thinking

This type of thinking resembles insightful solution in the, sense that ideas pour into our mind after much arrangement and rearrangement of symbols. The creative thinker, whether artist, scientist, or inventor, tries to achieve something new. He may be trying to solve a particular problem, or trying to express an idea in novel ways. In creative thinking the ideas seem to bubble up in almost spontaneous manner.

Several attempts have been made to obtain objective measures of creativity. Torrance (1962), Getzels and Jackson (1962), have used conventional intelligence tests to tap creativity but their attempts have been unsuccessful because although creativity is a dimension of intelligence it cannot be tapped by intelligence tests. There seem to be various stages involved in creative thinking. The steps involved in the thinking of outstanding creative thinkers have been studies by Wallas (1926), through interviews, questionnaires and introspection. Though each has his own way of thinking, the recurring pattern in creative thinking involves five stages: preparation, incubation, illumination, evaluation, and revision. In preparation, the individual formulates his problem and collects and materials relevant to his problem. During incubation the unconscious processes seem to be at work; many of the ideas that were interfering with the solution of the problem tend to disappear and individuals experiences may provide clues to the solution of the problem. In the stage of illumination, the thinker suddenly hits upon an idea. In evaluation he tries to determine if the idea that has suddenly dawned on him corresponds to the pertinent facts or not. Often the idea may be a wrong one and so he thinks it back where he started and in this process he revises his idea in order to come closer to the solution. The process of evaluation and revision is sometimes called verification.

LANGUAGE AND COMMUNICATION

Language serves two major functions: *(1)* it allows us to communicate with one another if the speaker and the listener share a common meaning of words and, *(2)* it provides a system of symbols and rules which facilitates our thinking. The study of language involves both linguistics and psychology. Linguistics is a subject concerned with a formal description of the structure of language, which includes speech sounds, their meanings and the grammar that relates sounds and meanings. Psychology studies the modes of acquisition of language and the way such a system functions. Since these two enterprises cannot be conducted separately, the field called psycholinguistics, which incorporates linguistics and psychological methods is undertaken to study the mental processes underlying the acquisition and use of language.

All languages are based on a certain number of elementary sounds called phonemes. Some languages use about 15 phonemes whereas others use as many as 85. The English language makes use of about 45 phonemes, which correspond to the different ways we pronounce the nouns and consonants of the alphabet. The smallest meaningful units in the structure of a language are called morphemes. Morphemes may be root words, prefixes, or suffixes and may consist of one or more phonemes. For example, the words talk, table, and strange are single morphemes. Strangeness, on the other hand, is made up of two morphemes, strange and ness, both of which have meaning; the suffix ness implies having the quality of.

The Meaning of Language. The primary purpose of language is to transmit information by communicating the meaning. The meaning of a message seems to be carried in two ways. One is by common experiences the individual has with words as they have been associated with things and events. A child comes to know the meaning of such words as doll, food, bed, etc. because these words are spoken when he is perceiving these objects directly. In this way, as we grow older we build up a large number of words whose meanings we think we know and understand when we communicate with each other. This kind of meaning, which can be verified by pointing to objects or events, has been called extensional meaning.

The second kind of meaning is derived from the first by using dictionaries. For example, if a child has never seen a zebra will have no extensional meaning for the word, but if he looks up in the dictionary, he will find it described in terms of words such as an animal that has stripes, that looks and runs like a horse, that it is about the same size as a horse and is usually found wild, for which the child will have extensional meaning.

Since language is used as a vehicle of communication between people, and since people manage to communicate only when the listener has roughly the same meaning for a word as the speaker, the only possible way to measure the meaning of a word is through agreement among people. The most fundamental fact about communication is that it serves as the basis of social relationships of all types. Communication is, as it were, the cement that binds people together in social systems like groups, communities, and cultures. The fact that two people are able to communicate with each other implies not only that they occupy positions in some kind of social system but also that some kind of relationship exists between them. The fact that they use a common language means that they share some percepts and may even be members of the same cultural or ethnic group.

Linguistic—Relativity Hypothesis

We have earlier seen that language symbols are the major mediating process used in thought. Most of us believe that reality exists independently of the ways in which we talk about it. For example, we believe that any idea expressed in one language can be translated into another language. However, Whorf, a student of American Indian languages, found that such direct translation is often impossible. One of the languages he studied makes no clear distinction between nouns and verbs; another blurs the distinctions of past, present and future; a third uses the same name for the colours grey and brown. These differences led him to believe that language, is not so much a system for reproducing ideas as it is a shaper of ideas and a guide for individuals mental activity. When most people would assume that language represents and is based on the way we perceive our environment, Wharf said just the opposite; according to him the way we perceive our environment is determined by the kind of language to which we are accustomed. Whorf's thesis known as the linguistic relativity hypothesis, which proposes that thought is relative to the language in which it is conducted, has been subject of much controversy among psychologists and anthropologists. Most of them agree that there is a correspondence between the language and the ways of conceiving the word, but they also are of the opinion that these experiences significant to the people affect the way things are expressed in language.

One study appears to support the Whorfian hypothesis; Susan M. Ervin (1964), asked subjects who were fluent both in French and in English (the bilinguals) to tell stories for standard Thematic Apperception Test (TAT) cards in both languages. She found that the stories her women subjects told in English were more likely to be marked by achievement themes and that stories told in French were more likely to be marked by verbal aggression and withdrawal as a way of coping with difficult interpersonal situations. In this experiment since the independent variables were the languages, it seems that the kind of language used by subject shaped their way of responding to the stimuli. From this and several other experiments based on linguistic-relativity hypothesis is that there is a close correspondence between language and thinking.

Development of Language

The commonsense view has been that the child learns to speak by imitation. He mimicks what his parents say, practices these speech forms and gradually modifies his speech until he is able to talk the adult language. This view, until recently, was held by many psychologists and it was thought that the acquisition of language could be explained by the principles of classical and instrumental conditioning. At present, due to research in linguistics and psycholinguistics, quite a different picture has emerged. According to the new view, a child possesses certain innate, or built-in mechanisms for processing language, which enable the child to construct his own rules for language usage. These rules seem to form the child's theory of how language works. The child goes on modifying his theory till he arrives at one that permits him to correctly generate adult language. Further, according to this view, the same rules appear in the same sequence for all children and are little affected by conditions in their environment.

During the first months of life vocalization is rather limited to generalized undifferentiated crying and perhaps some sort of grunting noises. Although it is difficult to tell from the cry just what is wrong, it seems that certain cries communicate distress of some kind. Similarly, gurgling and other such sounds may signify contentment and well-being. As the child grows older and the relevant muscles and brain structures mature, the child develops an immense variety of sounds, which is called babbling. During this babbling stage it is suggested that infants are able to produce most of the sounds that form the basis of language—including sounds used in languages other than their own. Experiments by Atkinson. Mac Whinney, and Stoel (1970), have shown that the babbling of a Chinese baby cannot be distinguished from that of a Russian or English baby during this period. By about nine months the range of babbled sounds narrows and the infant begins to concentrate on those sounds that will appear in his first words. In a sense, we can hypothesize that the child stops experimenting with sounds and concentrates on those syllables, which will form the initial words.

The first words consist of a front consonant p, m, b, or t produced with the tongue in front of the mouth and a back vowel, e or a produced with the tongue in the back. This perhaps is the reason why the words mama and papa are similar in many languages. This is also why English children say tut before cut.

Words and Meaning. Children learn to associate words with particular objects and events. The parents repeatedly name an object with which the child is familiar and through repeated pairing of the word with the object, the child learns to associate the two. For example, if every time the parent hands the child her doll by saying doll, the two being associated the child learns to name the object as doll. Although some of the child's early words may seem to have an adult meaning, research shows that the child's use an interpretation of most of his early words widely differ from those of an adult. As it was already stated the child overextends the word used to include much more than the adult meaning. However, gradually the child narrows his meaning by adding specific features.

Formation of Sentences. After the child has acquired some vocabulary he begins to form sentences. At first the child learns to use simple and short sentences and the words he selects are usually those that carry most meaning as well as those that receive the most stress or emphasis. For example, the child seldom uses articles or prepositions in his simple sentences and inspite of the brevity of sentences, the child's early utterances express most of the basic functions of language. Many of the first two-word sentences are devoted to naming objects (see car) and describing actions (car go). At this stage of language development the child seems to comprehend much more than he can express.

As the child grows, he progresses from two-word utterances to more complex sentences. By the time children are three years old, they are able to construct complicated sentences. For example, instead of saying want hat, he is able to say want daddy hat. Later, when the child begins to acquire regular verbs and learns the rule that past tenses are formed by adding ed, he tries to regularize the regular verbs. He will say mummy corned home or daddy tooked the book. At this stage the child is striving for a general rule and eventually he learns the correct usage of words.

Factors in Language Development

The rate of language acquisition depends upon several factors such as intelligence, sex and social environment.

Intelligence. Children who talk earliest are the most intelligent. Terman, *et al,* (1925), worked with gifted children with IQ's above 140 and found that such children began talking, on the average, 4 months earlier than average children. Subnormal children, on the other hand, are several months slower than the average child in beginning to talk.

Social Environment. How fast the child will learn depends upon the amount and type of stimulation he gets from his environment. The environment is a complex of several factors and people. The parents make up one important aspect of the environment. If the parents do not take the trouble to point out objects to him and pronounce their names, he will build his vocabulary rather slowly. Similarly, if the parents consistently use baby language of if they are sloppy in their pronunciation and sentence construction, the child will develop faulty speech habits, which will be very difficult to break.

Sex. Several psychological studies have shown that girls are slightly ahead of boys in most measures of ·language skill. Girls use more sentences than boys, they begin to talk earlier, they articulate better, they are more easily understood and have larger vocabularies, especially when they are young.

Bilingualism is another important factor in social environment, which affects speech development. If two languages are spoken in the home, or if the child is forced, to learn a foreign language when he is still learning his mother-tongue, he gets confused and his skill in both languages is retarded. Finally, studies have shown that there is a high relationship between the socio-economic status of the family and the rate of language development. Children coming from better homes, from well-educated parents are more likely to have books, pictures, and many more such facilities to improve their vocabulary. In short, we can say that the greater the variety of experiences the greater is his mental development in general and his language development in particular.

The order in which the child acquires his linguistic knowledge seems to follow a fixed sequence. To explain the universality in the stages of language acquisition, one possibility is that the human brain is innately programmed to process linguistic input. The child seems to operate on the language he hears and uses grammatical rules as various biological mechanisms mature. Some psychologists who hold this view have suggested that there is a biologically determined critical period for language development.

●●

10

Psychology of Abnormality

Abnormality is a subjectively defined characteristic, assigned to those with rare or dysfunctional conditions. Defining who is normal or abnormal is a contentious issue in abnormal psychology. There are several conventional criteria. One simple criterion is statistical infrequency. This has an obvious flaw—the extremely intelligent, honest, or happy are just as abnormal as their opposites. Therefore, abnormal behaviour is considered to be statistically rare as well as undesirable. A more discerning criterion is distress. A person who is displaying a great deal of depression, anxiety, unhappiness, etc. is defined to be abnormal. Unfortunately, many people are not aware of their own mental state, and while they may benefit from help, they feel no compulsion to receive it.

Another criterion is morality. This presents many difficulties, because it would be impossible to agree on a single set of morals for the purposes of diagnosis. One criterion commonly referenced is maladaptivity. If a person is behaving in ways counterproductive to their own well—being, it is considered maladaptive. While tighter than the above criteria, it does have some shortcomings. For example, moral behavior including dissent and abstinence may be considered maladaptive.

Abnormal behaviour violates the standards of society. When people do not follow the conventional social and moral rules of their society, the behaviour is considered abnormal.

However, the magnitude of the violation and how commonly it is violated by others must be taken into consideration.

Another element of abnormality is that abnormal behaviour will cause social discomfort to those who witness such behaviour. The standard criteria in psychology and psychiatry is that of mental illness. Determination of abnormality is based upon medical diagnosis. This is often criticized for removing control from the 'patient', and being easily manipulated by political or social goals.

The causes of abnormality are complex, and it is not always possible to isolate and evaluate the multiple factors involved. Some of the difficulties are.

(a) Psychological disorders are usually due to the interaction of two or more agents. It is frequently difficult to ascertain the relative importance of each contributory factor. In almost all forms of hereditary diseases, some account must be taken of environmental influences; and the inherent resistance level of the organism is a complicating factor in all diseases of physiochemical or environmental origin.

(b) There are many varieties of mental deficiencies, psycho-neuroses, psychoses, and antisocial personalities, and each variety tends to have an independent etiology. It is not a question of what is the cause of mental deficiency, psychoneurosis, psychosis, and antisocial behaviour, but rather what is the cause of each specific clinical type included under these general headings.

(c) The symptoms of the abnormal are not always tailored to fit standard disease entities. Often it is difficult to arrive at a definite diagnosis, and errors are quite common. These errors naturally complicate the task of evaluating the causes of specific diseases.

(d) The same symptom patterns may arise from a variety of different causes. Even when it is known that certain factors are responsible for a specific type of psychological disorder, it does not follow that these factors are always present in the same degree in all patients exhibiting similar symptoms.

Heredity

Heredity is the enigma of Psychopathology. Its importance is usually either exaggerated or underestimated. Almost every form of psychological deviation has been attributed by some writers to hereditary causes and by others to nonhereditary ones. Experimental data with respect to individual diseases are reported in subsequent chapters. A summary of these findings indicates that approximately three-fourths of mental defectives and one-third of psychotic individuals owe their condition mainly to unfavourable heredity.

Heredity is a contributory factor in an additional 15 per cent of psychoses, in many psychoneuroses, and in some, cases of chronic anti-social or criminal behaviour. It is relatively unimportant in juvenile delinquency and in most instances of mild or occasional criminality. One never inherits nervousness, anxiety, delusions, excitability, hallucinations, antisocial tendencies, convulsions, depressive states, urge to drink, or defective intelligence. All that one inherits are genes, which are submicroscopic chemical units that in some unknown way control the development of the nervous system and other parts of the body. The quality of the organs and tissues inherited in turn influences behaviour potentialities, since in the final analysis all psychological reactions have a physiological foundation. The final effect of any given set of genes is in no way absolute. A person who inherits genes that produce physiological structures favouring the development of some form of psychological abnormality is not necessarily destined to develop that abnormality. With such a hereditary handicap it will be easy for him to develop that disease, but whether he actually does or not will depend on the interaction of other genes and the external environment. Tuberculosis, for example, is a hereditary disease.

A person who has inherited genes that produce a favourable physiochemical basis for developing tuberculosis will probably develop the disease if he is exposed to the tubercle bacillus; but if he avoids infection, he will not develop it. Diabetes is also a hereditary disease, but a person who inherits the predisposition to the disease may avoid developing overt symptoms by insulin medication. In the field of psychological medicine the same situation prevails. A person who inherits a predisposition to a mental disorder runs a high risk of developing the disease, but if he is reared in a protected and simple environment, he may never exhibit overt symptoms Similarly, a person who inherits genes that predispose him to have convulsions may avoid having attacks, or decrease their frequency, through suitable medication. Where the controlling agent of some hereditary disease is unknown, however, it may be virtually impossible to prevent the appearance of symptoms.

Thus a child who inherits genes that favour the development of mental and physical characteristics associated with certain forms of mental deficiency will probably show these traits, not because they are inevitable but because preventive or curative measures have not yet been discovered.

Genetic Principles

A person's heredity is sealed at the moment of conception, when the male sex cell, or sperm, penetrates the female sex cell, or ovum. The ovum and sperm each contain 24 chromosomes, and their union provides the fertilised egg with 24 pairs of chromosomes.

The billions of cells that make up the human organism at birth are derived from the repeated division and redivision of the initial fertilised cell. Located in linear order in the chromosomes, like beads on a string, are the genes, which are directly responsible for the transmission of inherited characteristics. An important quality of genes is that each maintains its integrity, particular constitution and properties in unaltered form from one generation to the next. They are in no way affected by the life experiences of their temporary host. Traits, skills, and diseases that are acquired by the parent do not modify the genes he passes on to his children.

Like chromosomes, genes occur in pairs. For every gene present in the chromosomes released by the male sex cell, there is a corresponding gene present in the paired chromosome contributed by the female sex cell. Thus if a specific gene has to do with eye color, the gene located in the same position on the paired chromosome also is concerned with eye color. This double inheritance creates an important biological problem. Assuming: that a child inherits genes that produce blue-eyedness from the mother and genes that produce brown-eyedness from the father, what will be the eye color of the child?

Gregor Mendel, the father of genetics, offered a simple solution on the basis of his theory of dominant and recessive factors. Experimenting with peas in the garden of an Austrian monastery, Mendel noted that when yellow peas were crossed with green peas, all the first-generation peas were yellow. When the first-generation peas were crossed with each other, green peas reappeared in the second generation in the ratio of one green to three yellow peas. Meridel's findings, interpreted in terms of present-day knowledge, meant that the color-producing genes of the yellow peas, which may be indicated by the symbol DD, were dominant and held in check the recessive rr genes of the green peas. In crossing pure DD yellow peas with pure rr green peas, each of the D genes of the yellow peas was paired by chance with one of the r genes of the green peas, so that the first-generation peas had a hybrid Dr composition. For purposes of distinction, pure DD or rr'gene pairs are called homozygotes and hybrid Dr pairs are referred to as heterozygotes. On recrossing heterozygotic Dr peas with each other, one-fourth of the second-generation peas had an rr combination and were green; one-fourth had a DD combination and were yellow; and one-half were Dr and also yellow.

In the case of eye color, brown eyes tend to be dominant over blue eyes. When one parent is brown-eyed (homozygous) and the other is blue-eyed, the first-generation children are usually, but not always, brown-eyed. If the brown-eyed parent is heterozygous, resulting in a Dr x rr mating, one-half of the children, having Dr genes, should be browneyed, and the ent is heterozygous, resulting in a Dr x rr mating, one-half of other half, with rr genes, should be blue-eyed. Actually, these ratios are rarely pbtained.

One explanation that has been offered to account for exceptions to the Mendelian pattern is that some genes are only partially dominant or partially recessive. A second and perhaps more significant explanation is that although individual 'genes may play key roles in the production of certain inherited traits and defects, they do not exercise complete control. It has been experimentally demonstrated that each gene affects several traits, and every trait depends on the interaction of many genes whose combined influences are not always predictable on the basis of simple Mendelian ratios.

Psychopathology

With a few exceptions, hereditary forms of psychological deviations are of the recessive type. One important advantage of this fact is that the incidence of hereditary defects is much lower than it otherwise would be. If a disease were transmitted by dominant genes, the parent having such genes and a substantial number of his children would be affected even if the corresponding genes of the other parent were perfectly normal. On the other hand, if a disease were transmitted by recessive genes, the parents would not be affected, and the children would be, affected only if they received defective genes from both their parents and these genes were located in identical positions on paired chromosomes. Should the defective genes be located in different positions on the chromosomes of the two parents, the defective genes inherited by the child from one parent would be paired with dominant normal genes from the other parent, and no abnormality would be noted in any of the children.

A child whd receives defective paired genes from both parents runs a high risk, but he is not definitely destined to develop the disease in question. The reason for this is that the penetrance or manifestation rate of genes is far short of 100 per cent. In a substantial number of cases the latent predisposition is held in check by various biological and environmental influences. A disadvantage associated with having a disease transmitted by recessive genes is that the difficulty of eliminating it by eugenic measures is greatly increased. Because of recessive defective genes, it is possible for parents who are themselves apparently normal to have feeble-minded, mentally diseased, or otherwise defective children. Actually, most hereditary diseases are transmitted in this fashion. The great majority of children suffering from hereditary forms of psychological disorders have normal parents who are heterozygotic carriers of defective genes.

Investigation Methods

The evidence, in support of heredity as the cause of certain forms of Psychological disorders is based on family investigations and twin studies. The former method, which is more common, consists of ascertaining the incidence of a particular disease among the close relatives of patients. If heredity is important, one should find that the disease in question is more prevalent among the relatives of affected persons than in the general population, and more common among close relatives such as brothers, sisters, and children than among more distant relatives such as nephews, nieces, and grandchildren. However, except in rare instances, one should not expect to find more than a small proportion of the members of a family group to be affected, since each member, with the exception of identical twins, receives a different combination of genes and hence differs in his susceptibility to hereditary defects.

The importance of twins for studies in heredity rests upon the fact that there are two kinds of twins, identical and fraternal. Identical, or monozygotic, twins result from the fertilisation of one ovum by a single sperm. The single fertilised cell subsequently divides into two duplicate parts and each part becomes a separate individual. Since identical twins have identical genes, they closely resemble each other with respect to physical and mental traits and are always of the same sex Fraternal, or dizygotic, twins result from the fertilisation of two distinct ova by two different sperms. Fraternal twins are siblings who happen to be born at the same time. They have dissimilar sets of genes, may differ greatly in physical and mental traits, and may be of the same or opposite sex.

In hereditary studies based on twins, the procedure consists in locating a large number of unselected twins who have a particular disease and then determining whether the co-twin of each pair is similarly affected and whether the twin pairs are of the fraternal or identical type. If a significantly higher percentage of identical than of fraternal twin pairs are both affected by the same disease, heredity is probably an important factor; but if the disease is as prevalent among the co-twins of fraternal as of identical pairs, heredity is unimportant. One limitation of twin studies is the difficulty of determining whether a particular set of like-sexed twins are of the fraternal or identical variety. There is no infallible test, and errors in classification are not uncommon. Since twin investigations are usually based on a small number of cases, the incorrect classification of a few pairs may result in erroneous conclusions.

Constitutional Factors

As generally used in psychiatry, the term constitution refers to the total biological assets and liabilities of an individual, whether innate or acquired, that determine his reactive potentialities and his resistance or susceptibility to disease. Included under this heading are the more stable components of the individual's make-up, for example his bodily build, sex, and temperament, as contrasted with his social attitudes, habits, and other more changeable components. Constitution is mainly determined by heredity and endocrine function, but it is by no means fixed and unalterable. It is subject to modification by age and environmental factors, especially those that affect the physiology of the individual, such as diet and physical disease.

Personality and Physique

The intriguing game of classifying people into physical types and predicting personality on the basis of bodily traits antedates Hippocrates. About every half century it is "discovered" that individuals fall into certain physical categories and that there exists a close affinity between physique and personality. For a time, each new theory is enthusiastically received. Gradually it is discredited, but above the death knell of the rejected theory rises the birth cry of the succeeding theory, which is hailed as "original and penetrating." This, too is granted its hour of triumph and then discarded until again revived in new verbal dress a few years later. The repeated rejection and rebirth of the doctrine of physical types suggests that there is some foundation for it, but the foundation is shaky and will not bear too close investigation. In a very general way it is possible to classify many individuals as to whether they are primarily of the long-thin, short-stocky, or athletic-muscular build. However, this is obviously a rough classification since most individuals do not fit well into any of these groups, and even those who do so may differ greatly from others placed in the same category. Human physiques are not turned out from a few standard molds. Actually, they are infinitely varied, and in a strict sense there are as many types as there are individuals. This is only one weakness of the doctrine. When the proponents of type theories assign specific psychological attributes to various physical builds, they are really in deep water; for individual differences with respect to psychological characteristics are even more marked than for physical traits.

In addition, there is no scientific basis for assuming that physique and personality are intrinsically correlated. Long-thin or short-stocky individuals may have a wide variety of personalities, but here again there is a kernel of truth in that the same hereditary factors, which determine bodily build also contribute to the temperament or prevailing emotional tempo of the individual. Since attitudes and social adjustments are in part affected by physique and temperament, a case might be made for the theory that persons having similar physiques and temperaments tend to have similar life experiences and hence might be expected to develop similar personalities.

As a result of the interaction of their biological inadequacies and unfavourable social experiences, they may develop into quiet, sensitive individuals who are more interested in daydreams than in the realities of life. Conversely, individuals gifted with sturdy, attractive physiques and unlimited energy may, as a consequence of favourable social experiences, develop into good-natured, outgoing, enthusiastic realists.

The Nervous System

In describing the human nervous system, a distinction is usually made between the cerebrospinal and the autonomic system. The former consists of the brain and the spinal cord. The autonomic system is a semi-independent collection of nerve cells located mainly outside and along either side of the spinal cord. The two systems are closely interrelated structurally and functionally. Many of the nerve cells and fibers of the autonomic system lie within the cerebrospinal system. This structural relationship makes for functional interaction. In general, however, the cerebrospinal division is primarily concerned with receiving and organise sensory impulses, delivering motor impulses to the skeletal musculature, and engaging in higher mental processes. The autonomic system is more concerned with the control of the internal environment through stimulation of the endocrine glands, the heart, and the smooth muscles of the gastrointestinal, respiratory, and circulatory systems.

Spinal Cord

Apart from mediating simple reflex actions, the main function of the spinal cord is to conduct afferent, or sensory, impulses from various parts of the body to the brain and to conduct efferent, or motor, impulses from the brain to the muscles and limbs.

The Brain

As the "seat" of intelligence, judgment, memory, and integrative behaviour, and as the neural center for controlling excitation-inhibition and the experiencing of emotions, the brain undoubtedly plays an important role in almost all forms of psychological disorders. However, attempts to establish causal relationships between abnormalities in brain structure and abnormalities in psychological functioning have met with meager success. In anatomical detail, the brains of delinquents, criminals, and psychoneurotic individuals are indistinguishable from those of normal people. At most, only about one-fourth of mental defectives and one-third of psychotic individuals exhibit anatomical brain defects or injuries that might be interpreted as the direct cause of mental retardation or psychotic symptoms. The absence of structural brain abnormalities in most deviants does not necessarily rule out the importance of the nervous system, since it may be that the brains of abnormal people, though anatomically intact, may be distorted in their functioning.

The recent development of techniques for amplifying and recording the electrical potentials generated by the drain cells, popularly known as "brain waves," provided an unusual opportunity for exploring this possibility. The findings, however, have not been very encouraging. When electrodes are placed on various parts of the head, especially in the region of the occipital, parietal, and temporal lobes, the most prominent characteristic of the brain rhythms, or electroencephalograms, of normal people is an alpha wave having a frequency of 8 to 12 cycles per second. Characteristic abnormalities in brain rhythms have been observed among epileptic patients, but the deviations noted in all other forms of psychological disorders have been neither consistent nor specific.

The two parts of the brain that at present appears to have special significance for abnormal behaviour are the frontal lobes and the hypothalamus. The frontal lobes, which include that part of the cortex in the forehead region, are unusually large in man. Removal or destruction of the frontal lobes, especially if extended to both lobes, results in a marked impairment of the capacity for constructive planning. Intelligence, as measured by objective tests, is relatively unaffected, but the simple elements of a situation cannot be organised into a complex integrated whole. This defect is referred to by various observers as a lack of mental synthesis or a disturbance in planned administration.

A second outstanding characteristic following destruction of the frontal lobes is a loss of initiative. The patient may know what he should do but he is unable to carry out his plans. In their social reactions, individuals deprived of these lobes are tactless, unrestrained, and deficient in self-consciousness. Perhaps because of their inability to anticipate future events or comprehend the full significance of a situation, they are less troubled by anxiety and worry than before the operation.

They tend to be uncritical of their mistakes and are easily satisfied with a poor performance. Unproductive restlessness arid heightened distractibility are common. Emotions are uninhibited. Some patients arc euphoric and others are irritable, apathetic, or dejected. In all cases where both lobes have been removed because of tumor or infection, the patient has been handicapped to the extent of being unable to work for a living. The hypothalamus, which is located in the diencephalon, or middle brain, plays an important part in emotions. Injuries or lesions in this area are usually associated with disturbances in feeling and emotional expression. If all of the brain above the hypothalamus is removed, a eat will exhibit the physical signs of rage on the slightest provocation, hut if the hypothalamus is also removed, rage on the slightest provocation, but if the hypothalamus is also removed, rage responses can no longer be elicited. Further confirmation of the importance of the hypothalamus with respect to emotions is supplied by the fact that the hypothalamus is the integrating center for the autonomic nervous system, which is directly responsible for producing the physiological changes associated with emotional experiences.

Autonomic Nervous System

The autonomic nervous system consists of three parts, the cranial, the thoracicolumbar, and the sacral. The cranial division originates from the base of the brain; the thoracicolumbar from the middle portion of the spinal cord at about the level of the chest; and the sacral originates from the tail end of the spinal cord. The cranial and sacral divisions have similar functions and usually are combined into the craniosacral system. Although interdependent, the craniosacral and the thoracicolumbar systems have antagonistic effects.

In general, the function of the thoracicolumbar, or sympathetic, system is to mobilise the bodily resources for action. It stimulates the flow of adrenin, accelerates the heart, raises the blood pressure, directs the flow of blood from the interior to the periphery, inhibits gastric activity, and increases the amount of blood sugar available. The mental state associated with thoracicolumbar activity is one of diffuse excitement and tension. The craniosacral, or parasympathetic, system has just the opposite effect.

The contribution of the autonomic system to psychopathology is not definitely established. As the regulator of the internal environment, including the endocrine glands, the circulatory and digestive systems, and the sex organs, it probably exerts a greater influence on psychological adjustment than is generally recognised.

Kretschmer's Classification

Current interest in constitutional types is largely due to the brilliant writings of Kretschmer. According to this German psychiatrist, there are four main physical type—pyknic, asthenic, athletic, and dysplastic. Pyknic individuals have robust, well-rounded figures with a tendency toward shortness and stoutness. Trunk and body cavities are large. Chest and shoulders are rounded. The neck and limbs are short and stocky. The face is full, smooth, and shield shaped. Asthenics have thin, fiat, delicate physiques. They are slender individuals with long, lean limbs and flat, narrow chests. The head is often elongated and the facial features are sharp.

The athletic build is characterised by good muscular and skeletal development, including broad shoulders, large hands, and long, sturdy limbs. Dysplastics have malproportioned and atypical physiques. Placed in this category are the various abnormalities in physical development associated with endocrine dysfunction. The psychiatric significance of Kretschmer's classification was his observation that mental patients suffering from schizophrenia usually have asthenic or athletic physiques, whereas manic-depressive patients have pyknic builds. In personality make-up, schizophrenic patients are seclusive, apathetic, cold individuals who have isolated themselves from the external world by withdrawal into the self. Manicdepressive patients are essentially sociable individuals who are either extremely elated and excited or depressed and listless. On the basis of this finding, supplemented by general observation among normal people, Kretschmer concluded that the same germ plasm that leads to the formation of certain body types also favours the development of specific personality patterns. He maintained that individuals having asthenic or athletic physiques tend to be shy, seclusive, sensitive people who shun social contacts and spend much of their time daydreaming.

Healthy individuals exhibiting these characteristics to a mild degree are schizothymes. Borderline or abnormal persons showing these traits to a marked degree are described as having schizoid personalities. On the other hand, persons with well-rounded pyknic bodies are inclined to be genial, talkative, uninhibited individuals who enjoy social contacts. Their approach to problems is practical and realistic. They express their emotions freely and warmly, but at times they become unduly elated or depressed. Depending upon whether they exhibit these characteristics to a moderate or a severe degree, these individuals are classified as having cyclothymic or cycloid personalities, respectively. To prevent misunderstanding, it is well to emphasise that a person's physique has nothing to do with whether he becomes psychotic or not.

If an asthenic person becomes psychotic, he is more likely to develop schizophrenia than manic-depressive insanity, and conversely, an individual with a pyknic physique is more likely to develop a manic-depressive psychosis. The spectacular nature of Kretschmer's conclusions, with respect to the intercorrelation of physique and personality in normal people and the association of certain physiques with certain psychoses in the pathological field, led to a multitude of investigations on the subject. The net outcome of these studies appears to be that Kretschmer was partly right and partly wrong. Most experimental studies based on normal subjects have yielded negative or equivocal results.

Studies conducted with mental patients have been more favourable. Various workers have confirmed Kretschmer's finding that two-thirds of manic-depressive patients in mental hospitals have pyknic physiques and two-thirds of schizophrenic patients have either asthenic or athletic builds. However, it is now realised that these data are more or less invalidated by the age difference between schizophrenic and manic-depressive patients. Schizophrenia is primarily a disease of early adulthood, whereas manic-depressive psychosis affects primarily the middle-aged. The observed differences in bodily build between the two groups are mainly due to the fact that as individuals pass from early adulthood to middle age, they frequently put on weight and their physiques change from asthenic or athletic to pyknic.

Sheldon's Modification

Kretschmer fully realised that it is impossible to classify all individuals as pure asthenics, athletics, or pyknics. His writings contain many references to intermediate types and to individuals exhibiting a mixture of traits. Unfortunately, his attempts to integrate these intermediate and mixed types into his concept of trimodality were unsuccessful and left his work open to criticism. A second weakness of the Kretschmerian classification was its failure to specify precise anthropometric criteria for each type. Both of these criticisms have been ingeniously answered by Sheldon, an American investigator. Unlike previous workers who had unsuccessfully wrestled with the problem of reducing all physiques to a few standard types, Sheldon assumed at the outset that people differ in physical traits. He then suggested that these differences could be expressed as quantitative variations of three basic components.

Endomorphy refers to the relative predominance of softness and roundness throughout the body. When this component is high, the individual is fat and the digestive viscera are massive. Mesomorphy is characterised by a relative predominance of muscle, bone, and connective tissue. Individuals having a mesomorphic physique are massive, solid people with large bones, big joints, and heavy muscles. Ectomorphy means relative predominance of linearity and fragility. Individuals having a high ectomorphic component have slender limbs and bodies. As is apparent, these three components correspond approximately with the pyknic, athletic, and asthenic types, but an important new angle is now introduced by Sheldon.

On the supposition that all three components are present in varying degree in all persons, Sheldon rates individuals with respect to the amount of each component exhibited. His scale values range from 1 through 7, with 1 indicating a relative absence of that component. Numerical ratings are assigned on the basis of general inspection plus anthropometric measurements. This procedure makes it possible to describe an individual;; physique, or somatotype, by a three-digit number, the first digit representing the amount of endomorphy present, the second the amount of mesomorphy, and the third the amount of ectomorphy. Thus 163 would be a physique deficient in endomorphy, high in mesomorphy and moderate in ectomorphy. To date, 76 different physiques have been isolated and described, the most common among college students being 344 and 443. As to the origin of somatotypes, Sheldon is noncommittal. He mentions heredity, the endocrines, diet, and early environmental factors as possible determinants. Sheldon also recognises three components oftemperament, each component, like those of physique, having a scale value from 1 through 7. The three components of temperament are called viscerotonia, somatotonia, and cerebrotonia.

The extreme viscerotonic is characterised by a love of comfort and an interest in social gatherings and food. Individuals of this temperament express their feelings easily and their interests are outgoing. In brief, viscerotonics resemble cycloids. The extreme somatotonic is an active, energetic person who is self-assertive, aggressive, and somewhat noisy. He is most concerned with affairs of the present and is a doer rather than a thinker. The extreme cerebrotonic resembles a schizoid. He inhibits his feelings, is sensitive to distractions, shrinks from crowds, and meets his troubles by seeking solitude. Like Kretschmer, Sheldon maintains that there exists a close relationship between physique and temperament and between physique and psychosis.

Viscerotonia is the characteristic temperament of the endomorph, somatotonia is the typical temperament of the mesomorph, and cerebrotonia is the characteristic temperament of the ectomorph. According to Sheldon, the ectomorphic component predominates in certain types of schizophrenic patients, and the mesomorphic component is high in other types.

Psychological Types

The concept of psychological types, like that of physical types, has a long history. William James recognised two types, the tender-minded and the tough-minded. Tenderminded individuals are guided in their behaviour by abstract principles. They tend to be intellectualistic, idealistic, optimistic, religious, and dogmatic. Tough-minded individuals are realists whose actions are governed by facts. They are more interested in bodily sensations than in ideas, and they tend to be materialistic, pessimistic, irreligious, and skeptical.

Credit for popularise the doctrine of psychological types, however, goes to Jung, whose concept of introversion-extroversion has become common knowledge. Extroversion implies a turning outward of interests and energies, with highest values being placed on external, or objective, things. Introversion implies a turning inward of interests and energies, with highest values being placed on subjective, or personal, factors. Jung explicitly states that every individual possesses both tendencies. It is only the relative dominance of the one over the other, determined by outer circumstance and inner disposition, that decides whether a person will be an introvert or an extrovert. An "introvert" is an individual who habitually thinks, feels, and acts in such a way as to demonstrate clearly that the self is the chief factor of motivation and that the objective world is of secondary importance.

In evaluating Jung's classification, it is important to remember that the world is not made up of two distinct groups of people, introverts and extroverts. Only a few individuals characteristically react in an introverted or extroverted fashion. The overwhelming majority exhibit both tendencies in varying amounts and therefore are neither introverts nor extroverts but are ambiverts. It will be observed from the above description that introverts have many of the qualities of schizoids and that extroverts, in a general way, resemble cycloids.

The clinical significance of this similarity is that if introverts become psychotic they usually develop schizophrenia rather than manic-depressive insanity, whereas extroverts show a greater tendency toward the latter disorder. The main value of the doctrine of personality types in the psychoneuroses is that introverts and extroverts tend to develop different forms of psychoneuroses.

The Endocrines

The location of the endocrine glands of main psychological interest. Relatively small in structure, these organs have as their function the manufacture of chemical substances known as hormones. Hormones are internal secretions that are discharged into the blood stream, which carries them to various tissues. Though minute in quantity, they are unbelievably potent in their effect upon body structure and function. Two important characteristics of the endocrines are their inter-reaction and interdependence. An over-activity or under-activity of anyone of these glands generally has repercussions on the functioning of the others. Two or more endocrines may exercise joint control over specific functions. In the following analysis each gland is treated individually, but it must be remembered that they function as an interlocking unit, each influencing the others.

Thyroxine

The rate of living is determined by thyroxine, the hormone of the thyroid gland. A marked deficiency reduces the individual to a vegetative, imbecilic level; a marked excess may transform a previously normal person into a tense, unstable individual. More moderate secretory deviations produce changes ranging from lethargy and mental dullness to psychomotor hyperactivity and general alertness. The principal ingredient of thyroxine is iodine. Seafood, vegetables, and water with an iodine content constitute the principal natural sources. The amount of circulating iodine required for normal thyroid functioning is infinitesimally small.

Even so, there are many areas where the usual diet is deficient in this important chemical. The Great Lakes section in this country and the Swiss Alps in Europe are notable examples. Until comparatively recent years, when it was found that iodised table salt was a simple and effective preventive, these areas had a high incidence of cretinism, myxedema, and colloid goiters, the three diseases resulting from thyroid deficiency. The main distinction between cretinism and myxedema is one of age. Pronounced thyroid deficiency occurring in infancy or early childhood leads to cretinism; if it occurs in later life, the disease is called myxedema. Cretins are misshapen, feebleminded dwarfs. One is impressed by their heavy features and stupid expression. In appearance they are about what we might imagine a normal individual would look like if he were placed in a compressing machine and crushed to one-half normal size. If prompt and continued, thyroid medication often results in the elimination of physical symptoms and some mental improvement. 'Once firmly established, cretinism is incurable. Like cretins, myxedema patients are overweight, have puffed facial features, and are mentally sluggish. Because of the delayed onset of the disease, these individuals are usually of average height and are rarely feeble-minded. Prognosis following thyroid medication is favourable. Ranging from a mild swelling of the neck to the presence of large pendulous masses, colloid goiters are due to an enlargement of the thyroid gland. In a desperate attempt to compensate for the relative absence of iodine in the diet, the gland produces an excessive amount of thyroxine of poor quality.

The toll of the disease is slight. Some disfigurement of the neck and a tendency toward obesity are the principal symptoms. An excessive discharge of thyroxine accelerates the metabolic processes of the body, leading to loss of weight, rapid pulse, tremors, restlessness, and insomnia. The condition is sometimes referred to as Graves' disease. Intelligence is not affected, but the individual is irritable, nervous, and unstable. The gland may enlarge to form an exophthalmic goiter, so called because of the peculiar bulging outward of the eyes that gives the victim a startled expression. Relief may be obtained by expert surgical removal of a portion of the thyroid gland.

Adrenals

The two adrenal glands are found at the upper tip of each kidney. Each gland consists of two parts., an outer layer called the adrenal cortex and an inner core, the adrenal medulla. The two parts secrete separate hormones having different functions. The secretion of the cortex is cortin, a chemical compound essential to life. A deficiency of cortin produces Addison's disease, a disorder marked by increased fatigability, anemia, loss of appetite, listlessness, insomnia, irritability, and darkening of the skin. Over activity of the adrenal cortex stimulates the development of male sex characteristics in both sexes. Women who grow beards and develop masculine physiques suffer from an excess of cortin.

An over secretion of cortin during early life in boys hastens the puberty period. Although still infants in years, they attain the stature, strength, and sexual maturity of puberty. A child three or four years old may exhibit the physical and sexual maturity of an adult. Pubertas praecor is the name assigned to this form of precocious virilism. The mental development does not keep pace with the accelerated physical growth. Actually, most pubertas praecox patients are slightly retarded in intelligence. Their mean IQ, obtained by dividing mental age by true calendar age, is about 85.

Adrenin, the product of the adrenal medulla, is an emergency hormone. Under normal conditions, little, if any, adrenin is secreted, but in times of great emotional stress it is discharged in detectable quantities. As shown by Cannon in his classic experiments on fear, anger, and rage, adrenin has the unique power of mobilise the total resources of the body for vigorous action. Fear and rage situations demand that the muscles involved in flight or attack be plentifully and quickly supplied with fuel and oxygen for conversion into energy. For greater efficiency, waste products must also be speedily eliminated and unnecessary, distracting activities suspended. Adrenin accomplishes this feat by speeding up circulation, facilitating breathing and releasing sugar stored in the liver to replenish used-up food supplies. For greater efficiency, a considerable amount of blood, the vehicle for transmission of supplies, is detoured from the center of the body to the outer front lines. The activity of the digestive organs is suspended, a feature that incidentally accounts for the occurrence of gastrointestinal disorders during periods of prolonged intense emotion.

In primitive days, when it was possible to flee from or destroy threatening and thwarting objects and persons, this mobilising function served a highly useful purpose. Modern man, however, cannot run away from his fears or strike down his enemies with brute force. Threatened loss of position or savings, personal grievances, and frustrations still stimulate the flow of adrenin, but no appropriate outlet is available for the resulting energy. The individual is on edge and eager for action, but in constrained by social conventions to inhibit his impulses.

Parathyroids

The calcium equilibrium of the body is controlled by four or more tiny structures, the parathyroids, which are imbedded in the thyroid gland. Removal or destruction of the parathyroids results in tetany, a disorder marked by muscular tremors and twitches, cramps, and convulsions. The resulting chronic irritability of the nervous system makes for emotional instability and easily provoked outbursts of rage.

Symptoms may be checked by the injection of calcium salts or administration of parathyroid extracts.

Gonads

The testes or male sex glands have two important functions, the production of sex cells and the manufacture of hormones that accentuate the development of masculine physical and mental traits. Testosterone and androsterone are two of the principal male sex hormones that have been isolated. These hormones are secreted in abundance during puberty and are responsible for the growth of the sex organs, appearance of hair on the face and body, deepening of the voice, and gradual development of masculine musculature and body shape.

The female sex glands, the ovaries, are concerned with the manifold processes associated with ovum production, menstruation, and pregnancy. Like the testes, they also secrete hormones, classified as estrogens and progestins that promote sexual maturity and influence the development of physical and psychological sex characteristics.

In the late forties, women undergo a change of life called the menopause, or climacteric. In addition to physical symptoms, the menopause period is sometimes marked by psychological reactions. Irritability, restlessness, mental depression, and insomnia are common complaints. These are partly due to physiological causes, but there is also a psychological element in that women are often taught to expect difficulties during this period.

Pituitary

Because of its influence on other glands, the pituitary is sometimes referred to as "the master gland." It consists of two main parts, an anterior lobe and a posterior lobe. The posterior lobe exercises some control over blood pressure, kidney function, fat metabolism, and the contractility of smooth muscles. The anterior lobe has the greater psychological significance. It originates from embryological mouth tissue. Best known of its many hormones is somatotropin, the growth hormone.

If excessive somatotropin is secreted during the growing years, the child grows to be a seven-to nine-foot giant. Giants are usually sterile, have approximately average intelligence, and are short-lived. If the over activity of the growth hormone 18 delayed until adulthood, the maturity of the organism prevents further increase in stature. Growth is then limited to a general thickening and expansion of bony structure at the extremities. Over a period of years, the lower jawbone becomes elongated, the circumference o-f the head increases, the bones of the wrist, hands, and feet thicken, and the nose widens. This results in giving a previously normal individual a gorilla like appearance. The condition is known as acromegaly.

A deficiency of somatotropin dating from early infancy results in a midget. Unlike cretin dwarfs, midgets possess approximately average intelligence and their bodies are correctly proportioned. They grow up to be well-shaped miniature adults. Prepubertal destruction of the pituitary gland prevents gonadal development, and postpubertal destruction causes a sexual regression. Maternal behaviour, including lactation, may be experimentally induced in virgin female animals by the injection of prolactin, an anterior pituitary product. Still other hormones stimulate the thyroid gland and regulate the activity of the adrenal cortex.

Some involvement of one or both pituitary lobes is present in Frohlich's syndrome. The two outstanding symptoms are obesity and sexual infantilism. Although it may occur in either sex, the disease is most apparent in the familiar "fat boy" who has underdeveloped sex organs, a high-pitched voice, a girdle of fat about the hips, well-developed breasts, and a clear "peaches-and-cream" complexion.

Psychopathology and Endocrinology

Individuals with profound endocrine imbalance are rarely happy or well adjusted. In a small percentage of cases, the psychological symptoms are probably a direct result of hormonal dysfunction. The apathy of the hypothyroid, the anxiety and restlessness of the hyperthyroid, and the fatigue and irritability associated with cortin deficiency might be included under this heading.

More commonly, however, the only direct effect of glandular dysfunction is to produce physical anomalies that in turn provide fertile soil for the growth of distorted personalities. It is not easy for midgets, bearded ladies, giants, and obese persons to remain good-natured and mentally serene when they are continuously exposed to ridicule, jest, and social isolation. This harsh and unfair treatment makes many of them morose, hypersensitive, seclusive, depressed, and misanthropic. The extent to which the more severe forms of psychological disorders are due to endocrine disturbances is a controversial issue. Like other organ systems, the endocrines play an important part in bodily, mental, and emotional development, and if defective, they may constitute an added burden contributing to abnormal behaviour.

However, it is extremely doubtful that endocrinopathies, in themselves, are directly responsible for more than a small percentage of mental abnormality. A fair number of mentally defective, psychoneurotic, psychotic, and antisocial individuals do show physical anomalies of types common in endocrine dysfunction, but this is more likely an incidental than a causal relationship. Many normal individuals have similar physical anomalies.

11

Social Process

The actions and interactions of individuals in a group constitute a realm of behaviour of great proportions. A major part of any person's activity is carried on in a social context. Furthermore, our dealings with other people often involve such major processes as perception, motivation, learning, remembering, and problem solving. To some extent, then, we are studying all these topics in complex relationship when we investigate how people act and react in group situations.

Aims

Even a slight acquaintance with social psychology tends to suggest that a major aim of its research effort is to devise more effective techniques that groups may employ in striving toward their goals. Some investigators work consciously toward applicable principles for promoting group efficiency and harmony. Others seek basic knowledge, but the applications suggest themselves. The borderline between basic and applied research is thus insubstantial and devoid of any logical basis here as in other realms of behaviour science.

Much of the research directed at social processes is aimed at bridging the territory between the two disciplines of sociology and psychology. We seek to determine the psychological mechanisms that underlie social phenomena, which the sociologist may have observed in various groups in the community. Research efforts are often interdisciplinary. The specialists who pool their talents may come not only from psychology and sociology, but also from fields like economics and political science and from scenes of group action like government and industry, Our general aim of a unified science of behaviour is thus more prominent here than in some special areas in psychology.

Another aim of research in the social realm is to investigate processes like perception and learning at a more complex level than is attempted in the usual laboratory investigation. Behaviour science must work out the laws of behaviour in the complexity of their interactions as well as in their simpler manifestations. We need to understand how a person perceives other persons, and how he learns attitudes as a result of communicating with others, before we can consider the psychology of perception and learning to be complete.

Methods

With aims as broad and diverse as those, which we have briefly indicated, scholars who study behaviour in groups use many methods. Social processes are complex enough to be approached by various techniques, often used conjointly to supplement one another. We may profit by examining briefly some of the major methods employed.

Field Obsrvation. One way to study behaviour in group situations is to investigate the composition and activities of groups already in existence. Numerous aspects of this approach have been discussed by Whyte (1951) who used it in an intensive study of a street corner gang. Such studies generally involve a long-term investigation rather than a brief perusal of the group's activity. This general method of field observation may employ one or more special techniques for gathering information, in addition to direct observation at gatherings of the group being studied. Besides recording the interactions of group members, we may employ opinion polls, attitude scaling, and depth interviews to obtain a picture of the psychological forces at work. The technicalities of these approaches, beyond the scope of our discussion, must be understood and carefully considered if these methods are to enhance a research effort.

Sociometry. Sociometry, a method of analyzing the interpersonal structure of an existent group, requires that individuals choose or reject other group members as potential associates. As a basis for choosing, rejecting, or ignoring other persons, the individual is asked to consider a hypothetical situation where he might be associated with those he indicates as his choices This situation is often either a task requiring cooperative work or a period of leisure time, which may be shared with others.

A tabulation of each individual's choices and rejections provides the raw data in sociometry. Together with the pattern of cases where neither choice nor rejection was made between two persons, these data can be used to construct a sociogram, which is a graphic representation of group structure based on the data of sociometric choice. Each individual is represented at one point, or circular symbol, in the sociogram, with solid lines indicating choices and dotted lines rejection. This schematic representation is further refined by having distances between the person-points represent the different degrees of choice and rejection between pairs of individuals. Two people who mutually chose each other would be represented close together, whereas a pair who mutually rejected each other would be widely separated. Intermediate relationships, like mutual ignoring and non-mutual choice and rejection, would be shown as intermediate distances in the diagram of the group.

Persuasive Communications. A key role is played in social behaviour processes by communication of many sorts: an officer gives orders to his subordinates, a small boy pesters his uncle with questions, a popular singer charms his hearers with a new tune. Still another sort of social interaction is the communication of a message from a speaker to an audience. In many cases the person speaking is attempting to persuade the audience to change their opinions on some set of issues, whether he be delivering a keynote political speech, a sermon, or a football pep talk, to say nothing of a sales pitch.

One analysis of research on persuasive communication points to three major aspects of the process as places where experimental manipulations of variables have been undertaken. These are the communicator, the communication, and the audience. A typical study involves choosing a particular group to serve as the audience. Various social and psychological characteristics of this group are noted. A specially selected communication—a speech, a tape-recorded panel discussion, or perhaps a motion picture—is presented to them. The communicator is either present as an element in the situation or he, or they, may be identified for the audience. Since we are dealing with persuasive communication, another procedural detail is the assessment of opinions of audience members after the communication has been delivered.

Group Dynamic. The dynamic processes of interaction that occur when a small group of persons engages in a discussion or works on some assigned task have led to the development of a general method of study. Actually a set of methods, group dynamics refers to the careful observation and recording of the interactions of members as a group session proceeds. In its application to existing organized groups, this method overlaps with field observation. We shall concentrate on the use of group dynamics techniques in laboratory research.

Variations in this approach to behaviour in small groups are found principally in the kinds of observations that observers are required to make. The observers view the scene from behind a one-way vision screen, or else they sit taking notes in the same room with the group. In either case, group members usually know that a record is being made. Obviously, it is impossible to record everything that goes on in the way of discussion, gestures, and facial expressions. Sound motion pictures are usually too costly and tape recordings of conversation do not get the directed feature of many remarks that are made. Although these aids have sometimes been employed, the trend in group dynamics has been in the development of categories of interaction which an observer can use in recording. A prearranged plan indicating which facets of group processes are to be noted makes the trained observer an effective instrument in their study. Some recording systems concentrate on actions and statements, and others indicate the quality of the interaction-as friendly, hostile, mature, etc.

Experimental variations in the laboratory use of group dynamics have centered in the formation of the groups to be observed and the task assigned to them. Groups may be created somewhat randomly by employing whatever experimental subjects are available, or the group's composition may be guided by careful study of the individuals assigned to it. In some experiments one or more group members have to be confederates of the experimenter, trained to playa certain role in the group activity. Leaders are appointed for some groups, whereas other groups begin in an unstructured fashion with leadership allowed to emerge as it will. Generally, groups are permitted to engage in face-to-face discussion, but one class of experiments features limited channels of communication as an imposed characteristic of group structure.

Among the tasks assigned to laboratory subjects, the conducting of a group discussion is one frequently chosen. We might ask a group to discuss, for example, the relative merits of coeducational universities and separate colleges for men and women. In some studies we might collect individual opinions before, after, and even during the discussion. The participants might be required to reveal their views during the session and in some cases their task would be to arrive at a consensus, if possible. In these respects, experiments in group dynamics may have features in common with studies of persuasive communication.

Widely used as an alternative to requiring discussion is the requirement that a group of subjects cooperate in solving a problem. Discussion will naturally take place, but the direction of group activity will be partly determined by the nature of the problem. Whether problem solving or discussion is required, groups brought into the laboratory provide a wealth of social processes for careful study. There is admittedly a certain artificiality to this method, with subjects aware that their statements and actions are being monitored. However, experience has shown that people soon turn to the task at hand with considerable interest and communication among themselves.

PERSUASIVE COMMUNICATION

Social processes are communicative processes, to a great extent. We noted earlier that the basic format for research on persuasive communication offers three possibilities for introducing independent variables: communicator, communication, and audience. As we consider them, we shall also be concerned with the problem of measuring the dependent variable, opinion change in the audience. The illustrative studies we shall examine have come from a program of investigation at Yale University, reported in a volume by Hovland, Janis, and Kelley (1953).

Some Methodological Considerations

In considering many types of research we have noted that an experimental situation is typically quite complex, even where a design of elegant simplicity is adopted for a study.

Experimentation on persuasive communication might deserve our vote as one of the more treacherous areas in which to seek data that permit unequivocal interpretation. Hovland, Janis, and Kelley (1953, pp. 5-6) have noted that the generality of any relationships discovered in these studies must be tested in further experiments. The complexity of even a single study is such that a confounding of variables is virtually unavoidable. Additional testing serves to separate the relevant from the irrelevant factors.

The Communicator. If two or more communicators are brought separately into direct contact with the audience, any variable, which is assumed to be introduced by the way in which each one delivers his speech may be confounded with numerous variables of his personality as the audience reacts to it. If the same person plays different communicator roles, his portrayal of one speaker may be more valid than his impersonation of another type of communicator.

Often the complexities introduced by using a speech delivered in person are avoided by using a tape-recorded presentation. In this way, an identical communication can be attributed to two or more sources. It thus becomes the task of the experimenter to persuade the audience, for each presentation, that the communication is coming from the source he names. If his attributing of the message to some source should be doubted for any reason, then the outcome of the experiment might be questionable in proportion to the existence of this doubt in one or more of the audience groups.

The Communication. It would seem that devising a communication to be used in research might pose less of a problem than creating a communicator's role. However, this part of an investigation can offer difficulties of its own. Primarily, these may stem from the fact that a communication is a multidimensional pattern of stimulation. Among the facets of the message, which may represent important variables are its factual content, its motivational and emotional appeals, and its sequential organization as a series of persuasive arguments. For the investigator this wealth of variables again poses problems of interpreting results. It is unlikely that anyone class of factor can be manipulated without some shift in the value of other factors.

Even prior to planning how we will vary a communication to suit our experimental purpose we must make a decision on the general topic of the message. Usually we will want the message to be one, which has a fair amount of interest for the audience. Persuasion to the point of opinion change will hardly stem from exposure to a communication, which fails even to arouse interest. Picking a very interesting topic has its pitfalls too, however. Such a topic may have been widely discussed among the audience to be employed. This may mean that many individuals have firmly held opinions on the issues involved. There may be general knowledge of the group's views, with attendant pressure to conform. If the topic is timely, it introduces the risk that day-to-day news stories may affect opinion strongly.

The Audience. Having seen that a communication may be quite complex, we must now note that an audience is complex in the extreme. Each individual brings numerous perceptual, motivational, and associative predispositions to the experimental situation. We thus would face many unknowns if we tried to persuade even one person to alter his opinion on some matter. When we take great individual differences into account, we would face a formidable task if we tried to account in detail for the ongoing processes of the experiment. As in other research efforts in psychology, we take the easier course of treating group statistics, letting individual differences cancel out to some extent.

Most groups which constitute audiences for research in persuasive communication have a measure of homogeneity. Classroom groups, for example, would have a much narrower range on many psychological dimensions than would a random sample of persons from the general population. This similarity among individuals might even extend to the opinions, which entered into the experiment. A degree of such convergence of viewpoints might be appropriate for some studies, whereas other experiments would benefit more from employing a group whose views diverged markedly, covering a broad spectrum of opinion.

Besides selecting a communication that is appropriate to the audience, the experimenter must create plausibility for his request that it be given their attention. Why should they listen to this tape recording, and why should they fill out an opinion questionnaire on the topic? An ingenious investigator may invent some reason for conducting the experiment other than to see how the message causes opinion change. To admit his true purpose would invite resistance on the part of many people. Later, when the data have been collected, the experimenter may explain the study fully without danger of introducing distortion into his findings. The gaging of opinions must similarly be conducted in a way calculated not to alter response tendencies in an undesired way.

Measuring Opinion. An opinion may be defined as an evaluative response which a subject makes, or indirectly indicates his readiness to make. Being evaluative, opinions are measured through psychological scaling techniques such as we considered. Examples of items designed to assess an opinion are the following two:

Intercollegiate football . . .

1. should be given greater emphasis in college life.
2. should be maintained at the present level of emphasis in college life.
3. should be given less emphasis in college life.

Intercollegiate football should be abolished.

— Agree strongly

— Agree

— Neither agree nor disagree

— Disagree

— Disagree strongly

Either of these techniques for scaling opinion provides a means of measuring opinion change in a group. Some other scaling method, such as a graphic rating scale, might be selected instead if the experimental topic seemed to require it. In research on persuasive communication we may measure the average amount of shift along the opinion scale, or we may note the per cent of subjects who shift their opinion in either direction.

Opinion measurement cannot be regarded as simple to achieve. All stages of preparing and administering the testing instrument must be guided by the best technical advice available. Valid expressions of opinion must be encouraged by stressing the research orientation of the investigator. Anonymity may usually be promised to participants to elicit frank opinions. Communication topics may be chosen which do not arouse strong tendencies to shrink from revealing true opinions.

Design of the Experiment. We may conclude our discussion of methodology by considering the design of a study in persuasive communication. Our considerations will be guided in large measure by parts of an article by Campbell (1957). His paper deals broadly with experimental designs for investigations in social science, but many of his points seem particularly appropriate for research in persuasive communication.

Suppose that we wish to determine the effect of a communication, X, on the opinions, O, held by a group. It might seem that measuring opinions before and after the presenting of the communication to a group of subjects would provide the needed data. Any difference between pretest and posttest opinion measures might be attributed to the effect of the message. This design may be schematized as follows:

Only Group: O_1—X—O_2

where O_1 and O_2 represent the pretest and posttest of opinion, respectively, and X represents the persuasive communication.

This one-group pretest-posttest design has been shown by Campbell (1957, pp. 298-300) to yield data, which are virtually impossible to interpret with scientific rigor. The crux of the difficulty is that the possible effect of X may be confounded with one or more other effects. Procedural details of a study would make some of these more likely to distort the data than others, but each of them is a potential threat as we evaluate the design in general. In listing the possible confounding effects we shall follow Campbell's nomenclature for these extraneous variables:

1. History. Other events, besides X, which occur during the time from O_1 to O_2 may influence opinion change. This class of factors is particularly suspect when the interval is great, when subjects do not remain in the experimental situation, and when the topic: of the communication is one of current interest.

2. Maturation. This refers to any ongoing processes, which are not linked to specific environmental events. Between O_1 and O_2 subjects may experience an increase in hunger or the desire for a cigarette. Such factors might contribute to changes in expressed opinion on some topics. For example, frustration might lead to aggression toward whatever was being evaluated.

3. Testing. Responses on O_2 may be affected by previous experience with O_1. Many psychological tests induce reactions in those who are tested. Such reactive effects can arise, for example, when O_1 leads subjects to focus their attention on a particular topic. These reactions to O_1 may be more complete by the time O_2 is experienced, thus providing potential confounding with the effect of X.

4. Instrument Decay. As a measuring device is used repeatedly, it may undergo changes which affect the data obtained. This effect would be virtually absent in a printed questionnaire or rating scale. If items look different the second time the subjects see them, this may he classified as a reactive effect of the previous testing. However, an "instrument decay" effect might occur if we used judges to assess subjects' opinions in O_1 and O_2. The judges might be tired by the time O_2 took place, and this might affect their judgments.

The possible operation of one or more of these four types of factor—either introducing, augmenting, or reducing opinion change—leads Campbell to indicate that this plan for an investigation is not a true experimental design.

We shall briefly look at one more design in which a serious question of validity arises. An experimenter might present the communication, X, to one classroom group of subjects and try to compare their opinions subsequently with opinions measured in a different classroom group which had not been exposed to the message. This is a two-group design, which yields a static group comparison, according to Campbell (1957, p. 300). The two groups, constituted in some way other than by random assignment of individuals to them, are treated as represented in the following schema:

Experimental Group: $X — O_E$

Control Group: $— O_c$

where O_E and O_c represent the opinion measurement of the Experimental Group and Control Group, respectively, and X represents the persuasive communication.

The flaw in this design is that any differences in opinion revealed in the data of O_E and O_C may reflect differences in the two groups of subjects. This possible source of confounding is encountered whenever two ready-made groups are utilized or when groups are established on some basis which permits nonrandom factors to operate.

The schema we have just considered becomes the design for an acceptable experiment if we specify that the Experimental Group and Control Group are to be constituted by assigning individuals to them in a random fashion. A statistical test of a difference between O_E and O_c data is now valid because the analysis, perhaps a t ratio, is specifically intended to determine the likelihood that the difference might have stemmed by chance from the appointing of the various persons to serve in the groups.

It might happen that an experimenter would be forced to use existing classroom groups in a two-group study of persuasive communication. To be sure that differences of opinion at the end of the experiment were attributable to X and not to existing group characteristics, a pretest could be administered to both groups, as represented in this schema:

Experimental Group: O_{1E}—X— O_{2E}

Control Group: O_{1C} ——O_{2C}

In this design we would compare the change from pretest to posttest in the experimental group with the corresponding change in opinion data in the control group. That is, the difference between O_{1E} and O_{2E} would be compared with the difference between O_{1C} and O_{2C}. The latter difference is assumed to contain the effects of such potential confounding factors as history, maturation, testing, and instrument decay, which we discussed earlier. This control is effective only if conditions and temporal spacing of the opinion tests are arranged so as to be equivalent for both groups of subjects.

If we use this design with existent groups, it represents a compromise with a more effective plan of setting up both groups on a random assignment basis. With existent groups, the pretesting of opinion, O_{1E} and O_{1C}, permits us to see if equivalent states of opinion characterized the two groups used. If equivalence is evident, our analysis of opinion change becomes more meaningful. If not, we can only consider the data on change of opinion as tentative findings. The operation of confounding factors might not be the same at the two different levels of opinions, which distinguished the groups. There are additional complexities of the design problem in social science, which are discussed by Campbell, but the present discussion should be sufficient to alert us to possible pitfalls.

A Communicator Variable

As an illustration of how the communicator factor may be treated experimentally we shall review part of a study by Kelman and Hovland (1953). Their experiment dealt particularly with a delayed test of opinion change, administered three weeks after the communication, but we shall consider only the assessment of attitude immediately after presentation of the communication. Our interest centers in noting how the communicator variable was manipulated while communication and audience factors were equivalent in the different experimental conditions.

The persuasive communication was presented as a tape-recorded transcription of an educational radio program on juvenile delinquency. This interview between a moderator and a guest was prepared in three different forms, with the prestige and qualifications of the guest being varied. In one version, the guest was a positive communicator, introduced as a juvenile court judge of long experience. In a contrasting tape-recording, a negative communicator was established in the preliminary portion of the interview when it was brought out that the guest was a self-centered individual who had been in many scrapes with the law and was currently under indictment as a dope peddler. A neutral communicator was a guest who was presented as having been selected from the studio audience at random, with no information about him being given. After their identities and qualifications had been established in the first part of each tape-recording, the guests went on to give identically worded discussions of how juvenile delinquents should be treated. Their remarks advocated great leniency in treating such youthful offenders. Different classroom groups each listened to just one of the three tapes, involving either the positive, negative, or neutral communicator. It was predicted that the positive communicator would win more agreement with the advocated position than would the negative communicator, with the neutral speaker achieving intermediate success.

Ten classroom groups of high school students served as subjects with four classes listening to the positive communicator, four the negative communicator, and two the neutral guest. The content of the persuasive communication itself was identical in all cases. A questionnaire of eight multiple-choice items was given to all subjects before they heard their tape-recording. Analysis of these attitude indicators showed the different groups to be comparable in their attitude toward the treatment of juvenile delinquents. Immediately after hearing the recorded radio interview, subjects were given a set of twenty items from the Wang-Thurstone scale for attitude toward the treatment of criminals. These provided the data for assessing the effects of the different communicators. The different groups of subjects were also asked their opinions on how qualified the guest speaker seemed to be and how fair or one-sided they judged his remarks.

Analysis of the attitude scores showed that greatest agreement with the advocated position of leniency existed in the groups who had received the message from the positive communicator. A significantly lower degree of agreement was won by the negative communicator, delivering the same arguments. The neutral communicator achieved an intermediate degree of agreement as predicted, but the attitude level of these groups of subjects was much closer to that of the students who had heard the positive communicator, being not significantly lower. This neutral communicator did obtain a significantly greater measure of agreement than did the negative communicator. Attitudes toward the guest they had heard interviewed were similarly varied among the groups given the three experimental treatments. The speaker was judged to be highly qualified to discuss juvenile delinquency by 78% of those who heard the positive communicator, by 33% of those who heard the neutral guest, and by only 9% of the subjects who listened to the negative communicator. These data offer strong direct evidence that the communicators were perceived quite differently as intended. When asked for opinions on the fairness of the presentation, as opposed to one-sidedness, 73% of those who had heard the positive communicator responded favorably. Only 29% of those who had been exposed to the negative communicator felt that he had been fair, whereas this judgment of the communication was made by 63% of those who had listened to the neutral communicator. Again the evidence is that interrelated attitudes were being formed and shifted as the three different guests were introduced and as they gave the presentation.

A Communication Variable

Among the many variables, which constitute dimensions of persuasive communications is the extent to which the message is studded with stimuli designed to arouse emotion or motivation. One form of motivational arousal, which is widely employed is an appeal to fear or anxiety. Fear arousal may be employed in communications as diverse as "view-with-alarm" political speeches and "do-you-suffer-from" advertisements for patent medicines. What level of fear-arousal is most effective in bringing about sustained changes in attitudes and behaviour? This question was the focus of an experiment, which we shall review in concluding our discussion of research in persuasive communication.

Janis and Feshbach (1953) used three illustrated talks on dental hygiene, which differed in the kind and amount of fear-arousing material that they contained. The three messages were similar in presenting basic information about causes of tooth decay, and they all contained the same recommendations concerning proper care of the teeth. Different randomly assigned high school freshmen served as subjects in the three experimental groups to which Strong, Moderate, or Minimal fear-arousing forms of the communication were presented. A similarly constituted fourth group served in the Control condition, being exposed to a completely irrelevant message. In the Strong form of the dental hygiene talk there was repeated emphasis on the grave dangers of neglecting the proper care of the teeth and the illustrative slides portrayed serious cases of oral infection and tooth decay. For the Moderate degree of fear-arousal the slides showed milder cases of dental difficulties and the talk included far fewer references to the more serious dangers of improper care of the teeth. The Minimal fear-arousal involved very little threatening reference to oral pathology either in the message or the accompanying slides.

The attitudes and ideas of the subjects concerning the care of the teeth were assessed at three different points during the experiment. One week prior to the presenting of the different forms of the communication, a general health questionnaire was administered to all the students. It included key items on their attitudes and practices in the realm of oral hygiene. Immediately after hearing one of the recorded talks and seeing the accompanying set of slides, subjects filled out a questionnaire designed to test the amount of information they had acquired and their reactions as they heard the lecture. One week later, all subjects were given a questionnaire which resembled the one administered a week before the talks. This was intended to reveal any changes, which had occurred in the brushing of the teeth and in beliefs concerning proper dental care. The two post-communication tests of attitude were intended, of course, to reveal any differences among the three experimental groups is a result .of the Strong, Moderate, or Minimal fear-arousing stimulation incorporated in their messages. Also comparisons of these three groups with the Control Group could be made.

Equivalence of the four randomly established groups of subjects was noted in age, mean IQ, and number of boys and girls in each group. The pre-communication questionnaire further showed that the groups did not differ Significantly in their practices of dental care or in their attitudes on matters, which were to be tested after they had received the different presentations.

When tested immediately after hearing the communication and viewing the slides, all experimental groups scored about the same on an information test concerning proper care of the teeth. If the experiment had ended at this point, the conclusion might have been that the different levels of fear-arousal had produced no significant effect, at least in the imparting of the factual material common to all the messages. The groups did differ at this point in their attitudes toward the communications. The most favorable general appraisal of the illustrated talk came from the group who had been subjected to the Strong degree of fear-arousal. At the same time, this group was most critical of certain aspects of the presentation, specifically the unpleasant nature of some of the accompanying photographs. Mixed reactions were often expressed in response to an open-end question, with students stating that the fear-arousal was unpleasant but probably a good way of impressing the important message on the audience.

One week later, further testing was intended to reveal whether fairly long-standing effects on attitudes had been achieved and whether the magnitude of these effects was dependent on the level of emotion intended to be aroused by the Strong, Moderate, or Minimal forms of the communication. A major part of this assessment dealt with the subjects' reports on their current practices in brushing their teeth. Identical questions about personal dental care had been asked two weeks earlier, so the data permitted the investigators to determine if an individual reported increased conformity or decreased conformity with the tooth-brushing recommendations which had been given in the communication, or if no change was reported. The authors of the report point out that their data were based on reports by the subjects and not on observed behaviour. Any changes in reports may thus reflect only verbal conformity to the recommendations of the message.

In every group some subjects showed increased conformity with the methods suggested in the message, some showed decreased conformity, and some showed no change from their former report of tooth-brushing practices. Between 34 and 56% of subjects in different groups indicated no change in conforming to the advocated practices. Ignoring these, and subtracting the per cent showing decreased conformity from that showing increased conformity, the investigators obtained a per cent indicating net change in conformity in each group. For example, in the Minimal fear-arousal group, 50% showed increased conformity and 14% showed decreased conformity, so that a net change in conformity of 36% was calculated. This preponderance of subjects changing their reported habits in the expected direction was the greatest obtained in any of the groups. The Moderate and the Strong fear-arousal groups showed net changes in conformity of 22 and 8%, respectively. In the Control Group, 22% showed increased conformity and exactly the same per cent showed decreased conformity, so the net change in conformity for these subjects was zero. Statistical analysis supported the conclusion that the change in reported conformity with recommendations of the communication was significantly greater in the Minimal Group than in either the Strong or the Control Groups. These latter two groups did not differ significantly from each other. The Moderate Group fell between the other two experimental groups, not differing Significantly from either. This analysis of the data suggests a functional relationship, with reported changes in conforming behaviour becoming more frequent as the level of fear-arousal in the communication is lessened. Milder degrees of emotional arousal appear more effective in winning acceptance of recommendations. The report of the study includes proper cautions against generalizing this finding too broadly.

Another part of the final questionnaire tested the resistance of the different groups of subjects to counter-propaganda. In the communication presented to the three experimental groups a particular kind of toothbrush had been recommended. Just before taking the final test of opinion all groups were exposed to counterpropaganda in which a well-known dentist was reported as stating that any sort of toothbrush is effective if used properly. How many subjects would show more agreement with this statement now than they had two weeks earlier? In the pre-communication testing there had been an item on the adequacy of any sort of toothbrush but the statement of this opinion by a dentist had not been used.

It was found that a net difference of 20 per cent occurred in the Control Group when those agreeing more and those agreeing less with this dentist's statement were counted. A greater number changed to a position of greater agreement with the view that any toothbrush was adequate. Of course this group had not received the message on care of the teeth. In the experimental groups the net changes in agreement with this counterpropaganda of the dentist were all negative. In other words, more of the subjects were swayed by their memories of the illustrated talk to reject his statement. The greatest resistance to this counterpropaganda occurred in the group, which had been exposed to the Minimal fear-arousal form of the communication. In offsetting conflicting recommendations, then, as well as in eliciting reported conformity with advocated practices; the study indicates lesser emotional arousal to be more effective.

GROUP DYNAMICS

As we turn to group dynamics, the topic of communication as an important social process is by no means left behind. Rather, the one way communication of speaker to audience is replaced by multiple channels of communication. In most research, group members are brought into face-to-face contact and each person can converse with everyone else. In some studies communication is given special attention by limiting the channels by which group members may deal with each other. In either form of experiment, the frequency, direction, and content of "messages" sent and received are of considerable interest to the investigator. Earlier in this chapter we considered the general outlines of laboratory research in group dynamics. A small group of subjects is assembled, assigned a task, and carefully observed as interaction between group members continues. We noted that this general method is amenable to wide variation in the manipulation of experimental factors and in the observations and measurements, which are made.

Methods of Study

Our methodological discussion of group dynamics research will take the Simple form of considering first a sample of independent variables, which have been manipulated and, second, a number of dependent variables used in assessing the group's behaviour. We must omit any discussion of how group dynamics research is carried out in established groups in business and industry, in schools, and in the military. Within the domain of laboratory study of small groups assembled for experimentation, we shall further exclude from consideration those studies, which center on the personal characteristics of the group members—age, sex, intelligence, abilities, and traits of personality.

Size of Group. Among the early efforts in experimental social psychology were studies to determine whether individuals performing a given task would do better if they worked in a social setting, where others were similarly occupied, or in a solitary setting. The social setting proved to be facilitating for many performances. Somewhat different were attempts to determine if cooperative effort on a task like solving a problem would make a group more effective than an individual working alone. It was generally found that group problem solving was better than that accomplished by individuals. An extension of this sort of study is to determine what size of group is most effective in performing a given task cooperatively.

Taylor and Faust (1952) assigned a modified form of the Twenty Questions game as the problem to be solved by individuals and by groups of two and four experimental subjects. The groups tended to be superior to the individuals, but in most respects the groups did not differ, as a function of their size, in efficiency in solving the problems. The size of group made no difference, for example, in the number of questions asked or in the elapsed time before a solution was reached. One point at which a difference could be attributed to group size was in the number of failures. The groups of two persons failed to arrive at a solution in about 10 per cent of their attempts, whereas failures occurred in the groups of four subjects with less than half this frequency. With four people contributing ideas, a group was less likely to persist in pursuing an erroneous lead, as might be done by one or two persons.

In contrast to noting how size of group affects performance of the assigned task, some experimenters have sought the effects of group size on the ongoing processes of interaction as the group worked toward a goal. Hare (1953) assigned to groups of 5 and 12 Boy Scouts the task of discussing which items of camping equipment would prove most valuable to a scout sent out on his own into wild country. Each of the 18 discussion groups had to arrive at a consensus ranking of the 10 items of equipment. Individual rankings taken before and after the discussion provided correlational indices of how much general agreement had been engendered by the discussion. It was found that closer agreement was achieved in the groups of 5 than in the groups of 12. A questionnaire was employed to determine how the group leaders and followers had perceived their participation in the discussion. One perception that was widely shared in the groups of 12 was that there had been too little time available for discussion and exchange of views. Related to this was the judgment by members of groups of 12 that their own opinions had been of little importance as the group consensus was reached.

Pressure to Social Conformity. A social process of widespread occurrence is the tendency for individual opinions to be changed in the direction of group norms as views are exchanged in discussion. The mechanisms by which pressures toward conformity are exerted have been studied by three different methods with which we should be acquainted. In the first method, free discussion of a topic takes place among experimental subjects whose opinions are measured before and after the group exchange of views. Such experiments generally show the trend toward increased agreement, and they often reveal such aspects of the group interaction as the fact that most remarks tend to he directed toward those group members whose opinions are somewhat extreme.

A second experimental technique demonstrates the widespread extent to which individuals will abandon their asserted viewpoints or judgments in the face of divergent opinions expressed by others. In this type of study the experimenter often enjoys confederates who pose as subjects. These special assistants express judgments, which are divergent from the viewpoint of the individual who is the true subject in the experiment. On repeated trials, if not in a single occurrence, the real subject tends to follow the lead of the confederates, even to the point of denying his own perceptual experience. For example, a subject might agree that a line was curved when others expressed this view, even when it appeared perfectly straight to him.

In the third method one or more confederates are also employed, but the majority of the group members are valid experimental subjects. It is usually the role of the special assistant to express opinions that are fairly extreme, quite divergent from the consensus of the legitimate subjects. This special technique enables the experimenter to note the reactions of the true subjects to the one whose viewpoint is deviant. He may also observe the efforts they make to induce conformity with their views. This attempt on their part is encouraged by the experimental instructions that the group is to arrive at a single opinion on the matter under discussion.

Assigned Task. The tasks assigned to experimental groups have tended to fall into two main classes-topics to be discussed and problems to be solved. In some instances a discussion may have a problem-solving aspect, as when a group is required to arrive at a consensus on how some problem should be solved. In these cases there is usually no right or wrong answer, so that these discussions still differ from attempts to solve problems where an objectively correct solution exists. In some discussion groups, performance data are sought in the opinion changes registered by individuals. We noted this experimental approach when we discussed methods for studying pressure to social conformity in the preceding section. Other studies may involve little interest in the outcome of the discussion but may concentrate attention on the social processes taking place as the group members interact.

Many experiments on problem solving by groups have used the number of groups achieving the solution or the time taken to solve the problem as indices of effectiveness, while varying such factors as size of group or channels of intra-group communication. Such molar measures of performance have often revealed little of the processes taking place as the group solved the problem. Furthermore, when a principle as to the most efficient group size or structure was sought, discussion of experimental results has often included the unhappy conclusion that it depends on the type of task or problem involved. It is precisely in this lament that we can detect a powerful resource for the investigator of social processes in recent and future studies. If the outcome of a problem-solving effort and the group interactions leading to that outcome differ as a function of the type of problem assigned, then the experimenter should be able to use problem tasks of such variety as to create a wealth of interactions of various sorts among the members of the group. Putting the matter somewhat more empirically, an investigator may hope to find numerous aspects of behaviour varying as a function of the independent variables, which he manipulates in devising problem tasks and presenting them to his subjects.

Inspiration for the foregoing stress on the assigned problem as a pool of experimental variables has been largely derived from an article by Roby and Lanzetta (1958). These authors suggest the analysis of complex tasks into input variables of two kinds, those initiated by the experimenter and those, which arise as group members receive communications from each other. They would also deal with output variables of two kinds, the communicative acts and the actions directed toward solving the problem. This detailed task analysis should lead to the identification of critical demands made on the group by different problem tasks. A program of research may incorporate tasks, which feature different sets of critical demands so that different patterns of behaviour are elicited from the group members. Some tasks, for example, might place special demands on group members for perceiving and remembering the stimulus information, which might be gradually offered to them as the task progressed.

Communication Net. A general method for studying the interactions of group members as they solve a problem has been to establish different communication nets which restrict the sending and receiving of messages. Certain group members are permitted to send messages directly to others. Contrastingly, direct communication between certain persons in the communication net is prohibited. They may exchange information only indirectly, transmitting messages through intermediaries in the net. Two-way communication over each of the channels, which comprise the net is generally permitted, although one-way lines connecting certain persons may also be introduced as a variant in this method. Written messages are usually required so as to restrict communication to designated channels. This slows down the interaction processes and permits the experimenter to examine them in complete sequential detail. This experimental technique of restricting the interaction of group members contrasts markedly with the free face-to-face discussion that is permitted in many experiments on group dynamics.

Bavelas (1953) has discussed several communication nets, which have been compared with each other in a number of different experiments. Figure 1 illustrates three of the nets, which have been commonly used. In Pattern A the channels of communication make every individual equally accessible to the others in general. Each person can communicate directly with two others and can reach the remaining two of the five-man group by using just one person as an intermediary. In Pattern B the individuals on the ends of the chain are so remote that their communications with most other group members are accomplished quite indirectly. Pattern C features one person who can communicate directly with each of the other four. Further, this same person must be used as an intermediary by any other two who wish to communicate.

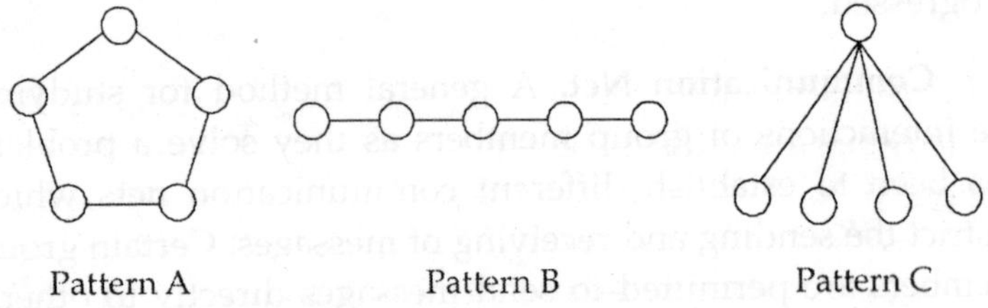

Fig. 1. Three sample patterns of communication net for a five-person group. Each circle is an individual and each line is a two-way communication channel. (After Bavelas, 1953.)

Task Performance Measures

Having noted several methods for varying independent variables in research on group dynamics, we now turn to a brief survey indicating some of the ways in which behaviour is assessed in the group situation. We begin by noting that the assigned task itself often provides measures of accomplishment, which indicate how effectively each group performed under the imposed condition. Among the more molar performance measures are frequency data Oil how many groups under each condition arrive at a solution to the problem assigned them. An experimenter might also employ measures like the time or number of messages used in solving a problem and the frequency with which erroneous solutions are proposed. Communicative actions involved in the course of discussion or problem solving are also amenable to quantification and categorization. This possibility for analysis is especially strong where written messages have been required, as in some studies of communication nets.

Observational Category Systems. Where a face-to-face interchange takes place among the experimental subjects, the common research practice is to use trained observers to note the various facets of their behaviour. These observers cannot be expected to obtain a verbatim record of all discussion. In some cases, tape-recording may be employed for this purpose. The observers task is, rather, to get a record of how the interactions among group members proceed during the session. The specific content of any interchanges of ideas is usually not noted, but attention is directed instead to the nature of the interactions. To accomplish this, the trained observers employ a system of interaction categories, which has been prepared to cover most of the aspects of group dynamics.

A set of interaction categories developed by Bales (1950) will acquaint us with some of the features of a systematic observational approach to group dynamics. The trained observers classify every interaction, which they note into one of these categories:

1. Shows solidarity, raises other's status, gives help, reward.
2. Agrees, shows passive acceptance, understands, concurs, complies.
3. Shows tension release, jokes, laughs, shows satisfaction.
4. Gives suggestion, direction, implying autonomy for other.
5. Gives orientation, information, repeats, clarifies, confirms.

6. Gives opinion, evaluation, analysis, expresses feeling, wish.
7. Asks for orientation, information, repetition, confirmation.
8. Asks for opinion, evaluation, analysis, expression of feeling.
9. Asks fur suggestion, direction, possible ways of action.
10. Shows tension, asks for help, withdraws out of field.
11. Disagrees, shows passive rejection, formality, withholds help.
12. Shows antagonism, deflates other's status, defends or asserts self.

Careful perusal of this list should convince you that an observer would require extensive training and practice before hoping to employ these categories in a reliable fashion. The observations are not oriented toward the content of the group's discussion but toward the social interaction processes, which comprise that discussion. Frequency tallies of the different interactions which take place, perhaps taken separately for different time periods, can reveal the quality of the dynamics exhibited by a group and by its individual members, Some groups may be strongly task-oriented and impersonal in their interactions, requiring an observer to make frequent use of Categories -1 through 9. Another group might evidence considerable negative emotionality, causing Categories 10 through 12 to be employed frequently. One individual might be seen in the frequency tallies as one who repeatedly asked questions, Categories 7 through 9, whereas a different person often showed reactions of a positive emotional tone, Categories 1 through 3.

Ratings. As a substitute or supplement for tallying the occurrence of various interactions, observers of a group may be required to rate the group on certain dimensions. This psychological scaling technique may be directed at the behaviour of individuals as well as at the group's functioning. Dimensions of the group, which might be rated include morale and degree of task orientation. Aspects of individual participation, which might be scaled are amount of leadership exerted and intensity of interest exhibited. Observers ratings of such a social-psychological trait as group morale can represent a facet of group dynamics which might not be readily apparent in tape-recorded group conversation or even in frequency counts of different interactions of group members. Of course, all the precautions concerning the use of ratings, which we discussed in "Psychological Scaling" apply to their employment in group dynamics research. Raters require especially intensive training and practice since they must rate so many aspects of a complex situation that changes moment by moment.

The selection of numerous dimensions to be rated does not mean that interactions between group members need be conceptualized in as complex a fashion as appearances might dictate. Carter (1955) has reviewed a number of empirical studies in which the inter-correlations of ratings on· various dimensions of individual behaviour were examined. Using techniques of factor analysis it was found that about three factors could generally account for an individual's participation in the group session. The factor names which Carter assigned to these three aspects of a person's social behaviour are Individual Prominence, the tendency to stand out from the group, Group Goal Facilitation, the tendency to promote group progress with the assigned task, and Group Sociability, a friendly interpersonal relationship to other group members.

Discussion and Decision-Making

A tremendous variety of possible experiments in group dynamics was indicated when our consideration of research methods revealed a number of ways of introducing independent variables and numerous techniques for describing and measuring behaviour in the group situation. In the realm of discussion and decision-making the research, which has actually been conducted has borne out the promise of this variety.

Interaction Profile as a Functions of Size or Group. Group size was the independent variable in a study by Bales and Borgatta (1955) who assigned similar discussion tasks to small groups of college students who met repeatedly for four sessions. Groups of two through seven men were formed from students drawn from a university employment bureau and paid for their time. Men previously acquainted were put into different groups. Once formed, every group was required to continue through four sessions, taking a new discussion task each time. Four different groups of each size were run.

Each discussion task was a case study or problem in human relations faced by an administrator. Copies of each problem were given to individual subjects to be read and were then put aside as the group discussion began. It was purposely not made clear whether the same range of facts had been presented to everyone. The discussion task was to bring all available information together, review the actions and motives of the people described, and decide a course of action, which ought to be followed by the administrator. After about 40 min the group was supposed to make a tape-recording of their proposed solution.

For their analysis of the group dynamics of discussion groups as a function of size, the investigators made use of the interaction categories devised by Bales (1950) which we reviewed as an example of an observational system in our discussion of methods. As the different interactions of individuals were tallied, how would these frequency tallies distribute themselves over the twelve categories of the system? To what extent would this distribution of interactions over the categories be affected by the size of the different discussion groups? This latter question was the heart of the investigation to which we shall devote our exclusive attention. Before reviewing the findings we need to note how the frequency data were combined and transformed.

In the principal analysis each individual's frequency tally over the twelve categories was first obtained by pooling all four sessions. Next, these twelve frequencies were converted to per cents for each subject. Then these per cents were treated by a mathematical transformation to obtain approximately normal distributions. Finally, a mean was computed, for each category of interaction, by pooling the individual's values according to the size of group in which they had participated. For example, mean values for each category were calculated for the twenty men who had been members of groups of five participants. Such means were compared within categories by tests of statistical significance to see how size of group affected the discussion process. We may take note of a few representative results.

As group size was increased, the investigators noted increases in the behaviours of exhibiting tension release (Category 2) and giving suggestion (Category 4). There were decreases in showing tension (Category 11) and showing agreement (Category 3). Such changes, occurring as the size of a discussion group grows larger, seem to reflect factors like the decreased talking time per participant which is available and the need to maintain good intra-group relationships as the number of persons interacting becomes larger.

The two-man discussion group showed a number of differences from the three-man group in the profile of interaction across the twelve categories. For example, the two-man groups were higher in frequency of showing tension (Category 11) but lower in showing disagreement (Category 10) and antagonism (Category 12). The authors suggest that this relative absence of overt antagonism in two-man groups is due to the need to proceed with caution when unanimity seems needed. In three-man groups such caution may be tossed aside when two participants arrive at a majority opinion and may hope to convince the third man of their view.

Although the two-man groups were fairly low in showing disagreement and antagonism, groups of four and six men were higher in these, Categories 10 and 12 respectively, than were the groups of three, five, and seven men, on the average. In this comparison, with the special two-man groups set aside, we need to ask why the groups containing an even number of men should generate more antagonism. The authors of the study suggest that it is due to the likelihood of even splits of opinion, which do not take place when an odd number of persons is involved in a discussion. In the latter instance, one view will have a majority, which keeps discussion moving and avoids prolonged conflict.

Social Scales of Judgement and Group Decisions. A quantitative group decision will be more accurate if it is derived from a broad, rather than a narrow, reference scale developed in the group discussion. This was one hypothesis tested in an investigation by Ziller (1955) which we shall review partially to illustrate a basic experimental format for the study of group decision-making. Although the experimenter used organized air crews as groups in the experiment, the research techniques are largely applicable to any small groul1s which we might assemble for research purposes. In this brief review we shall omit discussion of how the factor of military status entered into the investigation as the different crews were studied.

Thirty-six crews ranging in size from ten to fifteen men served as the experimental groups. A quantitative task was devised for which there was an objectively true answer, but which would elicit a variety of individual estimates as a starting point for the group decision-making. With each group seated in a face-to-face arrangement, the experimenter dropped into their midst a 16 in. X 21 in. card on which were scattered, evenly but irregularly, exactly 3155 dots. The card was in view for only 15 sec, longer exposure times having led to unduly accurate techniques of estimation. Each group was given the task of arriving at a crew decision about the number of dots that had been displayed.

Under Conditions A and B, the group discussion was preceded by a public poll in which the experimenter called on each individual to announce his own personal estimate. Under Condition C the group discussion began without this requirement for individual estimates. This condition was expected to lead to less accurate group estimates on the assumption that these groups would carryon their discussion with a narrower reference scale of estimates. Conditions A and B were expected to develop broader scales of judgment as a result of polling individuals, and the hypothesis we stated earlier predicts that more accurate group decisions should ensue. This same hypothesis was testable by fractionating the groups under Conditions A and B into those exhibiting a broad scale and those showing a narrow scale of judgment when initial individual estimates were examined. In addition to this approach to group decision-making, the investigator concluded each session by surveying individual opinion on the influences each person had felt and the degree of agreement with the final group estimate. We may note this extension of the experimental procedure even though we shall not be able to consider this part of the results.

When the various group estimates were examined, it was found that Conditions A and B, with individual estimates having preceded the group discussion, had given rise to mean errors of about 1000 and 900 dots, respectively. These error magnitudes were compared with a mean error value of about 1500 dots made under Condition C, with no polling of individuals prior to group discussion. Although this much larger mean error was in the predictoo direction, it was not statistically Significant in comparison with the means for Conditions A and B which had presumably come from broader scales of judgment.

All groups under these Conditions A and B were examined as to the SD of the original individual estimates as publicly expressed. The groups showing an SD above the median were then compared to those exhibiting an SD of preliminary estimates which was below the median. In other words, the groups having a broad scale of judgment were compared with those having a narrower scale established in the initial poll. It was found that the mean error of group estimates based on the broader scales was only about 800 dots, whereas groups using narrower scales showed a mean group error of about 1400 dots. The difference in this case was statistically significant, offering support to the hypothesis under investigation.

Problem Solving

Investigations in which groups are required to solve problems are as varied in content and method as are studies of group discussions. Since we are not attempting a representative survey, we shall omit examples of the more straightforward experiments in which a face-toface group is observed while it tries to solve an assigned problem. We shall look instead at some illustrative research featuring somewhat special methods.

Dynamics of Competitive. In contrast to the usual study, which calls for full cooperation in attacking a problem, Hoffman, Festinger, and Lawrence (1954) set up a situation in which three people bargained competitively to obtain points. Each individual was striving to earn points for himself, but the situation was arranged so that two people might form a coalition so as to win extra points. These points could then be shared in any way on which these two agreed. Such coalitions could be repeatedly formed and dissolved during a trial, so that the experimenters were afforded an excellent opportunity to see how competitive bargaining occurred under different conditions, which they imposed.

A special aspect of this study was that one of the three college students in each group of subjects was a paid collaborator, assisting in the research. His role in the competition for points and in the forming of coalitions was designed to bring out the motivational and problem-solving patterns of behaviour in the two bona fide subjects. Completing some geometric jigsaw puzzles was the first task required of the three persons, and on this task the confederate of the investigators always earned most points. On the subsequent four trials, points could be earned only if any two subjects pooled certain jigsaw puzzle pieces. This set the stage for forming two-man coalitions. The two real subjects could cooperate with each other to earn the available points to be shared as they wished. Alternatively, either could form a coalition with the confederate who already held a commanding lead in points. The confederate would usually be required to offer a larger share of the potential points before either subject would cooperate with him in earning them.

In their introduction of the subjects to the experiment, the investigators established two sets of conditions, which they felt would affect the bargaining for points and the forming of the two-man coalitions. One set of conditions involved an indication of the assigned tasks as either very important or somewhat inconsequential in nature. On the one hand great importance was attached to the session by presenting it as a social intelligence test with each of the three students being evaluated as they bargained among themselves. Alternatively the session was minimized in importance by indicating it to be a routine check of a test whose validity was seriously doubted by the investigators. The second set of conditions involved the apparent status of the collaborating student posing as a subject. Under the peer condition he was indicated to be about equal in intelligence to the other students. Under the non-peer condition he was shown to be their superior in intellectual functioning. The peer or non-peer relations were combined with the high or low importance conditions in a 2 × 2 factorial design. Seven groups were run under each of the four combinations of these conditions.

It was hypothesized that high importance attaching to the task would induce more coalitions between the two bona fide subjects in an attempt to compete with the third man who held the lead as a result of his initial success. A second hypothesis was that these two subjects would cooperate more if the other were seen as a peer-an equal against whom they ought to make a good showing. If he were perceived as clearly superior, as in the non-peer condition, then they should be less likely to cooperate in attempting to equal him. In this case, each of them should be more likely to join him in trying to beat the other regular subject who would appear to be appropriate competition.

Over the four critical trials the number of coalitions formed by the bona fide subjects under the two sets of conditions confirmed the two hypotheses we have stated. More coalitions were formed against the stooge subject when the task was considered to be very important. Likewise, more of these coalitions occurred under the peer condition in which the stooge was presented as a reasonable competitor for the others. These main effects were found to be statistically significant. The findings tended to be borne out by other data that were taken, such as the price in points, which the stooge had to offer in order to break up a coalition against him. A greater number of points was demanded of him in the bargaining when the task was perceived as more important and when he was perceived as a peer against whom the real subjects ought to compete successfully.

Three-Man Communication. A series of experiments by Heise and Miller (1951) involved a variety of communication nets achieved by using both one-way and two-way channels between members of the group. The five different nets, which were used are schematically represented in Figure 2. Among the features which distinguish these nets we may note that Net 1 permits each subject, A, B, or C, to communicate with each other person over a two-way channel; in Net 3 there is two-way communication between A and B as well as between A and C, but Band C are not joined directly by any channel; Net 5 involves three one-way channels, permitting A to communicate information to B, B to C, and C to A, without any chance for reversed communication over these three channels.

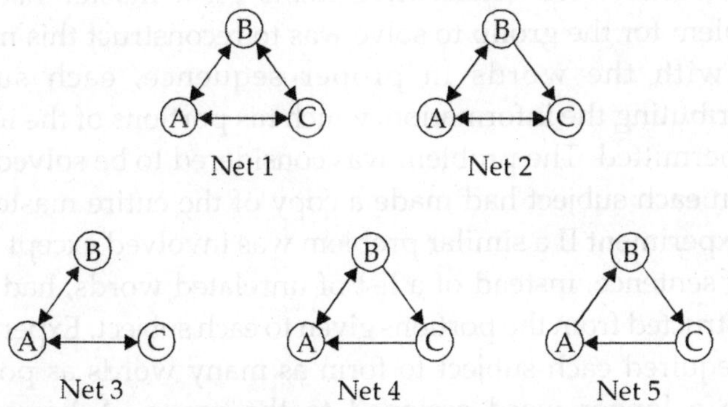

Fig. 2. Five three-person communication nets used by Heise and Miller (1951) with both one-way and two-way communication used in different net patterns as indicated by the arrowheads in the figure. (After Heise and Miller, 1951.)

Microphones and earphones were employed in setting up the required nets for communication among the subjects who were located in different rooms. The equipment was arranged to permit the experimenters to introduce three different noise levels into the channels of any net. This varying of signal-to-noise ratio constituted a second major independent variable in addition to the different nets. A high ratio, with little noise, permitted subjects to make themselves understood quite readily over the channels provided. A low signal-to-noise ratio made it difficult to transmit information, causing many errors to occur. In this brief review we shall not deal extensively with the signal-to-noise ratio as a variable. We may note merely that the lower ratios impeded the solving of the assigned problems by interfering with accurate communication. These difficult conditions of message transmission also accentuated the differences between the nets as certain tasks were attempted.

Three experiments in this study differed in the task assigned to the subjects. In Experiment I each subject was given a number of pairs of words. Pairing indicated that the two words were consecutive items on a master list. The problem for the group to solve was to reconstruct this master list with the words in proper sequence, each subject contributing the information, which his portions of the master list permitted. The problem was considered to be solved only when each subject had made a copy of the entire master list. In Experiment II a similar problem was involved except that a long sentence, instead of a list of unrelated words, had to be constructed from the portions given to each subject. Experiment III required each subject to form as many words as possible from a longer word assigned to the group. A bonus was offered for every word that was common to each of the three lists, which were constructed in this problem-solving task. The communication net could be employed to exchange information on words formed.

Just as research has shown that the different net patterns which are illustrated in Figure 1 affect problem-solving efficiency, these experiments demonstrated that the nets of Figure 2 also differ in the speed with which they permit some problems to be solved. In Experiment I the number of words spoken and the time taken in arriving at the reconstructed master list both showed Net 1 to be the most efficient and Net 5 the least. The performance data were in general agreement with an analysis of how" many spoken words would be needed to solve the problem, given each net with its own set of channels. Net 5, for example, does not permit any spoken word to reach two subjects at once, thus allowing no economy in transmitting information.

Experiment II, unlike Experiment I, showed Net 3 to be superior to Net 1. The experimenters suggest that the sentence construction task demands the sort of coordination which Subject A in Net 3 can supply. The more complete channels of Net 1 apparently introduce chaos, to some extent, when the sentence-building is attempted. The results for Experiment III contrast with those we have noted in that the nets did not differ in their effect on efficiency of performance. The task of constructing words did not require much exchange of information. Since each subject could go at the problem independently, the channels of communication played little differential role.

●●

Index

D

E

F

G